The Victorian Age

The Victorian Age

R. B. Mowat

SENATE

The Victorian Age

First published in 1939 by
George G. Harrap & Co. Ltd, London

This edition published in 1995 by Senate, an imprint of
Studio Editions Ltd, Princess House, 50 Eastcastle
Street, London W1N 7AP, England

ISBN 1 85958 161 7
Printed and bound in Guernsey by
The Guernsey Press Co. Ltd

TO

C. H. K. MARTEN

VICE-PROVOST OF ETON COLLEGE

WHO IN THAT HOME OF LIBERAL CULTURE

HAS MAINTAINED THE GREAT TRADITION

OF HISTORICAL STUDIES

PREFACE

HISTORIANS are bound to be impersonal, but in a preface it is permitted to depart a little from this wholesome rule, and even to indulge in the use of the forbidden first personal pronoun.

In the early years of the present century the Oxford Final School of Modern History (particularly in the teaching of the magnificent tutors of Balliol) was a splendid training, as it still is, exact, inspiring, vigorous. It was, however —this has been amended—almost exclusively a school of constitutional and political history. What Dr Gooch, whose mind embraces all aspects of history, has called cultural history was scarcely noticed. As the study of history ought to include all life—as history *is* life—society in its cultural, its 'leisured,' aspects demands as serious attention as any other part of history.

This truth was, perhaps, particularly impressed on me when I was professor in an American university; for American historians have always been attracted by the social aspects of their peoples' history. It was impossible to be on the faculty of the University of Wisconsin when Carl Russell Fish and Frederick L. Paxson were teaching without realizing that history was nothing if not social.

In *England in the Eighteenth Century, The Age of Reason, The Romantic Age*, a series of books issued by the late Mr George G. Harrap—surely one of the kindest and most courteous of the kindly and courteous race of publishers—I endeavoured to seize certain aspects of mainly cultural history, the last two volumes being concerned chiefly with the continent of Europe. When, however, I approached the rich Victorian Age I soon became convinced that only an encyclopædia could be comprehensive. It was essential to be strictly selective. The present work, accordingly, is concerned with a central period from about 1840 to 1870 or 1880. It corresponds to some extent with the period covered by the two handsome volumes of *Early Victorian England* (Oxford University Press, 1934), edited by Mr G. M. Young—a full and interesting work, which, however, is restricted to Great Britain.

The present volume, besides dealing with some aspects of Continental history, has five chapters which are mainly concerned with American history. This proportion, I must honestly confess, is partly due to my own personal interest in United States history. It is, however, also due to the fact that the people of the United States made a notable contribution to culture in this period, as has been delightfully recorded and assessed in Mr Van Wyck Brooks' *Flowering of New England* (Dent, 1936). Their politics also began to have considerable, if indirect, influence upon the Old World.

Although the theme of the book is the culture and comfort of the Victorian Age, it is not suggested that the people of this time were exceptionally cultured or comfortable. Mrs Browning's *Cry of the Children*, Tom Hood's *Song of the Shirt*, the *General Report on the Sanitary Condition of the Labouring Population* (1842), were based on only too good evidence. It is claimed merely that the general tendency of the age was progressive, towards higher and more diffused culture, increasing and more diffused prosperity; that the 'middle classes,' a minority, but continually increasing, substantially attained to the blessings of culture and a reasonably comfortable way of life; and not only they, but a good many 'working-class' families too.

Acknowledgment is gratefully made to Messrs John Murray for permission to use extracts from *The Letters of Queen Victoria* in Chapter XIII.

R. B. M.

CONTENTS

Chapter I

GOVERNMENT

THE historian Lecky, in *Democracy and Liberty*, wrote: " It does not appear to me that the world has ever seen a better constitution than England enjoyed between the Reform Bill of 1832 and the Reform Bill of 1867." [1] This somewhat sweeping statement may be explained by the fact that the middle class began to come into its own about 1832 in England (and also in France and certain other Continental countries), and that middle-class government was considered to correspond fairly nearly to the ideal of political philosophers. The Bill of 1832 gave the vote in England to the £10 householder in the towns and to the leaseholders—as well as the freeholders—in the country; and it suppressed all the privileged pocket boroughs. It added about half a million people to the voting list. In France, under King Louis-Philippe, every one who paid three hundred francs in direct taxes had the right to vote, but this ensured only about two hundred thousand people on the voting list; yet the system was considered by the eminent statesman Guizot to be a good middle way—the *juste milieu*.

Society had witnessed, since the last century of the Middle Ages, the steady process of dethronement of the feudal classes by the *bourgeoisie*. The benevolent despots of the eighteenth century all but completed the process. The Industrial Revolution of the first half of the nineteenth century did the rest.

Bourgeoisie is a better term for the new governors of Europe than 'middle class.' The so-called middle class

[1] W. E. H. Lecky, *Democracy and Liberty* (1899 edition), i, 21.

is not, and never was, between two other classes, high and low. How could a governing class be middle, in the sense of being under one class, though above another? It was not ' middle ' even socially, for on its arrival at high government its members had social prestige equal to that of any aristocrat. The cultured high *bourgeoisie* is equalitarian chiefly in the sense of recognizing its equality, political and social, with the former high feudal classes of the land.

Bourgeoisie is the right word, because the great middle class arose in the towns. It was the townspeople in the last century of the Middle Ages—and the kings relying on the townspeople—who began the crushing of feudalism. Gradually, however, the term *bourgeoisie* came to mean more than just townspeople: it included all people with a particular cast of mind. The *bourgeoisie*, according to André Siegfried, are " those who have reserves." It may be asked, reserves of what? Not of money only, or other kinds of property, but reserves also of culture. At the close of the Middle Ages the *bourgeoisie* profited by the breaking up of the universal Catholic Church, which had hitherto monopolized culture, and by the invention of printing, which put culture within the reach of any modest purse. And magnificently they used the opportunity! The literature of the age of Elizabeth, Cervantes and the Spanish novel, Bacon and Descartes, the architecture and drama of the age of Louis XIV, Voltaire and the brilliant *salon* life of the eighteenth century, were all *bourgeois* achievements. The Industrial Age of the nineteenth century gave the *bourgeoisie* further opportunities for interesting careers, high education, economic security. It was not a machine age. The machine was only an instrument making the higher life possible for ever increasing numbers of people. The ideal of the *bourgeoisie* of the nineteenth century was that all people should become *bourgeois*. In this sense they envisaged the possibility of a classless society united by culture, spirit, art, philosophy: " These are ideas from a *bourgeois* age." [1]

Government, according to the *bourgeois* ideal, was to be individualist, representative, responsible. It was to be individualist because, in spite of indispensable Government interference, the domain of the spirit, the individual's personality, must be left free and uncontrolled. It was to be representative because the *bourgeois* conception of justice and equality required that government should be derived from the people, though not directly operated by the people. And it was to be responsible—that is, ultimately controlled by the representative assembly—because justice demanded that the people should not be at the disposal of any arbitrary authority. For these reasons all the political effort of the middle nineteenth century was towards Liberalism—in the Continental sense of the word—towards government by cabinet of Ministers responsible to a representative legislature which was itself ' balanced ' by division into two chambers.

This balanced, *bourgeois* system of government was to be seen at its best in the United States. It was in 1831 that Alexis de Tocqueville, a young official in the French judiciary, visited the United States on a Government mission to investigate the penitentiary system. His great interest was philosophic history—the study of society, of politics. The result of his experiences in the United States was his *De la Démocratie en Amérique*, published in 1835. The observations and reflections contained in this book are as true concerning the Americans of 1865 as they were of the Americans of 1835. Indeed, James Bryce, writing in 1888, after prolonged travel and study in the United States, came to much the same conclusions as Tocqueville.

[1] Thomas Mann, " A Warning to Europe," in *The Spectator*, February 12, 1937, p. 261. Mann, writing in bitter comment on contemporary tendencies, says that culture, spirit, art, philosophy, are now regarded as " idealistic rubbish from the nineteenth century."

In no civilized country, writes Tocqueville, has less attention been paid to philosophy. Yet as all the Americans act in the same way it is clear that " they have a philosophy." Nevertheless, though there is a common basis of all their thinking, each American appeals to his individual understanding alone. It was in France that philosophers first began to subject everything in politics or religion to the test of private judgment. The Americans adopted " this freedom," though with some restraints and limitations on account of the strongly Christian basis of American society. The American belief is that all citizens can be raised to higher and higher levels of civilization. Aristocracies do not believe in the perfectibility of mankind, but democracies do, and " the Americans more than any." This explains why they do not construct ships or machinery to last: " they wish to keep up with the latest improvements." Tocqueville spoke with a sailor on this subject:

> I accost an American sailor, and I inquire why the ships of his country are built so as to last but for a short time; he answers without hesitation that the art of navigation is every day making such rapid progress, that the finest vessel would become almost useless if it lasted beyond a certain number of years. In these words, which fell accidentally and on a particular subject from a man of rude attainments, I recognize the general and systematic idea upon which a great people directs all its concerns.[1]

The minds of the Americans are fixed on practical objects, but they draw their theory from Europe:

> I cannot consent to separate America from Europe, in spite of the ocean which intervenes. I consider the people of the United States as that portion of the English people which is commissioned to explore the wilds of the New World; whilst the rest of the nation, enjoying more leisure and less harassed by the drudgery of life, may devote its

[1] *Democracy in America*, translated by H. Reeve (1862), ii, 39.

energies to thought and enlarge in all directions the empire of the mind.[1]

It may be said that in the middle of the nineteenth century Europe had entered the newspaper age. Tocqueville lived to see this: he died in 1859. He had seen it arrive earlier in the United States. The social equality of the Americans, he wrote in *De la Démocratie en Amérique*, and their desire to have their own opinions are the cause of the enormous number of newspapers there. The Industrial Revolution was spreading in America, for Tocqueville discerned a manufacturing aristocracy growing up there " under our eyes "—one of the harshest, but also one of the least dangerous. Tocqueville makes the curious remark that civilization in modern states is in peril, not, as in the ancient Roman Empire, from barbarians without, but from barbarians within. He concludes *De la Démocratie en Amérique* thus:

> The nations of our time cannot prevent the conditions of men from becoming equal; but it depends upon themselves whether the principle of equality is to lead them to servitude or freedom, to knowledge or barbarism, to prosperity or wretchedness.

Naturally the new political tendency towards equalitarian *bourgeois* rule showed itself most distinctly in the United States and the British Colonies, which had no old aristocracies in possession of power. In Great Britain, however, the *bourgeoisie* was becoming conscious of its claim, its ability, its future. The rise of Disraeli shows this, for that great admirer and describer of aristocracy was, and is, the hero of the conservative *bourgeoisie*. These people are not deluded by the arts of demagogy. Disraeli may have had some of these arts, but he had far more: he had genius and industry. Disraeli's novels are his " Confessions," and he can be traced from *Vivian Grey*

[1] *Democracy in America*, ii, 42.

in 1826, through *Coningsby* (1844), *Sybil* (1845), and *Tancred* (1847), down to *Endymion* in 1880. Vivian Grey was an attractive, thoughtful, sentimental youth, the darling of feminine society, in which, after a somewhat artificial, monastic education, he was spending all his evening hours.

> But Vivian Grey was a young and tender plant in a moral hothouse. His character was developing itself too soon. Although his evenings were now generally passed in the manner we have alluded to, this boy was, during the rest of the day, a hard and indefatigable student; and, having now got through an immense series of historical reading, he had stumbled upon a branch of study certainly the most delightful in the world, but for a boy certainly the most perilous—THE STUDY OF POLITICS.

The elder Grey, *blasé* clubman, still conscious of the existence and depressing weight of the aristocracy, takes a stroll with his son along Pall Mall, and gives him useful, if somewhat chilling, advice:

> We are, I hope, an improving race; there is room, I am sure, for great improvement, and the perfectibility of man is certainly a pretty dream. (How well that Union Club House comes out now since they have made the opening!) But although we may have steam kitchens, human nature is, I imagine, much the same this moment that we are walking in Pall Mall East as it was some thousand years ago, when as wise men were walking on the banks of the Ilyssus. Or when our moral powers increase in proportion to our physical ones, then huzza for the perfectibility of man!

Vivian, however, was not to be deterred by this cold reasoning. He felt that he had the making of a statesman in him, and he was sure that he would find the opportunity. "Now let me provoke my very soul," he said to himself. "Does my cheek blanch? I have the mind for the conception; and I can perform right skilfully upon the most splendid of musical instruments—the human voice."[1] It was this incomparable musical instrument—the human voice, mellow, resonant, clear—that was to charm the House of Commons and the audiences of the large halls, filled with rising, powerful, eager *bourgeoisie*.

In *Coningsby* (1844) the weight of the aristocracy is still balancing the rising *bourgeoisie*; an ambitious young man, if the highest political position is to be open to him, must have aristocratic support. The great *bourgeois* statesman, however, who had all but achieved the highest office before the Reform Bill of 1832, owed little to aristocratic support. Sir Robert Peel, it is true, entered the House of Commons through a pocket borough, and shared his first and second tenure of power with the Duke of Wellington; but after 1841 he was undisputed master of the legislature. Disraeli, in *Lord George Bentinck*, describes Peel's mastery. Not only the legislature, but even the Crown, now obeyed him, for on January 28, 1846, when a great debate on the proposed repeal of the Corn Laws was to be opened, "his Royal Highness the Prince Consort, attended by the Master of the Horse, appeared and took his seat in the body of the House." It was still a recognized convention, writes Disraeli, that "no Minister can introduce a measure into either House without the consent of the Crown." The coming of the Prince Consort, however, known to represent the Queen's views and decisions, was considered

> to be the unfair and unwise manœuvre of the Minister to give the semblance of the personal sanction of her Majesty to a measure which, whatever its result, a large portion, perhaps a majority, of her subjects deemed fraught with ruin to their interests.

Nevertheless the situation in the House of Commons

[1] The passages quoted from *Vivian Grey* are on pp. 18, 21, and 20 respectively of the "Bradenham Edition" (1926) of Disraeli's novels.

was easily controlled by the Prime Minister, Sir Robert Peel. Disraeli writes:

> This remarkable man, who in private life was constrained and often awkward, who could never address a public meeting or make an after-dinner speech without being ill at ease and generally saying something stilted or even ridiculous, in the Senate was the readiest, easiest, most flexible and adroit of men. He played upon the House of Commons as on an old fiddle. And to-night the manner in which he proceeded to deal with the duties on candles and soap, while all were thinking of the duties on something else; the bland and conciliatory air with which he announced the reduction of the impost on boot-fronts and shoe-leather; the intrepid plausibility with which he entered into a dissertation on the duties on foreign brandy and foreign sugar, while visions of deserted villages and reduced rentals were torturing his neighbours, were all characteristic of his command over himself, and those whom he addressed.[1]

A virtue of aristocrats is greatheartedness. They are not in politics for a living; they bear no malice. The Bill for the Repeal of the Corn Laws was carried in the House of Commons on May 18, 1846, and in the House of Lords on June 25. The Whigs, however, who had helped the Tory Sir Robert Peel to carry repeal, were not going to support him in a coercion Bill for Ireland. Such a Bill came to a vote in the House of Commons on June 25, 1846—the same day as the Corn Laws Repeal Bill passed the Lords. Whigs, and the Tory Protectionists too, voted against the Government. Peel looked on from the Treasury bench, impassive, as his former supporters passed out to the Opposition division lobby:

> It was impossible that he could have marked them without emotion: the flower of that great party which had been so proud to follow one who had been so proud to lead them. They were men to gain whose hearts and the hearts of their

[1] *Lord George Bentinck: a Political Biography* (1852), pp. 69–70.

fathers had been the aim and exaltation of his life. They had extended to him an unlimited confidence and an admiration without stint. They had stood by him in the darkest hour, and had borne him from the depths of political despair to the proudest of living positions. Right or wrong, they were men of honour, breeding, and refinement, high and generous character, great weight, and station in the country, which they had ever placed at his disposal. They had been not only his followers, but his friends; had joined in the same pastimes, drunk from the same cup, and in the pleasantness of private life had often forgotten together the cares and strifes of politics.

He must have felt something like this while the Manners, the Somersets, the Bentincks, the Lowthers, and the Lennoxes passed before him.

These were the " Gentlemen of England." As Peel watched

they trooped on: all the men of metal or large-acred squires, whose spirit he had so often quickened and whose counsel he had so often solicited in his fine conservative speeches in Whitehall Gardens. . . .

The news that the Government was not only beaten, but by a majority so large as 73, began to circulate. An incredulous rumour passed it along the Treasury bench.

" They say we are beaten by 73! " whispered the most important member of the Cabinet in a tone of surprise to Sir Robert Peel.

Sir Robert did not reply or even turn his head.[1]

That is how Victorian statesmen took the loss of " the proudest of living positions." Peel was of the middle class, but he had the stoicism and disdain for success which are aristocratic virtues. Yet even the most assured of aristocrats broke down, not over the loss of the Prime Ministership, but over the loss of a race. Their heart was on the Turf. Lord George Bentinck, writes Disraeli (his closest friend), " had become the lord paramount of that strange

[1] *Lord George Bentinck*, pp. 299–301.

world, so difficult to sway, and which requires for its government both a stern resolve and a courtly breeding." In 1848, the year of Continental revolutions, there was one of the longest Parliamentary sessions on record. Lord George Bentinck, now the undisputed leader of the Protectionist Tories, had been unremitting in his Parliamentary duties. A great horse-racer and breeder of horses, he had given up his stud, including his horse Surplice, solely in order to be able to devote himself without distraction to his public work. On May 24, 1848, Surplice won the Derby. Next day Disraeli met him in the library of the House of Commons. Lord George Bentinck was completely broken down:

> He had nothing to console him, and nothing to sustain him, but his pride. Even that deserted him before a heart which he knew at least could yield him sympathy. He gave a sort of superb groan.
>
> " All my life I have been trying for this, and for what have I sacrificed it! " he murmured.
>
> It was in vain to offer solace.[1]

Vivian Grey (1826) was Disraeli's first novel; *Endymion* (1880) was the last.[2] No longer simply Benjamin Disraeli, but Earl of Beaconsfield, the tired statesman, overwhelmingly defeated at a General Election, sat in the study at Hughenden and took up an uncompleted novel. " The long book was finished swiftly, as memories poured from his pen." [3] Louis-Philippe and Louis Napoleon are in it, Palmerston, Sidney Herbert, Cobden, and even " the youthful Dilke."

In *Endymion* Beaconsfield harked back to the time of *Vivian Grey*, or to the year after (1827), when Lord Liver-

[1] *Lord George Bentinck*, p. 539.

[2] Lord Beaconsfield left some nine chapters of an unfinished novel without a name. Mr Guedalla calls it *Falconet*, after the central character.

[3] Philip Guedalla, Introduction to *Endymion* (" Bradenham Edition "), p. viii.

pool had a stroke and retired from the Premiership, and Canning held this great office for a few months and then died. Between 1827 and 1880 the " great British middle class " had entered into its promised land:

> The great world then, compared with the huge society of the present period, was limited in its proportions, and composed of elements more refined, though far less various. It consisted mainly of the great landed aristocracy who had quite absorbed the nabobs of India, and had nearly appropriated the huge West Indian fortunes. Occasionally an eminent banker or merchant invested a large portion of his accumulations in land, and in the purchase of Parliamentary influence, and was in time admitted into the sanctuary. But those vast and successful invasions of society by new classes which have since occurred, though impending, had not yet commenced. The manufacturers, the railway kings, the colossal contractors, the discoverers of nuggets, had not yet found their place in society and the Senate.[1]

[1] *Endymion*, p. 22.

Chapter II

CONTINENTAL POLITICS

THE famous ' system ' of Metternich fell with him in 1848, though the astonishing old gentleman went on living with zest and with high interest in politics until his death at Vienna in 1859. He was then eighty-six years old; and though he had said he was " so weary " at sixty-five or seventy, he felt in his later years that spring-time was coming in Europe. With the death of the Tsar Nicholas I and the fall of Sebastopol in 1855 the Russian domination was ended, the incubus lifted. Poles and Italians and French and Spaniards felt that they could begin to breathe easily.

1848 was the great ' moment ' of Continental Europe in the nineteenth century. People felt (to apply to this time Wordsworth's reference to 1789): " Bliss was it in that dawn to be alive, but to be young was very Heaven." Carl Schurz, later an eminent American statesman, was a student at Bonn in 1848. On February 26 a friend rushed into his room shouting, " The French have driven away Louis-Philippe and proclaimed a republic ! " Schurz was writing a tragedy, *Ulrich von Hutten*, but he dropped his pen at once, and never touched the manuscript again. The shackles were breaking. The good time was at hand. And it was not to be like 1789. This time there was to be no violence. The *bourgeoisie* had been waiting and working over fifty years for this moment—ever since the Congress of Vienna in 1815—and now spontaneously the masses accepted them as leaders. The terrified monarchs everywhere (except in Russia) capitulated and hastily issued summonses for the election of constituent assemblies.

From Berlin and Dresden to Madrid and Lisbon newspapers blossomed into uncensored editions, and all the *cafés* were filled with the smoke and the talk of eager politicians. Nor did it all end in smoke and talk. In most countries the promised constituent assemblies met and drafted a constitution; but before the constitution was accepted or ratified the old Governments had recovered both confidence and strength. The Prussian Constituent Assembly, the Austrian, the All-German Frankfort Assembly, met the same fate: they were dispersed by soldiers and the doors were locked, after the manner of Oliver Cromwell and the Long Parliament. In the Italian states too the year of revolution ended only in renewed, if somewhat milder, despotisms. In France the Second Republic lasted a year or two longer, and then succumbed to the dictatorship of Louis Napoleon. Nevertheless, though the 1848 revolutions were a failure, they proved to be the turning-point in the political movement of the century: the *bourgeoisie* had asserted their power, exerted it for a time, then lost it, but they gradually took it up again over the next fifty years. Not everybody, of course, approved of this; not Karl Marx, whose *Communist Manifesto* was making the round of the world in 1848; not even Mazzini, though he was no Communist. "We could not foresee," he wrote in his autobiography, "that the doctrine of progress, which is the germ of the religion of the future, would be allowed to stop short so miserably with the organization of the *bourgeoisie*."[1] Here, however, Mazzini was referring to the *bourgeoisie* of the reign of Louis-Philippe, to the restricted middle-class franchise allowed by Louis-Philippe's *Charte*. He would have had to admit that the *bourgeoisie* in the latter half of the nineteenth century was not politically quite stationary.

"One of the great divisions of politics in our day,"

[1] G. Mazzini, *Life and Writings* (trans. 1891), i, 24.

writes Lecky, " is coming to be whether, at the last resort, the world should be governed by its ignorance or by its intelligence." [1] Everybody agrees that society should be governed by the intelligent people; but the aristocrats of the eighteenth century and the *bourgeoisie* of the nineteenth too easily assumed that they had a monopoly of intelligence. The progressive Disraeli, who appealed so successfully to the artisans to vote for the Conservative Party, and who gave them the franchise by the Reform Bill of 1867, regretted the loss of power by the high *bourgeoisie* in France when Louis-Philippe fell in 1848. " The subversion of the Orleans dynasty," he wrote in *Lord George Bentinck*, " was a great misfortune for France and for Europe. . . . Ancient communities like the European must be governed either by traditionary influences or by military force." He then proceeds to make the astonishing remark: " England is the only important European community that is still governed by traditionary influences." [2] He was writing in 1851, but before the *coup d'état* made by Louis Napoleon on December 2 of that year, the *coup d'état* which inaugurated a dictatorship.

The Italian philosopher Benedetto Croce seems inclined to the view that the Second French Empire which in 1852 followed the *coup d'état* was a kind of training-ground for the Third Republic.

> Liberty is a divine gift; and the gods sometimes take it away from men, who are eternal children, and remain deaf to their supplications, and do not give it back until they have once more become worthy of it.[3]

The French—this would seem to be Croce's view—became worthy of liberty by 1870. Napoleon III once

[1] *Democracy and Liberty*, i, 25.

[2] *Lord George Bentinck*, pp. 552, 554, and 555.

[3] *History of Europe in the Nineteenth Century*, translated by H. Furst (1934), p. 203.

said, "Liberty has never been able to found a lasting political edifice, but crowns it when time has consolidated it." Certainly the Third Republic which succeeded to the Second Empire proved itself to be a solid *bourgeois* state, even though it is based on a peasant population.

Lecky remarks in *Democracy and Liberty* that nationality is not necessarily a democratic idea: "Nations that value very little internal or constitutional freedom are often passionately devoted to their national individuality and independence." [1] Such, however, was not Mazzini's view. He could not conceive nationality without liberty; and without both he could not conceive that anything "vital" would be accomplished. Alluding to his own people, he wrote in his *Autobiographical Notes* (1861): "Without a country, and without liberty, we might perhaps produce some prophets of art, but no vital art." For Italians—so ran the words of the Manifesto of Young Italy (1831)—"every effort at emancipation shall proceed upon the three inseparable bases of unity, liberty, and independence." Nationalism, however, Mazzini contended, would not be an element of division, but, on the contrary, of unity. "The religion of humanity is love," declared the Manifesto of Young Italy. Oppressed, unfree people might have conflicts with one another; but free nations, because each was free and united, would have no other external interest than merely to co-operate harmoniously. In the *Autobiographical Notes* Mazzini wrote:

> I may, however, state that I was not influenced by any mere political conception, nor idea of elevating the condition of the single people whom I saw thus dismembered, degraded, and oppressed. The parent thought of my every design was a presentiment that regenerated Italy was destined to arise the *initiatrix* of a new life, and a new and powerful Unity, to all the nations of Europe.[2]

[1] *Democracy and Liberty*, ii, 475.
[2] Mazzini, *op. cit.*, i, 36.

Young Italy, Young Germany, Young Switzerland, and the rest would make Young Europe. In fact, Mazzini founded a society of Young Europe. " I saw regenerate Italy becoming at one bound the missionary of a religion of progress and fraternity, far grander and vaster than that she gave to humanity in the past."

Cavour too, the architect of Italian unity, was spontaneously liberal as well as national. An admirer of the July Revolution (1830) in France which produced the monarchy of Louis-Philippe and the *juste milieu*, Cavour was always a moderate, but always liberal. About this time, writes Croce, Cavour noted in his diary: " There is no great man who is not a liberal." Not to appreciate liberty was to him a sign of lack of culture. " The degree of love of liberty," wrote the young Cavour, " is proportionate in every man to the moral education attained by him." When after 1858 Cavour was able, step by step, to piece the fragments of Italy together he accompanied every step by a plebiscite, and extended the Statuto of 1848, the Constitution of the kingdom of Sardinia, over each new province. When he was Minister-President of only the small Sardinian kingdom he had worked for this liberal and national ideal:

> Fundamental was the formation, to which he then devoted himself, of an orderly Parliamentary activity, with parties that represented needs and collected their forces, and were able if necessary to unite for certain common ends, as he did by forming with Ratazzi and his men of the Left the so-called Connubio. The debates in the sub-alpine Chamber and Senate, the legislative and political activity that was carried on there, the speeches of Cavour, the Parliamentary combinations, the resolutions of the crises, offered examples of a correct and fruitful constitutional life, and served as a model and as a school to the rest of Italy.[1]

Indeed, it might be said that as Sardinia between 1850

[1] Croce, *op. cit.*, p. 211.

and 1870 was a model for the rest of Italy, so Italy was a model for the rest of Europe, in much the same way as France had been previously. The Italian movement—liberal, national—showed that the European revolutionary movement, of which France had been the representative since 1789, could be continued in an orderly, almost 'conservative' manner.

> If it were possible in political theory to speak of masterpieces as we do in dealing with works of art, the process of Italy's independence, liberty, and unity would deserve to be called the masterpiece of the liberal-national movements of the nineteenth century, so admirably does it exhibit the combination of its various elements—respect for what is old and profound innovation, the wise prudence of the statesmen and the impetus of the revolutionaries and the volunteers, ardour and moderation.[1]

The 'moderate' Italian movement, its constitutional monarchy, its orderly two-chambered Parliament, its conservation of the social structure, gave confidence to the *bourgeoisie* all over Europe.

Only in Russia did the future of politics seem to be undecided, though here too there were stirrings of the spirit. There was a *bourgeoisie* in Russia, though its numbers in proportion to the rest of the people were less than in other European countries. The Russian *bourgeois* was not class-conscious, for Peter the Great had established the principle that public service in the bureaucracy was the title to social position. The bureaucracy was like a national army in which all promotion is from the ranks. The infinite series of steps up which a civil servant, irrespective of birth, could rise in the bureaucracy had a unifying effect on the people. On the other hand, the absence of any system of national education kept the peasantry immobile—unlettered, ignorant, silent. Dostoievsky, who wrote novels of *bourgeois* life—*Crime and*

[1] Croce, *op. cit.*, p. 225.

Punishment (1866), *The Brothers Karamazov* (1880)—looked forward to all the people becoming *bourgeois*. He wrote:

> I never could understand the reason why one-tenth part of our people should be cultured, and the other nine-tenths must serve as the material support of the minority and themselves remain in ignorance. I do not want to think or to live with any other belief than that our ninety millions of people (and those who shall be born after us) will all be some day cultured, humanized, and happy. I know and firmly believe that universal enlightenment will harm none of us. I also believe that the kingdom of thought and light is possible of realization in our Russia even sooner than elsewhere, because with us, even now, *no one defends the idea of one part of the population being enlisted against the other.*[1]

The faith of the serious political thinkers of the nineteenth-century *bourgeoisie* was that the whole people would become "cultured, humanized, and happy," without sacrifice of private enterprise, liberty, property. That is, the *bourgeois* aimed at making all the 'proletariat' *bourgeois*, contrary to Karl Marx, who advocated making all the *bourgeoisie* proletarians. The *bourgeoisie*, be it noted, never used the horrible word 'proletariat'; it was the Marxians who invented and adopted it.

Even the Russian nobles, owing to the levelling effect of the bureaucracy in which most of them made their careers, were *bourgeois* in outlook and habit. Under Nicholas I Russian society was 'frozen'; discipline and stability were the ideals of that serious despot. Under Alexander II, however, the ill-educated Guards officer who as Tsar showed himself surprisingly liberally minded, the educated classes set forth to spread culture among the peasantry. Guards officers, gently nurtured ladies, professors and students, joined societies for founding schools

[1] Quoted by Laurence Irving, in his Introduction to *Crime and Punishment* in the "Everyman's Library" edition. The italics in the last sentence are mine.

in the countryside and for working among the people. The eager, glorious Tolstoi, of course, was awake to this movement and in advance of it.

Tolstoi had not the *bourgeois* outlook. He was a noble, and he was a socialist. He knew war, having been through the siege of Sebastopol. His experiences in the Russian army during war-time gave him a deep respect for the Russian peasantry—for those great, silent masses of men who stoically endured the long winter campaigns and gave their lives in a series of indecisive battles. He came to the conclusion that what really mattered in the long run in war and in politics was not the decisions of the generals and statesmen, not the futile battles nor the councils of statesmen, but the eloquent silence of the masses. They were the makers of history; in them the spirit of the time moved and worked. The achievements of the Cæsars, Napoleons, Bismarcks, would be enduring only if they expressed the silent views of the people. These so-called 'great men' were only fussy egoists making ripples on the ocean of time, but not controlling it. The truly great men were those who understood the silent masses, and who deliberately or unconsciously were the masses' agents.

In *War and Peace* Tolstoi interpolates chapters of historical comment on the Moscow campaign between chapters of narrative. The high generals, convinced that it was they who were directing the course of events, continually made wrong decisions. The way to defeat Napoleon's invasion was not to try to stop him with pitched battles, but to let him go on and bog himself in the middle of Russia. The only way in which the invasion could possibly succeed was by bringing the Russians to battle, with a chance of wiping them out and so obtaining a decision quickly. And this was the opportunity which the Russian generals were always giving Napoleon. They were always selecting places and dates at which to face Napoleon and let their men be futilely slaughtered. The battles did not alter the course of history, though they needlessly added to the sum of human misery. The fate of the campaign was decided by the Russian people expressing themselves through a general —one who, unlike the other generals, was in touch with the people. Old Kutusov, put in command of the Russian armies late in time, when the French were approaching Moscow, had, indeed, to fight one more battle—the Borodino—a delaying action—but after that he stopped. He gave the French no more opportunities of reaching a decision. His colleagues wondered what the old man was thinking about. He would sit for hours in a chair just watching the soldiers. This was how he came to his decisions, the decisions of the people.

War and Peace, which began to appear in 1865, is a useful corrective to the habit of worshipping great men. Doubtless there is a popular will, a persistent tendency of the people as a whole in one direction or another. It would be foolish, however, to ignore the influence of powerful individuals who can select a direction on which the people are not wholly decided, and who can then push them or lead them along that line. The years when *War and Peace* was coming out nearly coincide with the period when Bismarck—according to his own account—" made three wars "—the Schleswig-Holstein War (1864), the Austro-Prussian War (1866), and the Franco-German War (1870). From 1815 until Bismarck became Minister-President of Prussia in 1862 the Germans had lived at peace, without nationalism, their politics wholly domestic. After 1870 their outlook on domestic and foreign politics and their attitude towards the rest of the world were so different from their outlook and attitude of the pre-Bismarck period as to make them seem another people altogether. Bismarck may only have selected certain tendencies of the German mind and character, but he enormously strengthened these tendencies and weakened others. Nobody can deny the dynamic and enduring effect of his single personality on German history. And 'Bismarckism'—the doctrine of force, as distinguished from the doctrine of 'live and let live,' in the great affairs of the world—has become one of the cults of the twentieth century.

Bismarckism, however, was a late development in the Victorian Age, and had no popular response at all outside Germany. The year 1871, which saw the establishment of the German Empire, also witnessed the rise of the Third French Republic. This, though it coincided with the anguish of a lost war, was the triumph of the nineteenth-century *bourgeoisie*. The French people, in the previous eighty years—since the meeting of the Estates-General on May 5, 1789—had tried all known systems of government. They had experienced the grandeurs and servitudes of Cæsarism; the idealism and cruelties of the Commune; and between these two extremes they had tested varieties of 'representative' and 'responsible' government. They now chose the middle way, and have kept it. The Third Republic, inspired by the progressive yet conservative *bourgeoisie*, had proved itself to be solid. "*La République*," said Thiers in its first year, "*sera conservatrice, ou elle ne sera pas.*" ("The Republic will be *conservatrice* [this is not quite the same thing as 'conservative'], or it will not exist at all.")

The decade 1860–70 ended with the fall of the Second French Empire, the foundation of the Third Republic, with ultimately a moderate, balanced, *bourgeois* constitution, and the foundation of the German Empire, with a constitution only partly *bourgeois*. It might have been expected that the German Empire would gradually but fairly rapidly shed the more authoritarian elements in the constitution and develop the democratic features. This, however, did not happen. The Germans had 'representative,' though not 'responsible,' government; the electorate could, through the Reichstag, control legislation and the budget, but had no control over the executive authority, over the Chancellor and Secretaries of State. Germany was the exception in Central and Western Europe to the triumph of the *bourgeoisie.*

The year 1870–71, the year of the Franco-German War, really closes a well-marked period, and begins another with different characteristics. This latter period, the later Victorian Age, was in many respects a splendid one, but it had disturbing tendencies—rising tariffs, competition in armaments, a 'scramble' for colonies—with dangerous possibilities. The decade 1860–70 had more pleasing features. Croce calls the union of Italy "the masterpiece of the liberal-national movements of the nineteenth century."[1] These years, 1860–70, distinguished by the Anglo-French Commercial Treaty of 1860—the Cobden Treaty—were years in Europe of low or even falling tariffs. The problem of nationality—at any rate in the Great States—seemed to have been solved: union of Italy, union of Germany, Austro-Hungarian compromise, Russian liberation of the serfs. The Paris "Universal Exhibition" of 1867 was attended by "all Europe"; and "all Europe" admired and enjoyed the good things of the world, irrespective of national origin, whether it was Offenbach's *La Grande Duchesse de Gerolstein*, produced for the occasion, or the latest Paris mode or a German or British steel casting.

> There was a living and general consciousness of progress, not only as a concept of historical interpretation, but as a certainty that the royal road had been entered upon at last, that the human race now had acquired the mastery over things and, what was more important, over itself, and that it would not again abandon or lose this road, but would follow it for ever.[2]

[1] See above, p. 27. [2] Croce, *op. cit.*, p. 244.

The 'comfortable' assurance of progress which was fundamental in the faith of the Continental *bourgeoisie* down to 1870, and which lasted much longer among the English *bourgeoisie*, has now been shaken. In the early Victorian Age there was material and moral progress. Science, invention, industry, made better and better use of the material resources of mankind. The growth of political liberty and tolerance was progress in the moral sphere. The principle of authority in politics was represented by an Empire, reputed decrepit, like the Austrian, or another, reputed uncultured, like the Russian. The facts of 1870–71, however, made the liberal *bourgeoisie* of Europe doubt their own faith. For Prussia, a state based on authority, and the Prussian people, blindly following their rulers, were "obtaining such triumphs as no other state in Europe had the ability or the audacity to challenge." The Prussians were not uncultured, but on the contrary were versed in literature, music, art, "the best taught, the richest in knowledge and learning, of all the peoples of the world." The Prussian achievements, as Benedetto Croce says, were facts—big facts too—and facts, as Gibbon long since remarked, "are stubborn things."

The "stubborn facts," however, of the Prussian (or Bismarckian) achievement did not necessarily prove that the *bourgeois* faith was unjustified, though they might indicate that *bourgeois* thinkers had underestimated the importance of force in the great affairs of the world. Benedetto Croce, however, suggests that the significance of 1870–71 lies not in the Prussian triumph, but in the decline of philosophy and history, and in the concentration of attention upon the physical sciences. The grandeur of the early Victorian Age, of those years in Great Britain, on the Continent, in America, was expressed by the great speakers and, more permanently, by the great writers.

CHAPTER III

THOUGHT AND LITERATURE

AT an Oxford dinner-party in the afterglow of the Victorian Age, which persisted in the early twentieth century, talk turned upon the relative importance of various studies. A distinguished scientist, whose researches into power and heat had been applied with brilliant practical results in the sphere of mining and engineering, was asked how he would regard a life devoted, like that of the philosophy tutors of the University, to pure thought. " If I had my time to spend over again," the scientist said in his slow, cautious manner, " I would consider it the thing *most worth doing.*" A young history don who was present at the dinner-table was struck by this declaration of the greatest exponent of ' applied ' science of that time—a scientist, however (the young history don reflected), who had been originally educated in the ancient classical learning.

This incident, perhaps, suggests two things. First, that ' useless,' ' remote ' speculation, allied to philosophy, metaphysics, or abstract thought, may be as important in the life of mankind as any or all of the sciences, arts, or crafts. Second, that the decline of philosophy and of the place assigned to philosophy in modern society may be due to the decline of the ' useless,' ' remote ' ancient classical learning. The study of dead languages is unpractical. Greek particles and Latin verse, Homer's *Iliad* and Cicero's *Speeches*, have little obvious relation to the problems of to-day. Accordingly they are jettisoned, perhaps at the expense of the power of abstract thought, though with an increase in specialized knowledge.

It is true that by the time the Victorian Age was opened the great days of philosophy were over. Kant died in 1804, Hegel in 1831. Yet, though the greatest names were in the past, the new age lived upon the work of those grand thinkers. And they were not without eminent representatives in the new age—Victor Cousin, who lived and worked until 1867; Sir William Hamilton, who was on active service in his chair of logic and metaphysics until his death in 1856. Assuredly, too, Kant and Hegel exerted a profound influence for many years after their death.

Victor Cousin, who was contemporary with Hegel, and outlived him by over thirty years, was the great interpreter of Kant. Born in 1792, Cousin was educated in Paris under Napoleon, at the Lycée Charlemagne and the École Normale Supérieure. In 1815 he was appointed assistant professor to Pierre Royer-Collard, who, besides being a philosopher, was a politician, and had been an active member of the Council of Five Hundred under the Directory. Royer-Collard had an immense influence on French philosophy, diverting it from the sceptical, sensualist, materialist tendencies of the latter part of the eighteenth century, and giving it the stamp of idealism. His views were inspired by the "Scottish School" of metaphysicians, particularly by the work of the great Reid, Professor of Moral Philosophy in the University of Glasgow in the late eighteenth century. Cousin brilliantly expounded the views of the Scottish School—Hutcheson, Adam Smith, Reid, Beattie, Ferguson, Dugald Stewart, especially Reid, "*à nos yeux un homme de génie.*" In 1817 Cousin travelled in Germany, experiencing the political and intellectual excitement of German society in the "Congress period." He returned from Germany deeply interested in the Kantian philosophy, on which he proceeded to deliver regular courses of lectures. He retained, however, his enthusiasm for the Scottish philosophers, who by "a sound metaphysic, supported by a severe psychology," had corrected the effects of the prevailing philosophy of sensation of the eighteenth century, and had produced a sound system of morals and politics.[1] He had an excellent course of lectures on the *philosophie écossaise*, which appeared in book form in 1857. The gist of the lectures was issued in 1842 in an excellent book *Leçons de philosophie sur Kant*. This book was published in England, in an English translation ("Chapman's Quarterly" series), in 1854. Cousin's greatest work, *Du Vrai, du beau, et du bien*, was published in 1854, and went through over twenty editions in the next twenty years.

After the July Revolution (1830), the high cultured *bourgeoisie* of France seemed to have entered the Promised Land. Plato's ideal of philosophers becoming kings, or at any rate statesmen, was nearly realized. Royer-Collard, Cousin's teacher, was President of the Chamber of Deputies in 1828, and thereafter was actively in politics until 1842. Victor Cousin was nominated a peer of France in 1832, and thus sat in the Upper House in the monarchy of Louis-Philippe. Guizot, a philosophic historian, and one of the most brilliant lecturers in the University of Paris, had the portfolio of Foreign Affairs in the Soult-Guizot Ministry of 1840–47, and was Prime Minister from 1847 to 1848. Barthélemy Saint-Hilaire, Professor of Greek and Roman Philosophy in the Collègede France from 1839 to 1851, and author of important works in Aristotelian scholarship, was a member of the National Assembly in the Second French Republic (1848–51). Imprisoned by Napoleon III at the *coup d'état* of 1851, and keeping vigorously to his Aristotelian and Sanskrit studies under the Second Empire, Barthélemy Saint-Hilaire reappeared in politics as a member of the National Assembly of Bordeaux in 1871. A distinguished political career was crowned by his becoming Minister of Foreign Affairs in Jules Ferry's

[1] V. Cousin, *Philosophie écossaise* (1857 edition), pp. 10–11.

Ministry of 1880–81. Charles, Comte de Rémusat, author of philosophical studies on Lord Herbert of Cherbury, Bacon, Locke, and other English philosophers, was Minister of the Interior under Thiers in 1840. Thirty-one years later Thiers again called on him, this time to be Minister of Foreign Affairs in the Third Republic, a post which he held from 1871 to 1873. Abel-François Villemain, like Barthélemy Saint-Hilaire and Rémusat a pupil of Cousin, was Professor of Eloquence at the Sorbonne, and author of a celebrated *Tableau de la littérature française au XVIIIme siècle.* He was deputy and afterwards peer of France under Louis-Philippe, and Minister of Public Instruction from 1839 to 1844. Jules Simon, a pupil of Cousin, and himself a professor of philosophy at the Sorbonne, was a member of the Chamber of Deputies in 1848 and in the National Assembly of the Second Republic. One of the chief orators of the Parliamentary Opposition in the Second Empire, he held various official positions in the Third Republic, and was Premier from 1876 to 1877, when he had a celebrated contest with the President, Marshal MacMahon.

This impressive catalogue, which could be reinforced, applies only to France. Nowhere else was the philosopher in politics anything like so prominent, for most other states were managed by aristocrats or professional bureaucrats. The German people had some excellent scholars in politics. Droysen, Professor of History at Kiel, Jena, Berlin, historian of the Prussian state, was one of the leaders of the Liberal movement of 1848 both in Holstein and in the Frankfort Parliament; Eduard Simson, Professor of Law at Königsberg, was also a man of 1848, President of the Frankfort Parliament, and head of the delegation which offered the Imperial Crown, fruitlessly, to Frederick William IV; Savigny, founder of the " historical method " of jurisprudence, was Prussian Minister for the Revision of Legislation from 1842 to 1848; Moritz

August von Bethmann-Hollweg, Professor of Law at Bonn from 1829 to 1848, was in the Prussian Diet from 1852 to 1855, and Minister of Cults in the " New Era " (partly Liberal) Ministry of 1858–62. Great Britain in the mid-century had scholars in politics, but, except John Stuart Mill, no genuine philosopher was among them before John Morley and Arthur James Balfour, who came later in the century, and were not, in fact, primarily philosophers. Holland's most distinguished statesman, Prime Minister from 1849 to 1853, from 1862 to 1866, and from 1871 to 1872, was Jan Thorbecke, Professor of Law and Political Science at Leyden. Madwig, perhaps the greatest Latin scholar of the nineteenth century, was a Danish Minister of State from 1848 to 1851, and in 1855 was elected President of the Danish Parliament, a post which he occupied for many years. His scholarly interests, however, were in textual criticism, rather than philosophy. It must be admitted that in the connexion of abstract thought with politics the French easily win the palm.

In Great Britain the influence of philosophers on public life is discernible not through their active participation in politics, as in France, but through the attention paid to their writings and to their ' systems.' The impulse given by Jeremy Bentham to the theory and practice of scientific legislation continued after his death in 1832. Even if the facile principle, the greatest good of the greatest number, does not fairly represent the views of Utilitarians in the mid-nineteenth century, nobody will deny that Utilitarianism was a real thing, and a powerful influence in legislation. The Utilitarians, who were also known in politics as ' Philosophic Radicals,' were never fanatical. They deliberately aimed at conducting their private affairs, as they aimed at conducting public affairs, by the guidance of reason, of common sense, without any trace of mysticism or prejudice. Victor Cousin wrote that common sense (*bon sens*) was the characteristic feature of the thought of the Scottish philosophers. Concerning the latest of that great line, Sir William Hamilton, Cousin wrote:

> The recent death [1856] of Monsieur Hamilton is a calamity which does not stop at the frontiers of his country. It will be for long keenly felt by all those who from one end of the world to the other have consecrated their lives to the study of philosophy and its history. The University of Edinburgh has just given these men a reason for consolation and hope, in entrusting the chair of M. Hamilton to one of his favourite pupils,[1] who will doubtless make it a pious duty to follow the tradition of his illustrious master and to maintain the integrity of Scottish philosophy before the European public. What distinguishes this philosophy, and gives it a particular character and interest, is good sense; and what in the Scottish School ceaselessly nourishes and renews good sense is the assiduous study of human nature, the high rank attributed to psychology among all the other branches of philosophic science.[2]

Though John Stuart Mill, whose *Examination of Sir William Hamilton's Philosophy* was published in 1865, was a somewhat hostile critic of the master, it is fair to assume that he was influenced by a system of philosophy so carefully studied. In a letter to Professor Bain of Aberdeen Mill wrote (January 7, 1863): "My plan has been to go deliberately through the whole writings of Hamilton, writing down in the form of notes the substance of what I as yet find to say on each point."[3] Mill as a philosopher exercised a direct influence on his age, particularly by his *System of Logic* (1843), *Principles of Political Economy* (1848), perhaps most of all by his *On Liberty* (1859) and *Considerations on Representative Government* (1861).

It was undoubtedly a philosophic age. Auguste Comte

[1] Alexander Campbell Fraser.

[2] *Philosophie écossaise*, p. xii.

[3] *Letters of John Stuart Mill*, edited by Hugh Elliot (1910), i, 271.

completed his *Cours de philosophie positive* in six volumes in 1842, his *Système de politique positive* in 1854. In his preface to volume i of the *Politique*, written in 1851 from 10 rue Monsieur le Prince, Comte tells how he gradually arrived at his 'system,' Positivism, the religion of humanity, sociology. The great event had taken place about twenty-five years earlier,[1] at the end of a long period of training:

> It followed from my own law of the hierarchy of sciences that Social Philosophy could not assume its true character and make its full weight felt, except so far as it was seen to rest on the general results of Natural Philosophy as partially worked out during the last three centuries. The problem of direct reconstruction of the spiritual power started a train of continuous thought lasting for eighty hours, the result being the conception of a complete systematization of Positive Philosophy as a necessary preliminary to the task. . . . Such, then, was the result of this decisive crisis, which was speedily followed by serious cerebral disturbance.

In other words, Comte had a serious mental affliction, from which, however, he fairly soon recovered. He then went on constructing his "really complete synthesis," of which "Love is naturally the one universal principle." Still writing in 1851, Comte noted:

> Ten years ago, in the fifth volume of my Philosophy, I made the frank confession that the Positive School still essentially consisted of myself alone. Since that time the position of Positivism has radically changed. Throughout Western Europe men's thoughts and feelings are more and more occupied with it, in spite of the formidable obstacles to its popular dissemination interposed by our unworthy Press.

The basis of Positivism, the new religion of humanity, was the restoration of feeling to its proper position usurped by eighteenth-century rationalism; it was "the culture

[1] In 1826, when Comte was twenty-eight.

of the heart, purified by Positivism from the self-absorbing chimæras"; [1] the supersession of revealed religion by proved religion. As priest of humanity Comte in 1850 "conferred" three social sacraments connected with birth, marriage, death. Though "intended ultimately for all classes," Comte expected his "new doctrine" for a long time to find its chief adherents among the "philosophers and workers." [2] The Positive motto was "Love, order, progress." The 'system' was, in effect, a classification or hierarchy of sciences of which sociology was the crown, the last of the series. The Second French Republic, which existed from 1848 to 1851 (the year in which Comte published his *System of Positive Polity*), represented the principles of Positivism—love, order, progress. Republicanism subordinated politics to morals. As the supreme object of love and reverence Comte, in place of the Deity, offered humanity, past, present, future.

The eminent Littré, whose fame is for ever secured as the author of the *Dictionnaire de la langue française*, was one of Comte's earliest supporters, and is mentioned by him in the *Politique positive* of 1851. Littré wrote several large works on Comte and Positivism. In England John Stuart Mill was attracted to all Comtism, except Comte's religious ritual. George Eliot, Herbert Spencer, John Morley, Professor E. S. Beesly, and Frederic Harrison were more or less avowed Positivists. George Henry Lewes, in his *History of Philosophy from Thales to Comte* (1853), called Comte the greatest thinker of modern times. The Positivist Society of Paris, founded in 1848, had associated Positivist Societies in most of the chief cities of Great Britain and the western states of the Continent. Comte's direct influence lasted throughout the nineteenth century among select groups of men of severe morality and thought.

[1] This and the other excerpts from Comte, given above, are taken from the Preface to the *System of Positive Polity*, translated by J. H. Bridges (1875), i, pp. ix–xxv.

[2] *Ibid.*, i, 3.

The reading public of the age had the taste for philosophy. Herbert Spencer, whose *Social Statics* was published in 1850, *Principles of Psychology* in 1855, and *First Principles* in 1862, earned a reasonably good living by writing large books of philosophy in unadorned, closely reasoned language. They were soon translated into most European languages. Darwin's *Origin of Species*, first published in 1859, went into its third edition and seventh thousand copy in 1861—a respectable if not a great sale for a work of science and philosophic thought.

Hippolyte-Adolphe Taine has been called the *grand penseur* of the age. He was not the greatest abstract thinker, but his work embraced the most aspects of life, and he was probably appreciated more by the reading public than any other thinker of the time. His inexhaustible patience, industry, perseverance of thought, won him ascendancy in the world of letters, something like that of Voltaire in the eighteenth century.

> The result was that the historians esteemed Taine particularly for his literary works, the men of letters extolled him principally for his philosophic works, and the philosophers relished principally his works of history. And Taine thought; he thought repeatedly; he thought all the time. And that without mediocrity.[1]

A product, as are so many of France's teachers, men of letters, and officials, of the École Normale Supérieure, Taine taught in provincial *lycées* under the Second Republic, but had to resign his post on account of undisguised lack of sympathy with the dictatorship of Louis Napoleon. Risking his career in the literary world of Paris in 1853, he made a living, and in time a fair fortune, by works of high scholarship. He was able to travel in Italy, Spain, and England, and to have a villa at Annecy, where, like Voltaire on Lake Leman, he dispensed elegant hospitality enriched by conversation and learning. Taine had the

[1] J. Ernest-Charles, *Les Samedis littéraires* (1903), i, 237.

amplitude of an eighteenth-century scholar and man of letters, and he had the instinct or ambition of the mid-nineteenth-century scholars to view his fields of research as a whole, to construct a system. Thus he wrote, or attempted to write, a complete description, explanation, and criticism of English literature, of France under the *ancien régime* and the Revolution, of modern French philosophy; and all this was done without pedantry, without dullness, without sacrifice of distinction of style. Only his contemporary Renan could compare with Taine in erudition and charm of expression. Taine's influence remained on a notable list of critics and men of letters who acknowledged him to be their master: Brunetière, Faguet, Lemaître, Anatole France, Barrès, Bourget, Vogüé.

Taine's greatest works are *Les Origines de la France contemporaine* and *Histoire de la littérature anglaise*, which, Sainte-Beuve said, should be called "the history of the English race and civilization as expressed by literature." On holiday from his wide and profound researches, Taine still observed, reflected, noted. Accordingly his travel-books are admirable descriptions of places and people—mainly of people or of places as affected by people, for Taine's thought is always *social*. Three journeys to England (1861, 1862, and 1871) produced *Notes sur l'Angleterre*, which was published in 1872, after the modest manner of French books, in small octavo with yellow-paper cover. The repetition of visits gave Taine the opportunity of testing and controlling his first observations and reflections. The result is a remarkable picture—serious, reflective, judicious—of England and the English in the decade 1860–70, against a background, so to speak, of comparison with France and the French. Travel-books of this kind—literary, scholarly, philosophic—were popular in the Victorian Age. Most of them were written by Englishmen, Frenchmen, or Americans; most had for their subject either England, France, or the United States.

They reached their apogee in a great work which went far beyond the scope of a travel-book and comprehended history, law, and sociology in its treatment—Bryce's *American Commonwealth*, first published in 1888.

The taste for philosophy, evidenced by the vogue of such a work as *Sartor Resartus*, or *Society and Solitude*, or *The Ring and the Book*, is noticeable in the drama of the sixties and seventies. The philosophic drama, of which *Hamlet* is the supreme type, was born again in Northern Europe in the work of Ibsen. With him the drama was not a comedy of manners—it was a metaphysic, a search for the ultimate realities of life. Ibsen, after some chequered years spent as a chemist's assistant, a university student (at Christiania), and a journalist, became director of a theatre at Bergen in 1852, and director of the National Theatre at Christiania (now Oslo) in 1857. After seven years he left Norway in disgust with his countrymen's failure to support the Danes in the controversy with the Germans over the Schleswig-Holstein question. His residence abroad began in April 1864, shortly after the opening of the Schleswig-Holstein War. From this time Ibsen, who was unmarried, lived a somewhat solitary life of thought, in Dresden, Munich, Rome, which in those days were cosmopolitan centres of art and literature. *Brand* came out in 1866, *Peer Gynt* in 1867, *Emperor and Galilean* in 1873, *The Pillars of Society* in 1877, *A Doll's House* in 1879, *Ghosts* in 1881, and *Hedda Gabler* in 1890. These dramas were written in Norwegian, and appeared at once in translations in German, French, English.

Ibsen was not a rebel against society; he could scarcely even be called a satirist. In his dramas, like Shakespeare, he takes sections of life, as it might happen anywhere. Then, by simple delineation, brief dialogue, rare incidents, accumulative emotion, he makes his hearers see and feel the deep problems of humanity.

Chapter IV

PROPHETS

WEBSTER'S *Dictionary of the English Language* (of which the great revised edition came out in 1847) defines prophet as " one who speaks for another, an interpreter." The word has generally been reserved for those individuals who declare the ultimate verities, or—to express the same thing in religious language—who reveal the will of God. It may be, of course, that certain individuals have been considered by the people of their age to be prophets who were not, in effect, true prophets. There appears to be no infallible test; belief in the truth of a prophetic message is a matter of faith. Those individuals whom contemporary and subsequent civilized opinion regards as speaking eternal verities are entitled to be considered prophets. Not every age has such individuals. Not every age is sympathetic to prophets. The Victorian Age, however, was markedly sympathetic. All over the world the peoples were waiting, and when the man with a message came they could not hear too much from him. This attentiveness to prophetic message was a feature not only of European or American society. It existed among the Africans, who received the Christian message or experienced a Mohammedan revival. It existed in India, where Ram Mohan Roy founded Brahma Samaj.[1] Even the ' closed ' empires of China and Japan had the waiting and awakening attitude, responsive to prophets.

The British had many prophets. It was an idealistic age, quick to react to the prophetic spark, to the diverse

[1] Ram Mohan Roy (1774–1833) is buried in Arno Vale cemetery, Bristol, England.

messages of Carlyle, Ruskin, Tennyson, Browning, Kingsley, Seeley. The United States had Emerson, who was also a prophet to the British people, and Whitman and Abraham Lincoln. France had Hugo and Renan; Russia, Tolstoi, Dostoievsky; Italy, Mazzini. Germany's prophetic age had passed away with the death of Jean-Paul Richter in 1825 and Goethe in 1832.

A prophetic age is one which has people with messages which are received and discussed. The early Victorian British families read and discussed Mr Carlyle's latest pamphlet, Mr Ruskin's latest work on art, Mr Tennyson's or Mr Browning's latest poem. They read Emerson's essays, and felt inspired by them even though the content of the essays soon vanished from the memory.

Carlyle and Ruskin were the chief prophets of the British from 1840 to about 1880—in Ruskin's case, indeed, for a few years longer. By the end of 1840 Carlyle's period of struggle was over. He had long ago come to the conviction of the "Everlasting Yea" and the "Everlasting No." Since 1834 he had been settled with Mrs Carlyle at 5 Cheyne Row, Chelsea. In 1837 *The French Revolution* appeared. In 1838 *Sartor* was published in book form, and the lectures on "Heroes and Hero-worship" were delivered in 1840. Carlyle had now arrived at what is a well-known stage in a prophet's career, when he becomes finally confident of the power that is in him, of the conviction that moves him, or, as the phrase goes, when he is conscious of his mission. Doubtless Carlyle was helped towards his conviction of prophetic mission, as a man may be helped, by a friend. After *Sartor* had come out in *Fraser's Magazine*, and while Carlyle was wrestling with *The French Revolution*, Emerson wrote from Concord:

> Believe, when you are weary, that you who stimulate and rejoice virtuous young men do not write in vain. And whatever betide us in the inexorable future, what is better than

to have awakened in many men the sweet sense of beauty, and to double the courage of virtue?[1]

A prophet need not have only one message. He may have several, and they need not be consistent with one another. He must feel his messages intensely, and be able to command attention for them. Carlyle had three messages: contempt for shams, admiration for heroes, distrust of democracy—that is, of extreme democracy, for he was a decent *bourgeois* democrat himself.

The attack on shams is contained chiefly in the first four chapters—that is, Book I—of *The French Revolution.* There had once been reality in the French monarchy, when the King was "well-named the Kön-ning, Canning or Man that was Able." This was the time from "rough Clovis" to Louis le Grand. By the time, however, that Louis XV lay dying kingship was (according to Carlyle) quackery:

> But of those decadent ages in which no Ideal either grows or blossoms? When Belief and Loyalty have passed away, and only the cant and false echo of them remains; and all Solemnity has become Pageantry; and the Creed of persons in authority has become one of two things: an Imbecility or a Machiavellism? Alas, of these ages World History can take no notice; they have to become compressed more and more, and finally suppressed in the Annals of Mankind; blotted out as spurious—which indeed they are. Hapless ages: wherein, if ever in any, it is an unhappiness to be born. To be born, and to learn only, by every tradition and example, that God's universe is Belial's and a Lie; and the 'Supreme Quack' the hierarch of men![2]

Heroes attracted Carlyle because they were real men, and saw through or cut through shams and humbugs:

> Faith is loyalty to some inspired Teacher, some spiritual Hero. And what therefore is loyalty proper, the life-breath

[1] *The Correspondence of Thomas Carlyle and Ralph Waldo Emerson* (edited by C. E. Norton, 1883), i, 83.

[2] *The French Revolution* (1898 edition), i, 10–11.

of all society, but an effluence of Hero-worship, submissive admiration for the truly great? Society is founded on Hero-worship.[1]

The hero does not necessarily appear merely because he is wanted:

> Alas, we have known Times *call* loudly enough for their great man; but not find him when they called! He was not there; Providence had not sent him; the Time, *calling* its loudest, had to go down to confusion and wreck because he would not come when called.
>
> For if we will think of it, no Time need have gone to ruin, could it have *found* a man great enough, a man wise and good enough: wisdom to discern truly what the Time wanted, valour to lead it on the right road thither: these are the salvation of any Time.[2]

Carlyle will not have it, as Tolstoi held, that history is made by the common man, by the masses, who by their unspoken tendencies and judgments direct the course of events. He declares roundly: " The History of the World, I said already, was the Biography of Great Men." Yet, clearly, the great man could not do anything without the common man. The great thinker, the seer, " awakes the slumbering capability of all into Thought. It is ever the way with the Thinker, the spiritual Hero. *What he says, all men were not far from saying, were longing to say.*" [3]

So, after all, the age and the people have a good deal to do with the making, or at least with the development, of a hero. " The most significant feature in the history of an epoch is the manner it has of welcoming a Great Man." It will never welcome a sham—at any rate not for long. Stories of legerdemain may have gathered round the name of Mohammed, but they do not account for the prevalence of Mohammedanism.

[1] *Heroes and Hero-worship* (1898 edition), p. 12.

[2] *Ibid.*, p. 13.

[3] *Ibid.*, p. 21. The italics are mine.

A false man found a religion? Why, a false man cannot build a brick house! . . . A man must conform himself to Nature's laws, *be* verily in communion with Nature and the truth of things, or Nature will answer him, No, not at all! Speciosities are specious—ah me!—a Cagliostro, many Cagliostros, prominent world-leaders, do prosper by their quackery, for a day. It is like a forged bank-note; they get it passed out of *their* worthless hands; others, not they, have to smart for it. Nature bursts up in fire-flames, French Revolutions and such like, proclaiming with terrible veracity that the forged notes are forged.[1]

Napoleon Bonaparte was something of a hero up to a certain point, and then became a sham. His first work, achieving democracy—*la carrière ouverte aux talens*—was good:

Napoleon, in his first period, was a true Democrat. . . . Such a faith in Democracy, yet hatred of anarchy, it is that carries Napoleon through all his great work. Through his brilliant Italian Campaigns, onwards to the Peace of Leoben, one would say, his inspiration is: 'Triumph to the French Revolution, assertion of it against these Austrian Simulacra that pretend to call it a Simulacrum!' . . . To bridle-in that great devouring, self-devouring French Revolution. . . . Through Wagrams, Austerlitzes; triumph after triumph,—he triumphed so far. . . .

But at this point, I think, the fatal charlatan-element got the upper hand. He apostatized from his old faith in Facts, took to believing in Semblances; strove to connect himself with Austrian Dynasties, Popedoms, with the old false Feudalities which he once saw clearly to be false;—considered that *he* would found 'his Dynasty' and so forth; that the enormous French Revolution meant only that! The man was 'given up to strong delusion, that he should believe a lie.'[2]

The Duke of Weimar was right when he said, and kept on saying, that Napoleonism would not last, because "it

[1] *Heroes and Hero-worship*, p. 44.

[2] *Ibid.*, p. 241.

was unjust, a falsehood." In this comfortable faith, that the false would perish and the truth triumph, the early Victorians listened to Carlyle, himself a prophet. They were waiting: "I said, the Great Man was always as lightning out of Heaven; the rest of men waited for him like fuel, and then they too would flame." [1] He concluded these six lectures, delivered in Albemarle Street, Mayfair, in the month of May 1840. "The accomplished and distinguished, the beautiful, the wise, something of what is best in England, have listened patiently to my rude words." It was not exactly a democratic audience.

After *Heroes* came the pamphlets on democracy. Before he had written *Heroes*, however, Carlyle had already declared in *Sartor Resartus* his sympathy with the common man, whom he places in honour just below the artist and thinker:

> Two men I honour, and no third. First, the toilworn Craftsman that with earth-made Implement laboriously conquers the Earth, and makes her man's. . . . Hardly-entreated Brother! For us was thy back so bent, for us were thy straight limbs and fingers so deformed: thou wast our Conscript, on whom the lot fell, and fighting our battles wert so marred. . . .
>
> A second man I honour, and still more highly: Him who is seen toiling for the spiritually indispensable.[2]

Carlyle goes farther, and seems prepared to place highest of all the union of manual toiler and spiritual thinker:

> Unspeakably touching is it, however, when I find both dignities united. . . . Sublimer in this world know I nothing than a Peasant Saint, could such now anywhere be met with. Such a one will take thee back to Nazareth itself.[3]

Remembering the distinguished part that tailors and cobblers had taken in the radical politics of early nine-

[1] *Heroes and Hero-worship*, p. 77 (from "The Hero as Prophet," *ad fin.*).
[2] *Sartor Resartus* (1897 edition), p. 181. [3] *Ibid.*, p. 182.

teenth-century England, and thinking, perhaps, of Francis Place, breeches-maker of Charing Cross, Carlyle wrote:

> Turning the corner of a lane in the Scottish Town of Edinburgh, I came upon a Signpost, whereon stood written that such and such a one was 'Breeches-Maker to his Majesty;' and stood painted the Effigies of a Pair of Leather Breeches, and between the knees these memorable words, *Sic itur ad astra.* Was not this the martyr prison-speech of a Tailor sighing indeed in bonds, yet sighing towards deliverance, and prophetically appealing to a better day? [1]

No society, Carlyle said, ever existed without an aristocracy and a teaching class. And, writing in 1843 (*Past and Present*), he declared that the convulsive struggles of the last fifty years had made one thing clear:

> That Europe requires a real Aristocracy and a real Priesthood, or it cannot continue to exist. . . .
>
> Huge French Revolutions, Napoleonisms, then Bourbonisms with their corollary of Three Days, finishing in unfinal Louis-Philippisms: all this ought to be didactic! All this may have taught us that False Aristocracies are insupportable: that No-Aristocracies, Liberty-and-Equalities are impossible: that true Aristocracies are at once indispensable and not easily attained.[2]

This paragraph contained a correct prophecy about the transitory nature of Louis-Philippe's kingship, which ended five years later. As regards the kind of aristocracy that he wanted, Carlyle only insists that it must be a working aristocracy. The great landed nobles of England who maintained "insane Corn Laws," and who, in many cases, had incomes far larger than the rents and taxes of the Duke of Weimar, did nothing. Yet:

> The Duke of Weimar, with these incomings, had to govern, judge, defend, everyway administer *his* Dukedom.

[1] *Sartor Resartus*, p. 232.
[2] *Past and Present* (1897 edition), p. 241.

He does this as few others did; and he improves lands besides all this, makes river-embankments, maintains not soldiers only but Universities and Institutions;—and in his Court were these four men: Wieland, Herder, Schiller, Goethe.[1]

Carlyle reckoned that this Carl August of Weimar, who reigned from 1758 to 1828, " did more for the Culture of his Nation than all the English Dukes and *Duces* now extant." Carlyle did not wish to abolish the English aristocracy, but to indoctrinate it with the love of work. " *If* our Actual Aristocracy, appointed ' Best-and-Bravest,' will be wise, how inexpressibly happy for us! If not, the voice of God from the whirlwind is very audible to me." [2]

All this points to a kind of democratic aristocracy. Liberty, " the true liberty of a man," consists in finding out his proper life-work and then doing it. This is not democracy, " which means despair of finding any Heroes to govern you, and contented putting up with the want of them." Carlyle had not much faith in universal suffrage:

> The notion that a man's liberty consists in giving his vote at election-hustings, and saying, ' Behold, now I too have my twenty-thousandth part of a Talker in our National Palaver; will not all the gods be good to me?—is one of the pleasantest! . . . This liberty turns out, before it have long continued in action, with all men flinging up their caps round it, to be, for the Working Millions a liberty to die by want of food; for the Idle Thousands and Units, alas, a still more fatal liberty to live in want of work: to have no earnest duty to do in this God's World any more.[3]

In one passage of *Past and Present* Carlyle, perhaps feeling rather more atrabiliar than usual, seems to compare Parliamentary assemblies to the chattering of apes. Alluding to the " grand problem," the difficulty " of finding

[1] *Past and Present*, p. 284. [2] *Ibid.*, p. 285. [3] *Ibid.*, p. 219.

Government by your Real Superiors," he writes: "These Apes, chattering on the branches by the Dead Sea, never got it learned."

The Chartists, with their famous "Six Points" or demands—universal suffrage, payment of members, vote by ballot, annual Parliaments, abolition of property qualification, equal electoral districts—only impressed him as vehemently calling attention to the "Condition of the working classes." The new Poor Law (1834) had some value "as the probable preliminary of *some* general charge to be taken of the lowest classes by the higher." The solution of the "Condition of England Question" was not in votes and ballot-boxes, not in *laissez-faire*. Carlyle foresaw the social dangers and abuses from complete industrial *laissez-faire*. The solution of the Condition of England Question was that the aristocracy should attend to their duty, and not regard the rest of the people as bound to them only by the cash nexus. Surprisingly, Carlyle ends this discussion, his discussion of Chartism, with what would now be called a great imperialist plan, something which certain high minds to-day think that they have discovered:

> To the English People in World History, there have been, shall I prophesy, Two grand tasks assigned? . . . The grand industrial task of conquering some half or more of this Terraqueous Planet for the use of man; then secondly, the grand Constitutional task of sharing, in some pacific endurable manner, the fruit of the said conquest, and showing all people how it might be done.

He concludes:

> The Canadian Forests stand unfelled, boundless plains and prairies unbroken with the plough; on the west and on the east green desert spaces never yet made white with corn; and to the overcrowded little western nook of Europe, our Terrestrial Planet, nine-tenths of it yet vacant or tenanted by nomades, is still crying, Come and till me, come and reap

me! And in an England with wealth and means of moving, such as no nation ever before had.[1]

In 1867, when Disraeli's Representation of the People Bill was going through Parliament, Carlyle published in *Macmillan's Magazine* a warning and prophesy in a long essay called "Shooting Niagara: and After?" The Bill was a very modest one. Since the great Reform Act of 1832, which gave the Parliamentary vote to the "£10 householder," there had been no change in the franchise. The Bill of 1867 was to give the vote to the "£10 lodger." Disraeli himself, though it was his own Bill, called it a leap in the dark. In Carlyle's eyes it was "shooting Niagara." And what afterwards? He ventured on a prophecy, or, rather, three prophecies:

> Three things seem to be agreed upon by gods and men, at least by English men and gods; certain to happen, and even now in visible course of fulfilment.
>
> 1. *Democracy* to complete itself, to go to the full length of its course, towards the Bottomless or into it . . . till we have seen where it will lead us to, and whether there will *then* be any return possible or none.
>
> 2. That in a limited time, say fifty years hence, the Church, all Churches and so-called religions, the Christian religion itself, shall have deliquesced—into Liberty of Conscience, Progress of Opinion, Progress of Intellect, Philanthropic Movement, and other aqueous residues, of a vapid, badly scented character;—and shall, like water spilt upon the ground, trouble nobody considerably thenceforth, but evaporate at its leisure.
>
> 3. That in lieu thereof, there shall be Free Trade, in all senses, and to all lengths: unlimited Free Trade,—which some take to mean, 'Free racing, ere long with unlimited speed, in the career of *Cheap and Nasty*.'[2]

The fifty years (and more) within which Carlyle prophe-

[1] *Chartism* (1839 edition), *ad fin.*

[2] "Shooting Niagara: and After?" in *Critical and Miscellaneous Essays* (1899 edition), v, 1–2.

sied that these things would happen have passed. Have they happened?

1. Complete democracy—that is, "count of heads to be the divine court of appeal on every question"—has not been brought about, for democracy (wherever it exists) recognizes certain checks and balances, and operates through some kind of governing class.

2. The Churches, the Christian religion itself, have not "deliquesced" amid universal tolerance.

3. There is anything but universal Free Trade. And it is in countries least open to Free Trade, in countries aiming at economic sufficiency, that goods, though not cheap, are nastiest. For there people have to be content with 'substitutes,' instead of the foreign articles which could be obtained under conditions of Free Trade from more favourable soils and climates.

To recognize that the prophecies have not been fulfilled is not necessarily to condemn Carlyle. The course of events is not predestined, and prophets are not infallible. What is important in shaping the course of history is that men and women who have a message should speak it forth, and that the 'public' should attend to messages, discuss them, consider them, criticize them. The grand quality of the early Victorian Age was that it was (with other qualities) an age of prophets—men with a message, and not disregarded. Thus the age had the springs of progress in itself. Carlyle, in spite of his assurance and dogmatism, was not without hope, which he placed in the aristocracy—the titular aristocracy, "a body of brave men and of beautiful polite women," and the *aristocracy of nature* (speculative and practical), infinitely the more interesting. There is always this second kind of aristocracy, and democracy exists solidly and functions harmoniously so far as it recognizes this. Carlyle placed such faith as he had in this recognition, so that mankind should have guidance. The guides of the future should comprise the traditional governing class, the aristocrat by title " coalescing nobly with his two brothers, the Aristocrats by nature"—the man of genius, speculative and practical. " By nature and position they are visibly a kind of Kings." [1]

[1] " Shooting Niagara: and After? " in *Critical and Miscellaneous Essays*, v, 45–46.

Chapter V

HISTORIANS

"It is part of my creed," Carlyle wrote in his first letter to Emerson, "that the only poetry is history, could we tell it aright." [1] Benedetto Croce does not make quite so sweeping a statement as this, but he calls history an "eternal poem."

It is a remarkable fact that before the eighteen-forties there was very little history written. The educated gentry of the seventeenth century read Livy, Cæsar, Xenophon, and Plutarch, in the original or in translation. Some knowledge of English history they got from the chronicles of Stow or Holinshed, which provided Shakespeare with the facts for his historical plays. The eighteenth-century gentry read ancient history in the classics, and there was Clarendon's *History of the Rebellion*, Burnet's *History of My Own Times*, Voltaire's *Charles XII* and *Siècle de Louis XIV*. Scholars, even schoolboys like the precocious Gibbon, could find material in the dusty folios of Renaissance historians, learned treatises or collections on the Greek or Roman or early Christian world. There were also the "Quarto Historians"—Hume on England, Robertson on Charles V, Orme on India, and the majestic Gibbon himself. Gibbon was at once translated into French, German, and Italian. The early nineteenth century produced Alison's *History of Europe* (from the French Revolution to the restoration of the Bourbons). This was published in ten volumes between 1833 and 1842. Disraeli said that it was written to prove that Providence was on the side of

[1] *Correspondence of Carlyle and Emerson*, i, 25. The following Croce reference is from *The History of Europe in the Nineteenth Century*, p. 36.

the Tories. Nobody reads Alison now. A contemporary historian, with a genius for describing battles, was William Napier, who, after having served in the Peninsular War, wrote its history, published between 1828 and 1840. And there was Scott's *Napoleon* (nine vols. in 1827), and *Tales of a Grandfather* in 1828; and Hazlitt's *Napoleon* in 1828; and Lockhart's *Napoleon* in 1829. The first volume of Bancroft's *History of the United States*, now long ago superseded, though still good reading, was published in 1834. Of the whole lot of histories written from the time of Hume down to Lockhart's *Napoleon* only Gibbon is really read at the present time, though Hallam's *Constitutional History of England* is well worth the attention of any scholar or other citizen.

In the eighteen-forties a different account is rendered; or, rather, the era of great historians begins a little earlier, for it had a forerunner in Carlyle, whose *French Revolution* was published in 1837. Thiers' *Histoire du Consulat et de l'Empire* began to appear in 1845. Ranke's *German History in the Time of the Reformation* (*Deutsche Geschichte im Zeitalter der Reformation*) came out from 1839 to 1847, but his *History of the Popes* (*Die Römischen Päpste, ihre Kirche und ihr Staat im 16 und 17 Jahrhundert*), still very readable (and historically valuable), if not much read, had been issued from 1834 to 1837. Sybel's *History of the First Crusade* (*Geschichte des ersten Kreuzzuges*), a brilliant small work, was published in 1841. In 1859 Sybel founded and produced the first volume of the great quarterly *Historische Zeitschrift*. Palacky's *History of the Bohemian People* (in Czech and German) began to appear comparatively early (1836), though it was not completed until 1867. Macaulay's *History of England*, the most magnificent work of literature and scholarship since Gibbon, and without any other peer in English literature, was published (first two volumes) in 1848. Carlyle's *Frederick the Great* came out at intervals from 1858 to 1865. Parkman's histories of the English and French in North America started with *The Conspiracy of Pontiac* in 1851. Kinglake's *Invasion of the Crimea* began to appear in 1863. Froude's twelve volumes of the *History of England from the Fall of Cardinal Wolsey to the Defeat of the Spanish Armada* were published from 1856 to 1870. After this the era of great historians who were great men of letters was past, though John Richard Green's *Short History of the English People* (1874) had the magic of genius, as well as scholarship, in it, and later Treitschke, Sorel, de la Gorce, Churchill, and Trevelyan wrote in the tradition of the "grand style." No other period, however, in England or on the Continent could match the period from the late thirties to the early seventies, distinguished by Carlyle's *French Revolution* at the beginning and Froude's *History* at the end. These mid-century historians were men of genius, scholars, men of letters; and their works were read by the general public. They wrote 'definitive' works, in many volumes, and were widely read. Yet there was one historian, one of the most learned, John Acton (raised to the peerage as Lord Acton in 1869), who had published nothing but some essays in *The Rambler* before 1877, and who never, indeed, had a large body of published work.

What caused this great outburst of historical writing, this period of thirty-five years (1835–70) when history was written on the grand scale, and was literature? It is impossible to say what causes produce the rise of great literature. It may be possible, however, to indicate why great writers turned their attention to history, and studied it thoroughly and with imagination: that they did this was owing to Sir Walter Scott. The Wizard of the North, who published *Waverley* in 1814, aroused the historical sense of all Europe and America. History ceased to be a chronicle—a dreary chronicle: it was seen as a romance, the "eternal poem" of mankind on this earth.

Alongside of the historic-romantic movement of the

late eighteenth and early nineteenth century, in which Scott was the most prominent figure, there was a great revival of philosophy through the teaching of Kant and Hegel. Philosophy, the "love of wisdom," is also the search for reality, for truth. History too is the quest for reality, the search for truth. History is philosophy directed to the search for truth and reality in the life of man as he has lived through the ages. The 'Age of Great Historians' (1835–70) would not have taken place without Gibbon's *Decline and Fall of the Roman Empire* (1776), Kant's *Critique of Pure Reason* (1781), Scott's *Waverley* (1814). The impetus of these men produced the great collections of historical documents, the materials of historical study—Pertz's *Monumenta Germaniæ Historica*, begun in 1826, Guizot's *Mémoires relatives à l'histoire de France*, in 1823, the British Rolls Series, in 1858.

Under the pen of the historian, it may be said, as Macaulay says of Milton's poetry, the past becomes present and the distant near. Indeed, for the historian there is no essential difference between past and present, or, rather, everything that he deals with is past—recent or remote past. The present, by the time he starts to write about it, has become the recent past. It is only more vivid to him than is the remote past because the 'documents' are better. He has himself experienced the recent past by living in it, and so he feels this recent past to be 'present.' The remote past, however, becomes equally present to him if he can find enough documents about it and time to study them sympathetically. Italy in the Age of the Antonines or Romulus Augustulus was as 'present' to Gibbon as the France of the Consulate and Empire was to Thiers. Anybody who reads the third chapter of Macaulay's history will realize that English society of the reign of Charles II was as 'present' to Macaulay as was the English society of William IV or Victoria which Creevey and Greville were describing in their 'contemporary' histories day by day. Croce explains this:

> If we look more closely we perceive that this history already formed, which is called, or which we would like to call, 'non-contemporary' or 'past' history, if it really is history—that is to say, if it really means something and is not an empty echo—is also *contemporary*, and does not in any way differ from the other. As in the former case, the condition of its existence is that the deed of which the history is told must vibrate in the soul of the historian, or (to employ the expression of professed historians) that the documents are before the historian, and that they are intelligible. That a narrative or series of narratives of the fact is united and mingled with it merely means that the fact has proved more rich, not that it has lost its quality of being present.[1]

Sir Walter Scott, a great historian, had in his historical novels taken the facts of contemporary or remoter Scottish history and found that, under the spell of his imagination, they yielded a rich harvest of romance. They yielded this harvest because he read deeply in the documents of Scottish history, and so experienced the past as vividly as the present. The facts "vibrated in his soul"; the past was present and the distant near. As a novelist he added more facts—fictitious ones—to the authentic narratives disclosed or suggested in the documents. But the great historians in the post-Romantic Age—Carlyle, Thiers, Macaulay, and the rest—had no need to invent facts in order to enrich their narratives. As they studied the documents the 'past' became more 'present' to them. Their romantic and philosophic minds selected, reproduced, and interpreted the section of past life which was the object of their study. Therefore the public of the mid-nineteenth century read the great historical narratives of Carlyle, Thiers, or Macaulay as the previous generation had read the historical novels of Scott; but in reading the histories

[1] *On History*, translated by D. Ainslie (1921), p. 12.

they surely came rather nearer to the reality, to life itself, than the previous generation had done by reading only the novels. For history *is* life:

> Once the indissoluble link between life and thought in history has been effected the doubts that have been expressed as to the *certainty* and the *utility* of history disappear altogether in a moment. How could that which is a *present* producing of our spirit ever be uncertain? How could that knowledge be *useless* which solves a problem that has come forth from the bosom of life? [1]

Except for Gibbon's *Decline and Fall*, Carlyle's *French Revolution* was the first work of genuinely imaginative—that is, living—history written in England. It was published in 1837, and took the public by storm. There were still people alive who remembered the terrible times of the French Revolution, and they recognized the vibrant reality of Carlyle's work. The public took to reading history with the same zest as that with which they had read Scott's novels. The first and second volume of Macaulay's *History of England from the Accession of James II* (so called, but actually from the accession of Charles II) came out early in December 1848. The booksellers took up the whole of the first edition of 3000 copies on publication. Within six months it had gone into its fifth edition. It is believed that about 200,000 'pirated' copies were sold in the United States within twelve months. There was no profit to the author on pirated editions, but Macaulay did very well out of the English editions. A cheque for £20,000, sent to him by Messrs Longmans in March 1856 on account of his royalties on volumes iii and iv is believed to have been the largest single sum sent to any author down to that time. The *History* was in the best sense of the word popular, though anything but superficial. Macaulay's method of research has been thus described:

[1] Croce, *On History*, p. 15.

To the making of every paragraph went the reading of perhaps a score of books and a hundred pamphlets, correspondence with the possessors of facts and figures which could not be gleaned from the printed page—foreign antiquaries, custodians of manuscripts, registrars of births and burials—and often a visit in person to some obscure or remote spot which he was describing. We see him toiling up the slope of Killiecrankie, testing the time the English army took to climb the pass, or knocking at the doors of Londonderry cottages to inquire of aged inhabitants traditions of the siege told them by their fathers, and filling all the while his teeming notebooks. Most of all we picture him in that book-lined upper room in the Albany, working from seven in the morning till seven at night, or surrounded by pamphlets in the King's Library in the British Museum.[1]

Carlyle, curiously, did not share the public approbation of the *History*. He wrote to Lady Ashburton after reading the first two volumes:

> I was, if anything, a little disappointed; little of the Book, except that chapter on the old state of England, quite equal even to men's hopes of Macaulay. Pleasant, easy reading too; clear, definite, every corner of it, but without concentration, modulation, a formless *flat*—flat like a Russian Steppe; pleasant grass to gallop on, but without stream, without mountain, without feature, grass, grass to the uttermost horizon: in fine, *no story* to be told, and nothing but a *Whig Evangelist* to tell it us! I was not sorry to end, and shall not burn to begin again! The true " History of England," so far as England has a *History* in those scandalous years, will turn out to be very brief (I apprehend) and to lie leagues below all that—where T. My., I perceive, will never find it or seek it.—Did men ever look at such a series of empty *clockcases* as these " characters " one and all are? *This* is *not* their likeness, I say; why take their likeness at all?

This is pretty hard hitting, though even Carlyle excepts from his adverse criticism the celebrated Chapter III—

[1] Arthur Bryant, *Macaulay* (1932), p. 95.

which he calls " on the old state of England "—the perfect chapter on social history which has restored to us the England of 1685.

Macaulay was a Whig, and his popular history, in four quarto volumes, fortified the British *bourgeoisie* in their attachment to Parliamentary government and the *limited* monarchy derived from the principles of 1688. Carlyle was not a Whig. He had great confidence in Sir Robert Peel, and was a curious, but not altogether uncommon, combination of Toryism and Radicalism, with, like Edmund Burke, a great respect for the territorial working aristocracy. He tried to show forth his doctrine of history as the work of great *men* (as distinct from shams or what Burke called " solemn plausibilities ") in *The History of Frederick the Great*, Friedrich or Frédéric, as he variously calls his hero. The British public, and the German public, read *Frederick*, the first two volumes of which came out in 1858, with pleasure. The English public learned through *Frederick* to have some understanding of Prussia and sympathy with the Prussians such as they had not had before. This, however, is not its particular merit, which is nothing less than that of being the epic of the eighteenth century.

Frederick took thirteen years in the writing. Carlyle started making studies for it in 1851, and for the next three years " read himself " into the eighteenth century through a dreary mass of dull historians, starting with Preuss's five-volume *Friedrich der Grosse: eine Lebensgeschichte*. To Lady Ashburton he wrote (November 14, 1851): " Frederic, the more I know of him, pleases me the better; a Man and King whose love of *reality* was instinctive and supreme. . . . I find him the last of our Kings." He continued to wrestle for thirteen years with his Preuss, Schlosser, Podewils, Archenholz, and all the rest. What a labour! To Emerson he confides in 1853:

> I have sat here in my garret, wriggling and wrestling on the worst terms with a Task that I cannot do, that generally seems to me not worth doing and yet *must* be *done*. These are truly the terms. I never had such a business in my life before. Frederick himself is a pretty little man to me, veracious, courageous, invincible in his small sphere; but he does not rise into the empyrean regions, or kindle my heart round him at all; and his history, upon which there are wagon-loads of dull bad books, is the most dislocated, unmanageably incoherent, altogether dusty, barren and beggarly production of the modern Muses as given hitherto. No man of *Genius* ever saw him with eyes, except twice, Mirabeau, for half an hour each time. And the wretched books have no *indexes*, no precision of detail; and I am far away from Berlin and the seat of information;—and, in brief, shall be beaten miserably with this unwise enterprise in my old days; *and* (in fine) will consent to be so, and get through it if I can before I die.[1]

Frederick and Voltaire (Carlyle wrote to Emerson), were " the celestial element of the poor eighteenth century." In 1855 the Ashburtons put Addiscombe Farm at Carlyle's disposal. He found a complete edition, sixty volumes, of Voltaire at Addiscombe, and he spent long, delightful hours reading in the clear light of that genius. This was a relief from the dreary chaos of histories of the wars of Fritz. He was at Addiscombe " as in La Trappe." Mrs Carlyle stayed at home in Cheyne Row, coming out now and then by train to see how Carlyle was faring; and Carlyle rode in to Cheyne Row on his nag when his wife bade him come to be present at luncheon or dinner with some visitors—with Browning or Clough. The Voltaire part of *Frederick* is one of the most lively, sparkling, and romantic. The rest of the writing seems to have been one long, frightful struggle; two years after it was all over Carlyle wrote to Emerson (January 27, 1867): " The truth is, I was nearly killed by that hideous book on

[1] *Correspondence of Carlyle and Emerson*, ii, 246–247.

Friedrich." When publication was well under way, and volume succeeded volume, Emerson, to whom Carlyle sent presentation copies, wrote:

> You have lighted the glooms, and engineered away the pits whereof you poetically pleased yourself with complaining, in your sometime letter to me, clean of it, according to the high Italian rule, and have let sunshine and pure air enfold the scene.

Emerson continued, perhaps over-enthusiastically:

> It is Mankind's Bill of Rights and Duties, the royal proclamation of Intellect ascending the throne, announcing its good pleasure, that, hereafter, as *heretofore*, and now once for all, the World should be governed by Common Sense and law of Morals, or shall go to ruin.[1]

The great work proceeded fairly steadily. There was a portentous amount of reading to be done in the soundproof room which Carlyle had constructed (1853) at the top of his house in Cheyne Row, and in the British Museum, where apparently he found better books on German than on English history. " I had much much rather have had an English hero, if it pleased Panizzi and Company—which alas it does not nor can do! " Anthony Panizzi, an exile in London since the Piedmont insurrection of 1821, was Keeper of Printed Books at the British Museum. Carlyle continues:

> I find Panizzi—the preposterous Panizzi mismanaging the British Museum Library, and already known to us—the true representative of English dilettantism, Pedantry, Babblement, and hollow dining and drinking Museum of so-called " Literature " in this epoch.[2]

The long hours' study made his liver worse, but he kept going by riding in and around Chelsea and when he was on a visit in Surrey with the Ashburtons. He conceived a

[1] *Correspondence of Carlyle and Emerson*, ii, 278–279.

[2] October 14, 1851; in D. A. Wilson, *The Life of Carlyle* (1929), v, 23.

great admiration for Prussian soldiery, after reading so much about them and having seen something of them when he visited Germany in 1852. To Emerson he wrote (June 25, 1852): " I confess also to a real love for Frederick's dumb followers: the Prussian *Soldiery*. I often say to myself, ' Were not here the real priests and virtuous and martyrs of that loud-babbling, rotten generation? ' " In Germany he had liked " their intelligent *silence*, with the touches of effective Spartanism I saw or fancied in them."

While the English historians of the Macaulay, Carlyle, Froude, school were making literature in the grand style there was another great school of historians in France whose works had European fame. These men were all contemporary, all born in the Revolutionary-Napoleonic era: Augustin Thierry (1795–1856), François Mignet (1796–1884), Adolphe Thiers (1797–1877), Jules Michelet (1798–1874), Henri Martin (1810–83). Guizot was older than all these: he was born in 1787, just before the Revolution, and lived until 1874. Not a literary genius, less imaginative than the other five, Guizot nevertheless is the only one of the group whose work is still regularly used in Great Britain. The Modern History School in the University of Oxford has in the last thirty years had Guizot's *Lectures on the History of Civilization* or his *History of Oliver Cromwell and the English Commonwealth* among its prescribed books of study.

All these French historians were by profession either teachers or lawyers, and all of them supplemented their modest incomes by doing a good deal of journalism, without detriment to their scholarship. They were enormously industrious, produced, each of them, twenty or thirty large volumes of learned history, and yet had time to contribute fugitive articles to the Press, to engage in politics, to attend the brilliant *salons* which occupied the evenings of fashionable and intellectual Paris society.

Thierry was their master. His *Conquête de l'Angleterre* (1825) is an exhibition of vast learning and minute investigation into the origins of medieval society. He narrated the life of a people for five centuries or more, writing epic history from a minute study of chronicles and legends, and aiming not only at eloquent narrative, but at philosophic exposition and comment. In the bewildering multitude of facts of the past he saw one age after another assume distinct character and tendencies; the forces and laws which, for good or ill, governed society became clear to the eye of the scholar.

Mignet was an austere historian, an archivist, who wrote an admirable *History of the French Revolution* (1824). Michelet, who was a teacher at a boys' school, the Collège Rollin, and later professor in the Collège de France, wrote a nineteen-volume *History of France* (1833–67), which Lanson calls a veritable "resurrection of the past."[1] Michelet was passionate and poetic. With vast erudition, minute examination of sources, he had colour, imagination, a vibrant style. He was not *bourgeois* like the rest, but a man of the people, filled with love and sympathy for the people, weeping and rejoicing with them: "*son histoire est un chef-d'œuvre de l'art romantique.*"[2] His story of the life of Joan of Arc is a grand poem. Compared with Michelet's glowing pages, Henri Martin's sober fifteen-volume *History of France* (1833–36) seems to offer little attraction; yet it is an informing history, and the reader acquires a firm grasp of French life and institutions convincingly displayed through the ages by Martin's competent pen and mind.

Thiers, however, is the grandest figure in this great historical group. The squat little man with the thin, harsh voice had indomitable spirit, industry, knowledge. Seven years old at the end of the Consulate, when Napoleon was

[1] G. Lanson, *Histoire de la littérature française* (1898 edition), p. 1006.
[2] *Ibid.*, p. 1009.

proclaimed Emperor, eighteen when the Empire fell, he would remember the things he wrote about. The Consulate, the Empire, the Continental System, the wars in Germany, the Moscow expedition, the Hundred Days, Waterloo—he had lived through these events. The people themselves—Napoleon, the marshals, councillors of State, Pope and priests, conscripts, citizens—he knew them, as it were, personally, even if he had not seen them all.

In 1815 Thiers went to the law school at Aix in Provence, was called to the Bar, and in 1821 went up to Paris with his fellow law student Mignet. He made a living by journalism, wrote articles for the *Constitutionnel*, attracted the attention of eminent people, including Talleyrand. The *salons* began to open to him. He studied prodigiously in the Royal Library. He talked with men who had attended the Estates-General at Versailles, who had seen Louis XVI executed, who had followed Napoleon to Austerlitz, to Moscow. In 1823 the first two volumes of his *History of the French Revolution* appeared; the tenth and last volume was published in 1827. In the fateful year 1830 Thiers, with Casimir Périer, Armand Carrel, and Laffitte, was one of the makers of the second French Revolution.

There followed ten years of incessant political activity. Thiers became deputy in Parliament, Minister of State, Prime Minister (1836 and 1840). Despite his poor person and voice he was famous as an orator. The chancellories of Europe were filled with reports about M. Thiers; he nearly made a great European war in 1840. This was too much for King Louis-Philippe, who dismissed his bellicose Radical Minister and took Thiers' rival, the Conservative Guizot. Thiers' dismissal gave him eight years of leisure, until 1848, when he became Prime Minister for the third time, but for two days only; he could not save the house of Orleans, to which he was devoted.

Thiers had been using these years of leisure (1840–48) to work on his great book *The History of the Consulate and*

Empire. The first volume came out in 1845. The revolution of 1848 scarcely interrupted his studies. Under Louis Napoleon and Napoleon III he was in political opposition, with plenty of time for study. Steadily the grand volumes were completed and published, the last, the twentieth, in 1862. As each appeared it was bought or circulated through libraries; and the French public settled down in their easy-chairs to read the stout volumes in the long, delightful hours of a still fairly leisurely age. Some of Thiers' chapters (which he calls *livres*, ' books ') have over a hundred pages.

Here is history in the grand style, on the great scale—ample, copious narrative, majestically describing empire, church, people, commerce, finance, campaigns. It is history of personalities and events, with commentary—shrewd, penetrating, common-sense commentary of the man of the world, the scholar, the statesman. There is, it must be admitted, no great literary distinction, none of the thunder of Carlyle, nor the eloquent harmonies of Macaulay. There is just good, straightforward French narrative, simple words, lucid sentences, all in full-bodied paragraphs. There are few or no character-studies: the personalities exhibit themselves—and like flesh and blood too—just in the unfolding of events. No conversations, nothing imagined; only that is put on the page which is known to have happened. There is absolutely no straining after effect; yet the effect is there, simply because the writer has knowledge—ample, convincing knowledge, given out in his copious, coherent, easy narrative. There are no references, no appendices; just a few personal reminiscences in a very occasional footnote. Documents, printed books, and the memories of men and women were Thiers' sources. The result is narrative in which the men of the Consulate and Empire live, and the events of the time—events of the kind that the gazettes noted—occur.

The taste for reading long histories—ten to twenty volumes—in the eighteen-fifties and -sixties, was like the taste for reading long poems. It is a taste lost in the twentieth century. It is difficult to imagine people becoming excited over five quarto volumes of Gibbon's *Decline and Fall* or twenty octavos of Thiers' *Consulate and Empire*. Perhaps they were not exactly excited by *The Consulate and Empire*, but at any rate they read it, were informed, interested. So interested were those who read the volumes in the eighteen-forties that they absorbed the 'Napoleonic legend,' and, perhaps unconsciously, sighed for the order and grandeur of the first Napoleon, so that they easily accepted the promises of order and grandeur coming from the third Napoleon. For Thiers was invincibly *bourgeois*, and though his copious, clear narrative shows Napoleon in error as well as in achievement, the Emperor nevertheless is the *great man* throughout, and his period the *great period*—a *bourgeois* point of view. The cultured *bourgeoisie* read Thiers' work with avidity. Yet if they learned to despise Louis-Philippe's reign as dull in comparison they could see too, when the third Napoleon came, that *his* reign was a poor imitation. Thus Thiers by his grand presentation of the Consulate and Empire helped to bring about the fall of two monarchs.

Between 1860 and 1870 Thiers was a powerful critic of the Second Empire in the Corps Législatif. When the Empire fell after the battle of Sedan, and the Government of National Defence was formed, he went on mission to the neutral Courts of Europe on behalf of the French people. In extreme difficulties the French people have the habit of turning for guidance to the old men. Thiers, aged seventy-four, became President of the Third Republic, with the task of making the final peace treaty with the Germans, paying the war indemnity, and liberating the country from the German army of occupation; but before these things could be accomplished he had to face the terrible insurrection of the Communards. The French people (or perhaps the French politicians), as they have the habit in time of extreme national stress of calling upon an old man for guidance, when the crisis is past have the habit of at once letting the old man go. Thiers, after some stormy debates in the National Assembly, resigned the Presidency of the Republic on May 24, 1873, with France in peace and prosperity. He was now seventy-six years old. His house and library in the Place Saint-Georges had been burned by the Communards in 1871, but were by this time restored. He did not, however, confine himself even in his last years to his library: he remained in politics—there was no tradition, nor is there now, against a former President of the Republic doing this—until the end of his life (September 3, 1877).

Thiers, who was not regarded as a great man in his own time, nor is now so regarded, had a unique career in the history of mankind. He held the highest offices in the State, under monarchy and republic, and he wrote one of the biggest books in the world—and one of the clearest, most informing, and most readable—the twenty-volumed *Consulate and Empire.*

Even if Thiers was not a great man (whatever that is), there is only one other man, universally acknowledged to be among the greatest, who had a career like him. This was Julius Cæsar, who held the highest offices under the Roman Republic, was the founder of the Roman Empire, and was the author of one of the best histories ever written. The noble Roman with the majestic presence, the little squat journalist-politician of the Bourbon Restoration, are peers in statesmanship and historical literature.

Chapter VI

CARLYLE AND EMERSON

LETTER-WRITING, an almost forgotten art, is practically the only way of maintaining friendship in spite of distance. One of the largest, and certainly one of the most interesting, collections of letters between two eminent men is *The Correspondence of Thomas Carlyle and Ralph Waldo Emerson.* The total number of letters in the collection is 173. They are all good-sized letters; no 'scraps,' though they become shorter towards the end of the series. They are a beautiful expression of the mutual regard of two great souls. Carlyle and Emerson met only four or five times—in 1833, 1847, 1872, and 1873—and only for a few hours on each occasion. The correspondence went on from May 14, 1834, to April 2, 1872.

The friendship began with a visit of Emerson to Craigenputtock. He was then thirty years old. He was a man of good New England stock, "a long line of educated and respected ministers." He had been through the Boston Latin School and Harvard College. "Young Ralph Emerson took Pascal's *Pensées* to church to read during the sermon."[1] He kept school, studied divinity, and became a Unitarian minister at Boston. One of his sermons, on the Lord's Supper, met with so much disagreement on the part of his congregation that the young minister resigned in 1832, after holding the charge for three years. In the same year (1832) his wife died. For the rest of his life he maintained himself, in serene liberty, by writing essays and delivering lectures.

Carlyle was seven and a half years older than Emerson.

[1] Van Wyck Brooks, *The Flowering of New England* (1936), p. 14.

He was a very different man from the tranquil, sunny New England philosopher. Carlyle came of Scottish peasant stock. Life was a hard struggle for such a man, but he was given a good education, though when he went to the University of Edinburgh he had to walk thither from his native place, Ecclefechan, a hundred miles, on foot. He taught in school for a time, hated it—he had no vocation for teaching—and thought of emigrating to America in 1818. Instead he set up as a private tutor at Edinburgh, and managed to make some kind of a living. After some farming with a brother at Hoddam Hill and Scotsbrig, near Ecclefechan, he married Miss Jane Welsh and settled down at 21 Comely Bank, Edinburgh. In 1828 they moved to a small property belonging to Mrs Carlyle at Craigenputtock, near Dumfries. There Carlyle wrote his magnificent essays on Burns, Goethe, Johnson, Voltaire, Diderot, Schiller. Not all by any means of his literary work was accepted by editors, and he became very dejected. On August 24, 1833, he wrote in his journal: "I am left here the solitariest, stranded, most helpless creature that I have been for many years. . . . Nobody asks me to work at articles." He felt, in any case, that he had much more in him than the making of some articles. He noted: "In *all* times there is a word which, spoken to men, to the actual generation of men, would thrill their inmost soul. But the way to find that word? The way to speak it when found?" He was a rugged-faced, bilious-looking man with a bad digestion and inclined to pessimism. Emerson, always cheerful and optimist, had a marvellous digestion. David Alec Wilson writes:

> He deserved it too. He had 'hitched his waggon to a star,' and avoided hurry and worry, the prime causes of most bodily ills; and seldom, indeed, had he a sorrow that could hinder him from enjoying pie at breakfast in comfort that was complete.[1]

[1] *Op. cit.*, vi, 267–268.

In 1833 Emerson, having given up his ministerial charge and lost his wife, came on a long visit to England. He met the three people whom he wanted to meet—Coleridge, Wordsworth, Carlyle. When he went to Craigenputtock Carlyle invited him to stay the night. They went for a long walk on the hills, discoursing of the immortality of the soul. " Christ died upon the tree," said Carlyle to Emerson, " that built Dunscore Kirk yonder; that brought you and me together." When Emerson left next morning Carlyle did not accompany him part of the way. Carlyle noted in his journal: " I saw him go up the hill. I did not go with him to see him descend; I preferred to watch him mount and vanish like an angel." On Emerson's return to Boston he started the correspondence.

The first letter, Emerson to Carlyle, is dated May 14, 1834, and begins " My dear Sir." It is a long letter, and gives the history of his interest in Carlyle:

> Some chance wind of Fame blew your name to me, perhaps two years ago, as the author of papers which I had already distinguished (as, indeed, it was very easy to do) from the mass of English periodical criticism as by far the most original and profound essays of the day.

Next comes a warm-hearted reference to the visit to Craigenputtock: " Drawn by strong regard to one of my teachers, I went to see his person, and, as he might say, his environment at Craigenputtock." Then follows a fairly long—and fairly severe—criticism of *Sartor Resartus*, which was then appearing as a serial in *Fraser's Magazine*. " I am glad," wrote Emerson, " that one living scholar is self-centred, and will be true to himself, though none ever were before. . . . And it is good to have a new eye inspect our mouldy social forms, our politics and schools, and religion." He added, however: " Has literature any parallel to the oddity of the vehicle chosen to convey this treasure? " *Sartor* is a very wonderful book—and it must have been a wonderful magazine that admitted it as a serial—but it is written in extraordinary, a sort of hobgoblin, style. Emerson explained this very fully to Carlyle in that first letter. Yet in the end he declared, " in spite of this grotesque, Teutonic, apocalyptic strain," that Carlyle was " perhaps now the best Thinker of the Saxon race."

Carlyle took the criticisms of *Sartor* in very good part. By the time Emerson's letter arrived Carlyle and his wife had moved from Craigenputtock to London—5 Cheyne Row—" for the best of reasons," he wrote to Emerson, " to seek bread and work." Whenever Emerson cared to come again to England he would be warmly received: " Understand too that your old bed stands in a new room here, and the old welcome at the door." Carlyle might even himself go to America—a not very serious intention, never fulfilled:

> It occasionally rises like a mad prophetic dream in me, that I might end in the Western Woods! . . .
>
> And so here, looking dimly over the water, let me repeat once more what I believe is already dimly the sentiment of all Englishmen, Cisoceanic and Transoceanic, that we and you are *not* two countries, and cannot for the life of us be; but only two *parishes* of one country, with such wholesome parish hospitalities, and dirty, temporary parish feuds, as we see; both of which brave parishes *Vivant! vivant!* [1]

The letters did not succeed one another very rapidly. Emerson's answer to the letter of August 4, 1834, is dated November 20. It contains more discussion of *Sartor* (which Emerson playfully alludes to as Teufelsdröckh). To a query of Carlyle about himself Emerson writes:

> Account me ' a drop in the ocean, seeking another drop,' or God-ward, striving to keep so true a sphericity as to receive the due ray from every point of the concave heaven. . . . Now as to the wholesome hint that you might come to America, it shall be to me a joyful hope. Come and found

[1] Carlyle to Emerson, August 4, 1834.

a new Academy that shall be church and school and Parnassus, as a true Poet's house should be.

Carlyle's reply was dated two and a half months later. It showed fairly clearly that he did not intend to go to America: "As for America and Lecturing it is a thing I do sometimes turn over, but never yet with any seriousness." He continued in this frame of mind to the end of his life, interested in the United States, reading a good deal about it, but never really meaning to go there; whereas the placid Emerson, who seemed so rooted to his pleasant house and garden at Concord, paid two more long visits to Britain and the continent of Europe. Their correspondence was much more important to their friendship than their few and brief meetings were. It began in the days of sailing-ships, a fact which accounts for the long intervals between the answering letters, and also for their length. Writing on February 3, 1835, Carlyle says:

> Your letter, written in November, did not reach me till a few days ago. . . . On the whole, as the Atlantic is so broad and deep, ought we not rather to esteem it a beneficent miracle that messages can arrive at all; that a little slip of paper will skim over all these weltering floods, and other inextricable confusions, and come at last, in the hand of the Twopenny Postman, safe to your lurking-place, like green leaf in the bill of Noah's dove?

The low charge of twopence for a letter from America —letters were paid for on delivery then—is explained in a subsequent letter of Carlyle to Emerson. There were three 'packets' monthly from New York to London, and the masters of these ships carried letters for anybody free of charge to London and put them into the post-office. From this point the letters were carried by the postman to their destination, and the ordinary charge was collected according to the distance in Great Britain. All this, of course, was before the penny postage and Rowland Hill's reforms of 1839. Carlyle in the same way deposited his letter for Emerson at the North America or South America Coffee House, paying twopence for it as a 'ship-letter.'

Books and high thoughts are the subject-matter of the correspondence. Carlyle tells of his literary struggles—not struggles to secure publication, but simply to write. For, curiously to this giant among men of letters, literary composition was a labour and an agony—at least, so he told Emerson many times. The travail of his soul is obvious to all readers of, for instance, *Past and Present* or *Chartism*; yet he must have had pleasure in the achievement of his artistry. In Carlyle's correspondence with Emerson there can be traced the conception and writing of *The French Revolution* and *Frederick the Great*, two of the grandest historical works of the nineteenth century. Carlyle writes (February 3, 1835):

> *The Diamond Necklace* has not been printed, but will be, were this French Revolution out; which latter, however, drags itself along in a way that would fill your benevolent heart with pity. . . . It is the dreadfullest labour (with these nerves, this liver) I ever undertook.

Curiously, too, Carlyle felt himself lonely in London: "I suffer also terribly from the solitary existence I have all along had; it is becoming a kind of passion with me to feel myself among my brothers." Emerson was a brother, his peer in spirit and intellect; and almost his only male friend after the death of John Sterling.

Carlyle, though he found writing a terrible labour, liked lecturing: "I may say that Lecturing (or I would rather it were *speaking*) is a thing I have always had some hankering after." Emerson replies at once to correct Carlyle's impression that America is without opportunities for this:

> Boston contains some genuine taste for literature. For a few years past we have had, every winter, several courses of lectures, scientific, miscellaneous, even some purely literary, which were well attended. Some lectures on Shakespeare

were crowded. . . . The fee to the lecturer is inconsiderable, usually $20 for each lecture.[1]

In one of the early letters Carlyle relates simply, without any bitterness, the frightful tragedy of the destruction of the manuscript of the first volume of *The French Revolution*: " A Friend borrowed this volume of Manuscript—a kind Friend but a careless one—to write notes on it which he was well qualified to do. One evening about two months ago he came in on us, distraction (literally) in his aspect." The manuscript, left carelessly out, had been torn up as waste paper, and, all but three or four tatters, was clean gone. " I could not complain, or the poor man seemed as if he would have shot himself: we had to gather ourselves together, and show a smooth front to it; which happily, though difficult, was not impossible to do." The " Friend," whose name Carlyle chivalrously withheld, was John Stuart Mill. When we reflect on the agony with which Carlyle wrote, the passion infused, red-hot, into the first volume of *The French Revolution*, and the accumulated learning in it, we can realize something of the large-heartedness and stoicism with which Carlyle and his wife received Mill's terrible news, and the heroism with which Carlyle set to work to compose the whole volume over again.

Information like this—intimate messages about their literary composition—is the subject-matter of much of the correspondence, with many references to friends—Wordsworth, Longfellow, Clough. They had the literary world, even the political world, and all the realms of high thought in common. They made good resolutions: " Please God," Emerson wrote in 1838 (October 7), " I will never again sit six weeks of this short human life over a letter of yours without answering it "—a resolve which even this lofty soul did not completely live up to.

The subject-matter of this converse across the Atlantic was books, people, ideas, with just a little high-standard

[1] Emerson to Carlyle, April 30, 1835.

gossip or details of daily life. Carlyle chronicles the progress of composition of *The French Revolution*, of *Heroes*, of *Frederick the Great*. About *The French Revolution* he tells Emerson: "It is a wild, savage, ruthless, very bad book." As the work progressed under his blustering pen a withering contempt for his fellow-creatures consumed him. He often felt (he says) tempted to flee from London and its huge population to Emerson's village of Concord. "There are hardly three people among these two millions, whom I care to exchange words with, in the humour I have. Nevertheless, at bottom, it is not my purpose to quit London finally till I have, as it were, *seen it out*." It was a terrible struggle, and reduced Carlyle to a state of complete exhaustion; but "in two months more this unblessed book will be finished. . . . As for the results of the Book, I can rationally promise myself, on the economical, pecuniary, or otherwise worldly side, simply *zero*." His incessant labour was almost without profit, though in the same letter (November 5, 1836) he announces to Emerson the acceptance of *The Diamond Necklace* by Fraser for £50; the essay on Mirabeau had been published and would be paid for. "I think it is the first shilling of money I have earned by my craft these four years: where the money I have lived on has come from while I sat here scribbling gratis, amazes me to think." He must have been living on savings and the small income that Mrs Carlyle had from the sale of Craigenputtock.

In the next letter, early in the following year (February 13, 1837), Carlyle announces the completion of "the unutterable *French Revolution*":

> You, I hope, can have little conception of the feeling with which I wrote the last word of it, one night in early January, when the clock was striking ten, and our frugal Scotch supper coming in. I did not cry. I did not pray: but could have done both. No such *spell* shall get itself fixed on me for some while to come.

The two friends always sent each other their books. *The French Revolution* duly arrived in Concord (October 1837); Emerson's verdict was swift and generous: "*You have broken from all books and written a mind.*" He added: "It is a brave experiment, and the success is great. We have men in your story, and not mere names." More comment followed this. Emerson, however, was much more than the appreciative friend and man of letters. This ethereal philosopher, who had hitched his wagon to a star, and who lived a simple village life on a small income, arranged at his own risk for the publication of *The French Revolution* in Boston, obtained subscribers to the edition, and in the next two years remitted to Carlyle a profit of about £200. Later Emerson arranged for publication in Boston of a collection of Carlyle's "fugitive" essays in five volumes under the title of *Miscellanies*; this appears to have been his own idea. Part of the American edition was sent over to England and sold there. Carlyle, who suffered from dyspepsia and found horse-riding the only thing that did him any good, bought a hack with £20 out of the American profits, and went for a week's ride over Surrey and Sussex. After arriving home again, "a right weary man," he sold the nag and finished writing the lectures on "Heroes."

Emerson's presents of books were not so substantial as Carlyle's—just an essay now and then, the essay of a poet. Compared with the physically dyspeptic, mentally storm-tossed Carlyle, wrestling with demons of thought amid the huge roar of London, Emerson had an amazingly tranquil life in Concord. He was happily married again, living in the pleasant Massachusetts village, in a roomy house—white-painted, timbered, with veranda—with in all two acres of ground, orchard, meadows, by the slow-flowing Musquetaquid. He planted his trees, and himself did a little digging, for he held the sower and grower to be the *universal* workman: "He solves the problem of life, not for one, but for all men of sound body." Emerson seems to have been one of the few really happy and contented men who ever lived. He had a gentle wife, two fine children, a charming house and garden in a beautiful village, some delightful scholarly society in the village, with Harvard and Boston within easy reach. His income from investment was about £250, and his winter lecturing, which he found enjoyable and a pleasant change, brought him in another £150 or so. Bronson Alcott, "a majestic soul with whom conversation is possible," came to live with his wife and three children (among them Louisa, the future authoress) in a cottage at Concord. He was a kind of Pestalozzi, an "educationalist," who made no great success in life, but whose fertile mind and spirit were a resource to Emerson. Later Hawthorne took up his residence in Concord. On one occasion there was a little dinner at Cambridge (Mass.), described by Charles Eliot Norton, at which Emerson, Longfellow, Hawthorne, Oliver Wendell Holmes, James Russell Lowell, and Norton were together.

The first essay that Emerson sent to Carlyle was *Nature.* This was issued as a small volume, anonymously, in 1836. "Your little azure-coloured Nature," wrote Carlyle (February 13, 1837),

> gave me true satisfaction. . . . You say it is the first chapter of something greater. I call it rather the Foundation and Ground-plan on which you may build whatever of great and true has been given you to build. It is the true Apocalypse, this when the 'Open Secret' is revealed to a man.

Carlyle rejoiced in the "glad serenity of soul" with which Emerson looked out upon the world, and listened to the everlasting melodies—the *ewigen Melodien.* Harriet Martineau said that Emerson was "the only man in America" who had quietly settled down on a competence to follow his own path and to do the work prescribed for him by his own will. Carlyle considered this to be a magnificent example to mammon-ridden England and America. New England was showing the better way to old England and old Europe.

The next little work which came to Chelsea was the famous Phi Beta Kappa oration "The American Scholar," delivered by Emerson at Harvard in 1837. Emerson's message about this was: "I shall send you an Oration presently, delivered before a literary society here, which is now being printed." Carlyle was carried away—as every sensitive scholar is carried away—by his first reading of this masterpiece. Carlyle, amid the "infinite jangling and jabbering" of his time, was feeling more and more alone, intellectually and morally:

> And lo, out of the West comes a clear utterance, clearly recognizable as a *man's* voice, and I *have* a kinsman and brother: God be thanked for it. I could have *wept* to read that speech; the clear high melody of it went tingling through my heart. I said to my wife, "There, woman!" She read; and returned, and charges me to return for answer, "that there had been nothing met with like it since Schiller went silent."[1]

It deserved all its praise. Samuel Rogers, whom Carlyle called "a grim old Dilettante," was heard saying, "It is German poetry given out in American prose." James Russell Lowell, who was an undergraduate at Harvard at the time, and heard the oration, declared later that "it was an event without former parallel in our literary annals." Carlyle was able to do, though not in the same opulent manner, with Emerson's essays what Emerson had done with Carlyle's *French Revolution* and *Miscellanies*: he arranged for their publication by Fraser in London on the "half-profits" system. On the edition of 750 copies Emerson's share of profits would be £10. Carlyle wrote a preface for the book.

Carlyle had more to say about society than Emerson,

[1] Carlyle to Emerson, December 8, 1837.

although Emerson must have met a good many interesting people besides Bronson Alcott. Trying to tempt Emerson over on a visit, Carlyle writes (November 15, 1838):

> Come if you dare; I said there was a room, house-room and heart-room, constantly waiting you here, and you shall see blockheads by the million. *Pickwick* himself shall be visible; innocent young Dickens reserved for a questionable fate. The great Wordsworth shall talk till you yourself pronounce him to be a bore. Southey's complexion is still healthy mahogany-brown, with a fleece of white hair, and eyes that seem running at full gallop. Leigh Hunt, "man of genius in shape of a Cockney," is my near neighbour, full of quips and cranks with good humour and no common sense. Old Rogers, with his pale head, white, bare and cold as snow, will work on you with those large blue eyes, cruel, sorrowful, and that sardonic shelf-chin—This is the man, O Rogers, that wrote the German Poetry in American Prose; consider him well!

London, the "Wen," as Carlyle (after Cobbett) called it, was in Carlyle's view the metropolis for Anglo-Saxondom, including the Americans:

> I reckon that this huge smoking Wen may, for some centuries yet, be the best Mycale [1] for our Saxon *Panionium*, a yearly meeting-place of "All the Saxons" from beyond the Atlantic, from the Antipodes, or wherever the restless wanderers dwell or toil. After centuries, if Boston, if New York, have become the most convenient All-Saxondom, we will right cheerfully go thither to hold such festival, and leave the Wen.

London still was, and still is, the annual, or, indeed, the continual, gathering-place of people from the British and American Commonwealths. In the same letter (June 24, 1839) that Carlyle wrote to Emerson about the Wen as the Mycale of Anglo-Saxondom he described a meeting with one of America's great men:

[1] Mycale was an island in the Ægean Sea where the ancient Ionian Greeks met for a yearly festival.

Not many days ago I saw at breakfast the Notablest of all your Notabilities, Daniel Webster. He is a magnificent specimen; you might say to all the world 'This is your Yankee Englishman, such Limbs *we* make in Yankee land.' As a Logic-fencer, Advocate or Parliamentary Hercules, one would incline to back him at first sight against all the extant world. The tanned complexion, that amorphous crag-like face; the dull black eyes under their precipice of brows, like dull anthracite furnaces, needing only to be blown; the mastiff-mouth, accurately closed:—I have not traced as much of *silent Berserkir-rage* that I remember of, in any other man. "I guess I should not like to be *your* nigger"—Webster is not loquacious, but he is pertinent, conclusive; a dignified, perfectly bred man, though not English in breeding: a man worthy of the best reception from us; and meeting such, I understand.

There is a picture by a master-hand. Carlyle's characters stand out, living, speaking, doing. Emerson's genius was not for this. He was a poet, and believed that there was "room for a poet—in this great, intelligent, sensual, and avaricious America." His lectures helped "the circulation of thought" there—a modest aim, a modest man of genius. Such was the outlook of Emerson, trimming roses in his garden at Concord, or writing quietly in his study to the dynamic Carlyle overseas.

Chapter VII

CARLYLE AND EMERSON—*continued*

CARLYLE and Emerson corresponded with each other over a period of about thirty-eight years. The correspondence, however, is divided into two halves of unequal numbers of years. In the edition of Charles Eliot Norton the letters of the first eight years fill volume i. The second volume contains all the balance—the letters of nearly thirty years. In this last period the letters tended to diminish in length, and the intervals between them to become a little longer. After April 2, 1872, the letters ceased altogether, although Carlyle lived for nearly nine years more. He died on February 4, 1881. Emerson died on April 27, 1882. One of the most difficult things in life is to maintain a correspondence with anything like its original frequency and its original zest. Carlyle and Emerson, it must be admitted, did fairly well, in corresponding for thirty-eight years. Nevertheless the silence of the last nine years of their joint lives mars what looked like being a perfect series.

The great interest of the letters lies in the converse of two great minds and in the association of two literary 'capitals'—the British metropolis and the New England village. Contact was made through occasional personal visits as well as through correspondence. On July 19, 1842, Carlyle writes to Emerson about a visit from Bronson Alcott:

> He has been twice here, at considerable length; the second time all night. He is a genial, innocent, simple-hearted man, of much natural intelligence and goodness, with an air of rusticity, veracity, and dignity withal, which

in many ways appeals to one. The good Alcott: with his long, lean face and figure, with his grey worn temples and mild radiant eyes, all bent on saving the world by a return to acorns and the golden age; he comes before one like a venerable Don Quixote, whom nobody can even laugh at without loving.

Alcott was a rather ineffective man, a gentle philosopher highly thought of by his friends, contributing to the distinguished literary society of Concord, and yet never quite convincing the public, or perhaps even himself, of the soundness of his educational views. His literary daughter Louisa, a young woman of mental vigour and strong character, was probably as much influenced by her reaction against Bronson's inertia as she was by her attraction to his literary gifts. Emerson always maintained that he himself owed much to converse with his neighbour Bronson Alcott. " He is a great man," Emerson wrote to Carlyle, " and was made for what is greatest, but now I fear he has touched what best he can."

At this time (1842) Emerson was helping with a magazine called *The Dial*. It was edited by Margaret Fuller, later Marchioness Ossoli. It was a serious magazine, and though it lasted for less than four years it seems to have represented an important stage in the intellectual and moral development of New England.

Emerson wrote to Carlyle (October 15, 1842):

For the *Dial* and its sins I have no defence to set up. We write as we can, and we know very little about it. If the direction of these speculations is to be deplored, it is yet a fact for history that all the bright boys and girls in New England, quite ignorant of each other, take the world so, and come and make confession to fathers and mothers—the boys that they do not wish to go into trade, the girls that they do not like morning calls and evening parties. They are all religious, but hate the churches; they reject all the ways of living of other men, but have none to offer in their stead. Perhaps one of these days a great Yankee shall come who will easily do the unknown deed.

Emerson himself was the great Yankee who was restoring to the Americans faith, not in dogmatic theology, but in goodness and truth. At the same time Carlyle was preaching faith in great men. In the exchange of their literary news he writes (October 31, 1843):

> As for myself, dear Emerson, you must ask me no questions till—alas, I know not when! After four weary years of the most unreadable reading, the painfulest poking and delving, I have come at last to the conclusion that I *must* write a book on Cromwell: that there is no rest for me till I do it. This point fixed, another is not less fixed hitherto, that a book on Cromwell is impossible.

It was done nevertheless, and put Cromwell on the pinnacle where he still stands, and seems likely to do so for ever.

At this time Tennyson was coming into fame, and the British people's taste for reading poetry—now, it seems, absolutely lost—continued to grow. Carlyle had a great admiration for Tennyson, as, indeed, all England had until recently. Alfred, he writes to Emerson, " is one of the few British or Foreign Figures (a not increasing number I think!) who are and remain beautiful to me;—a true human soul, or some authentic approximation thereto, to whom your own soul can say, Brother! " He complained that Alfred " skips me in his brief visits to Town," that, in fact, Alfred skipped everybody, being a man solitary and sad. The poet seemed to dwell in an element of gloom, and to carry about with him a piece of chaos " which he is manufacturing into cosmos." Carlyle must have piqued Emerson greatly with his description of Tennyson as a native of moated granges and the green fat pastures of Lincolnshire. Having a small annuity, the poet on leaving Cambridge chose, instead of going into law or the ministry, to club together with his mother and sisters and to live unpromoted and write poems. The family lived now here, now there, always within reach of London, but never in it. On Tennyson's rare and brief visits he lodged in some old comrade's room.

> One of the finest-looking men in the world. A great shock of rough dusty-dark hair; bright-laughing, hazel eyes; massive, aquiline face, most massive, yet most delicate; of sallow brown complexion, almost Indian-looking; clothes cynically loose, free-and-easy;—smokes infinite tobacco.[1]

Carlyle said that Tennyson, "alone of our time," had proved that *singing* was possible in the English language. Twenty-five years later, however, Carlyle wrote to Emerson (January 27, 1867) that he had not found the *Idylls of the King* wholly satisfying. He had read them aloud with a friend, Miss Bromley-Davenport, "with a profound recognition of the finely elaborated execution and also of the inward perfection of *vacancy*." He felt impatient that Tennyson was treating his readers like infants, "though the lollypops were so superlative." Reading aloud Emerson's *English Traits* was found to be a satisfactory corrective.

Emerson's second visit to England took place in 1847. In Liverpool a letter was delivered to him addressed to "R. W. E. on the instant when he lands in England." The letter contained a warm invitation to Cheyne Row. So Emerson went to London, and at 10 at night found himself on the doorstep of No. 5. The door was opened by Mrs Carlyle, "and the man himself was behind her with a lamp in the hall." Emerson saw that they had changed very little since he left them at Craigenputtock, fourteen years earlier. "Well," said Carlyle, "here we are shovelled together again." They had long talks and walks, Carlyle being as great a walker as he was a talker, "melting all Westminster and London into his talk and

[1] Carlyle to Emerson, August 5, 1844.

laughter as he goes." Emerson noted in his journal—and this is important in view of charges made later—" Carlyle and his wife live on beautiful terms." It was on this visit to England that Emerson made the notes and observations for his *English Traits*. When he returned to America he gave Carlyle news about *English Traits*, and also about " American Traits," in which Carlyle was greatly interested. On a visit, for lecturing, to St Louis and the Mississippi valley Emerson found that " Working-men, ability to do the work of the River, abounded "; but nothing higher was thought of: " America is incomplete. . . . 'Tis a wild democracy, the riot of mediocrities, and none of your selfish Italies and Englands, where an age sublimates into a genius." He seemed to think that America could not produce geniuses (though he was one himself): " Our few fine persons," he wrote, " are apt to die."

Two wars naturally occasioned considerable comment in this correspondence—the Crimean (1854–56) and the American Civil War (1861–65). Carlyle had nothing good to say of the Crimean War, which, indeed, is now generally regarded as a blunder on the part of the British and French Governments. He called it " the Turk war," and said that it seemed an enterprise " unworthy of Bedlam." He called the British General, who was Lord Raglan, " a mere sash and cocked hat "; the Emperor Napoleon III " a gentleman who has shown only house-breaker qualities hitherto "; and Marshal Saint-Arnaud, French Commander in the Crimea, " a commander of the Playactor Pirate description, resembling a General as Alexander Dunn does Dante Alighieri." He admired, however, the persistence of the British in face of difficulty and disaster—" There is something almost grand in the stubborn thick-side patience and persistence of this English people "—and he thought that they would " work themselves through in one fashion or another." The fashionable phrase now would be Rosebery's " muddle through." Carlyle even held that some good might come to the British from " this astonishing slap on the nose to their self-complacency before all the world."

Emerson and Carlyle were not likely to disagree over the Crimean War, but the American Civil War was a different sort of thing. Emerson had always been an anti-slavery man, an Abolitionist, though never violent or fanatical. Carlyle, on the other hand, was—from Emerson's point of view at any rate—unsound on what he called " the Nigger Question."

Carlyle's views on this were of long standing and were very pronounced. His pamphlet *The Nigger Question* was published in 1849. It was written with reference to the emancipation of the West Indian slaves, effected in 1833. The result, Carlyle says, had been that " poor Quashee," being freed from the necessity of working, had taken to growing just as much pumpkin as would keep him comfortable in the sunshine; and thus the land and the planters, deprived of labour, were going to ruin. The only remedy would be to compel the black man to work " and to do his Maker's will who had constructed him with such capabilities."

When the Southern Slave States seceded from the Union in 1861 and the war of North and South began Carlyle was, naturally, quoted in the South to prove the naturalness and social utility of slavery. In his letters to Emerson Carlyle kept clear of the subject of slavery, and wrote mainly about his writing of *Frederick the Great*, which he was gradually completing, though it " nearly killed " him. Emerson was more explicit. He wrote (September 26, 1864) that if Carlyle had carried out the visit so often mentioned in their correspondence " it would have made it impossible that your name should be cited for one moment on the side of the enemies of mankind." Ten days' residence in America, says Emerson, would have made Carlyle " the organ of the sanity of England and of Europe." American nationality was in the Republican party—that is, the Union or Northern and Western States —"and I hold it not less certain that . . . the battle for Humanity is, at this hour, in America. . . . Ah! how gladly would I enlist you, with your thunderbolt, on our part!" Emerson discerned good even in war itself, despite the havoc it was making in the land and in the hearts of people. "I shall always respect war hereafter. The cost of life, the dreary havoc of comfort and time, are overpaid by the vistas it opens of Eternal Life, Eternal Law, reconstructing and uplifting Society."

The great correspondence was drawing to a close now. Carlyle seems not to have sent any direct answer to this "Civil War" letter of Emerson's of September 26, 1864. His next letter, not written from Cheyne Row, but from Cummertrees, Annan, Scotland, where he had gone for a holiday after finishing *Frederick*, is dated June 14, 1865, two months after the end of the American Civil War. He makes no allusion whatever to it. He was now seventy years old, and his hand shook as he wrote. "In the first days of February I ended my weary book, a totally worn-out man, got to shore again after far the ugliest sea he had ever swam in." It is a pleasant letter, about his holiday, "sauntering about in Devonshire, in Chelsea, hither, thither, idle as a dry bone." He was now at his eldest living sister's farmhouse, "one of the most rustic farmhouses in the world," situated on dry, waving knolls, with the finest water he ever drank anywhere, except at Malvern; around him the mountains of Galloway and Cheviot; beyond Solway brine and sands the mountains of Yorkshire and Cumberland. Carlyle spent his time partly in "sauntering moodily in thin checkered woods," or "galloping about, once daily, by old lanes and roads, oftenest latterly on the wide expanses of Solway shores." This is, in fact, as good a letter as Carlyle ever wrote.

There are ten more of Carlyle's letters in the series, and nine of Emerson's. These last letters from one side and the other of the Atlantic are not alternate: Carlyle's Annandale letter of June 14, 1865, is followed by two of Emerson's (January 14 and May 16, 1866); these by three of Carlyle's (January 27, 1867, November 18, 1869, and January 4, 1870). The series continues irregularly until the last, from Carlyle, dated Chelsea, April 2, 1872.

Carlyle had lost his wife, as the result of a carriage accident in 1866. He wrote to Emerson in January of the following year; this is the letter from Mentone already quoted about Tennyson's *Idylls of the King*. By the death of his wife, Carlyle writes to Emerson, " I lost my little all in the world." To this letter Emerson made no answer —surely a very extraordinary lapse, particularly in view of his old correspondent's bereavement. Nearly three years passed, and then, on November 18, 1869, Carlyle wrote again. He evidently kept a tally on the letters that he wrote, for he mentions in this one: " It is near three years since I last wrote to you; from Mentone, under the Ligurian Olive and Orange trees." It is a remarkable letter, Carlyle with obvious sincerity excusing Emerson's failure to reply: " That you made no answer I know right well means only, *Alas, what can I say to him of consolatory that he does not himself know?* " Now among all the lights that had gone out for him he counted this with frequent regret: " That our correspondence (not by absolute hest of Fate) should have fallen extinct or into such abeyance: but I interpret as you see; and my love and brotherhood to you remain alive, and will while I myself do." He then proceeds to carry into effect an idea which had been for many years in his mind: " Of testifying my gratitude to New England (New England acting mainly through one of her Sons called Waldo Emerson) by *bequeathing to it my poor Falstaff Regiment, latterly two Falstaff Regiments of Books.*" These comprised Carlyle's collection of books on

Cromwell and Frederick the Great—the sources of his great historical works.

Curiously, Carlyle received no reply to this letter, so he wrote again on January 4, 1870. To this second letter Emerson replied at once (January 23, 1870), explaining his delay by the fact that he had undertaken "to write a book for a given day," and that he could now write only by spasms. This time he wrote a proper letter, and concluded by saying that after his "long contumacy" he believed that he would quickly write again. Naturally the bequest for books for Harvard was gratefully accepted.

The resumed correspondence went on quite vigorously throughout 1870, Emerson good-naturedly saying: "I think I must mend myself by reclaiming my old right to send you letters." Carlyle was rejoiced. "If you *will*, at the eleventh hour, turn over a new leaf, and write me letters again—but I doubt *you won't*. And yet were it not worth while, think you. *Νὺξ ἔρχεται* ['Night approaches']." Emerson was touched. He wrote:

> There is no example of constancy like yours, and it always stings my stupor into temporary recovery and wonderful resolution to accept the noble challenge. But 'the strong hours conquer us,' and I am the victim of miscellany—miscellany of designs, vast debility, and procrastination.

Four letters seem to have passed in 1871, one of them a good account from Emerson of his Californian journey in that year.

In 1872 it was Emerson who wrote twice, "two beautiful letters," Carlyle confessed, and had to wait long for an answer. In November 1872 Emerson, on his way to Egypt, visited Carlyle in London, and again in 1873, on his way back to America; but they exchanged no more letters with each other.

Chapter VIII

THE NEW ENGLAND RENAISSANCE

IT would be stupid to regard any country by itself in the nineteenth century, particularly in the middle period. Ideas passed from continent to continent, and culture was pooled among the civilized peoples of the world. German romanticism deeply influenced Carlyle, and both deeply influenced Emerson. The cold, dogmatic Calvinism of New England was dissipated, or, it might be said, changed, by rationalism combined with poetry and just a touch of mysticism. Negative and pallid as it was, the new religion sprang from an atmosphere that was favourable to the flowering of the mind.[1] Emerson, high-minded, tolerant, serene, in tune with Nature and the Infinite, made New England culture 'Transcendental'; the village of Concord, twenty miles from Boston, became a home of Transcendentalism. New England literature flowered in a veritable renaissance. High thought made for devotion to great causes. Of these causes the most absorbing in the middle years of nineteenth-century New England was Abolitionism—the Slave Question. So New England produced *Uncle Tom's Cabin* in 1852, against which Southern propaganda novels could effect nothing. Yet there was a fine culture in the South. Aristocratic society has seldom anywhere shown to better advantage than it did in Charleston between 1830 and 1860. Yet it produced nobody anywhere approaching Emerson's calibre, nor even Harriet Beecher Stowe's. Southern society, the Southern view of life, had to wait until the third decade of the twentieth century to find the reply to *Uncle Tom's Cabin*

[1] Van Wyck Brooks, *op. cit.*, p. 12.

in Margaret Mitchell's *Gone with the Wind.* This was read with zest equal to *Uncle Tom.*

Emerson, the greatest American thinker and prose-writer, was the leading Transcendentalist. In 1842 he read a lecture on "The Transcendentalist" at the Masonic Temple, Boston. He began his explanation with these words:

> The first thing we have to say respecting what are called *new views* here in New England, at the present time, is that they are not new, but the very oldest of thoughts cast into the mould of these new times. The light is always identical in its composition, but it falls on a great variety of objects, and by so falling is first revealed to us, not in its own form, for it is formless, but in theirs; in like manner, thought only appears in the objects it classifies. What is popularly called Transcendentalism among us is Idealism; Idealism as it appears in 1842. As thinkers, mankind has ever been divided into two sects—Materialists and Idealists.

The Transcendentalist, accordingly, is the Idealist.

> The Transcendentalist adopts the whole connexion of spiritual doctrine. He believes in miracle, in the perpetual openness of the human mind to new influx of light and power; he believes in inspiration and in ecstasy. He wishes that the spiritual principle should be suffered to demonstrate itself to the end, in all possible applications to the state of man, without the admission of anything unspiritual; that is, anything positive, dogmatic, personal. Thus the spiritual measure of inspiration is the depth of the thought, and never who said it? And so he resists all attempts to palm other rules and measures on the spirit than its own.

Emerson lived 'Transcendentally,' with perfect serenity, in his house and garden at Concord for forty-eight years, dying there, quite tranquilly, in 1882. His garden extended down to the Musquetaquid, which flows into the Merrimac river, and he was able to buy a grove of white pines on the near-by Walden Pond, and a large tract with a rocky pinnacle on the farther shore. So he could sing:

> My garden is a forest ledge
> Which older forests bound;
> The banks slope down to the blue lake-edge,
> Then plunge to the depths profound.

Though steeped in Latin and English nature-poetry, he found, when he settled down in the country, that he knew nothing of poetry's fine things—of flowers, birds, mountains, sun, and moon. "If I go into the forest I find all new and undescribed. . . . Every man that goes into the woods seems to be the first man that ever went into a wood." His wife would rather have set up house at Plymouth, her town, but Emerson knew what he owed to his vocation. "Wherever I go," he told her, "I guard and study my rambling propensities with a care that is ridiculous to people, but to me is the care of my high calling." His high calling was to "sit apart, write; let them hear or let them forbear, the written word abides, until slowly and unexpectedly and in widely sundered places it has created its own church." He combined speaking with writing, for most of the things that he wrote were also delivered as lectures. He made most of his living—his wife and himself had some small means of their own—by lecturing to "Lyceums," the "mutual improvement" societies which existed in the middle decades of the nineteenth century in nearly all New England towns and villages, and, though less numerously, in the Middle West. "Lyceums," he said, "are as good a pulpit as any other." Emerson had once, as a young Unitarian minister, had a pulpit of his own, but gave it up owing to his scruples against administering the sacrament of the Lord's Supper. His lectures to Lyceums necessitated a good deal of travelling, so that his forty-eight years at Concord were varied by many excursions; and he had three trips to England. He was a member of the celebrated Saturday Club of Boston, and at

Concord he had some congenial society, especially that of the unpractical philosopher Bronson Alcott.

The New England Transcendentalists made two co-operative ventures in witnessing to their views. One was Brook Farm—its proper name was the West Roxbury Association—founded by George Ripley in 1841. It was to be a commonwealth, a Utopia, with a reminiscence of the Greek city-state (but no slavery), and more than a reminiscence of Fourierism. Brook Farm had land, and bakery and school and nursery; and, according to the proper Fourier plan, a phalanstery, or public edifice where its indoor activities could be carried on. Emerson did not join George Ripley's "colony of agriculturists and scholars," though he admitted, "I am gently mad myself." Nathaniel Hawthorne, who never seemed mad at all, did join the Brook Farm community. It lasted only until 1846, when the phalanstery was burned down.

The second joint venture of the Transcendentalists was *The Dial*, a monthly periodical which was issued from July 1840 to April 1844. Its first editor was Margaret Fuller; its second and last Emerson, who made forty contributions to it in prose and verse, including the essay-lecture called "The Transcendentalist." Other contributors were Margaret Fuller, Bronson Alcott, George Ripley, James Freeman Clarke, Theodore Parker, William Ellery Channing, Henry Thoreau, and Eliot Cabot. Most of the best minds of New England helped to make *The Dial*, and it was carried on with boundless enthusiasm; but all this could not ensure it four years of life.

In 1857 Boston embarked on another literary venture, *The Atlantic Monthly*, with James Russell Lowell as editor. Longfellow wrote a poem for the first number. Emerson made twenty-eight contributions to *The Atlantic Monthly*, more than half of them poems. Not directly connected with the magazine, but comprising much the same group as started it, was the literary circle called the Saturday Club, of which O. W. Holmes has left a pleasant description in his life of Emerson. It dined on the last Saturday of every month at the Parker House.

> During its first decade [from about 1857] the Saturday Club brought together, as members or as visitors, many distinguished persons. At one end of the table sat Longfellow, florid, quiet, benignant, soft-voiced, a most agreeable rather than a brilliant talker, but a man upon whom it was always pleasant to look—whose silence was better than many another man's conversation. At the other end of the table sat Agassiz, robust, sanguine, animated, full of talk, boy-like in his laughter. The stranger who should have asked who were the men ranged along the sides of the table would have heard in answer the names of Hawthorne, Motley, Dana, Lowell, Whipple, Peirce, the distinguished mathematician, Judge Hoar, eminent at the Bar and in the Cabinet, Dwight, the leading musical critic of Boston for a whole generation, Sumner, the academic champion of freedom, Andrew, " the great War Governor of Massachusetts," Dr Howe, the philanthropist, William Hunt, the painter, with others not unworthy of such company. Along with these, generally near the Longfellow end of the table, sat Emerson, talking in low tones and carefully measured utterances to his neighbour, or listening and recording on his mental phonograph any stray word worth remembering. Emerson was a very regular attendant at the meetings of the Saturday Club, and continued to dine at its table until a year or two of his death.[1]

The movement for emancipating slaves attracted most of the eminent literary men of New England. Emerson sat on platforms of meetings called to support the movement; he even occasionally spoke in public on this subject, though he felt that on the whole he must keep himself to his scholar's business. Abolition did not find an

[1] O. W. Holmes, *Ralph Waldo Emerson* (1912 edition), pp. 222–223.

eloquent and wholehearted literary advocate until Mrs Harriet Beecher Stowe appeared on the scene.

Mrs Stowe was a minister's daughter, a minister's wife, and had six brothers in the ministry. She was born at Lichfield, Connecticut, in 1811, and was brought up there and at Boston. Her husband was a professor at Lane Seminary, Cincinnati, Ohio, a 'free' state, but bordering the 'slave' state of Kentucky. She took an active part in the relief of fugitive slaves who came to Cincinnati. In 1850 Professor Stowe was called to Bowdoin College, Maine, with a salary of thirteen hundred dollars a year. Mrs Stowe added to this by writing. In one of her letters she says:

> I can earn four hundred dollars a year by writing, but I don't want to feel that I must, when weary with teaching the children, and tending the baby, and buying provisions, and mending dresses, and darning stockings, sit down and write a piece for some paper.

The year 1850, when the Stowes removed to Bowdoin College, was the year when the Fugitive Slave Bill was passed in Congress, and received the signature of President Fillmore. This commanded Federal commissioners, upon complaint from owners, to arrest fugitive slaves in whatever state they were, and to restore them to their owners. Edward Channing, in his *History of the United States*, says that the Fugitive Slave Bill became law "without much opposition and with slight notice." It received plenty of notice, at any rate, in the Beecher family, and one of Harriet's sisters said to her in a letter: "If I could use a pen as you can I would write something to make this whole nation feel what an accursed thing slavery is." Mrs Stowe was struck by the suggestion, and offered to write weekly sketches about "Uncle Tom's Cabin" in the *National Era*, a journal edited in Washington by Dr Gamaliel Bailey. The offer was accepted. The first sketch or chapter appeared in June 1851; the last in April 1852.

A Boston publisher, Mr Jewett, had noticed it in its serial issue, and offered to bring it out in book form. He published an edition of three thousand copies on March 20, 1852; the edition was exhausted immediately. No amount of Southern literary propaganda—and much was attempted—could check the influence of *Uncle Tom's Cabin*, which became immediately the most-talked-of book in the United States and outside. Even Lord Palmerston, not much given to 'causes' or to sentiment, read it three times in quick succession. Three hundred thousand copies were sold within one year, and it was translated into twenty-three languages.

The people of the middle decades of the nineteenth century are often accused of sentimentalism. It is true that they were sentimental, though in effect not much more than the people of the present age; only their sentiment took different directions from that of the present time. It was concerned more with domestic life, with the pathos of frail childhood, like that of Little Nell, or of gallant youth cut off before its prime, like Mrs Ewing's Jackanapes, or with the loves of virtuous young men and young women whose marriage stabilized their romance for good and all, and therefore usually brought the story to an end.

Uncle Tom's Cabin is full of this wholesome kind of sentiment—loving husbands and wives, innocent, charming, unfortunate children, kind masters and mistresses, brutal exploiters, good, religious old men. Let anyone, however, to-day read the whole book and ask himself if it strikes him as overcharged with sentiment. It is a well-told story, and one of the few propaganda novels written with the unconscious artistry of genius. Topsy is a more natural child than Little Nell, and the death of Uncle Tom is told with restraint, like that of Colonel Newcombe.

The *Key to Uncle Tom's Cabin*—what historians would call the *pièces justificatives*, and policemen the *dossier*—was compiled by Mrs Stowe in 1853, after the publication of the novel; but obviously most of the material in the *Key* was in her mind when she wrote *Uncle Tom's Cabin*, and the authenticity of her charges has never been seriously challenged.

More of a child of nature than the serene, nature-loving, but predominantly bookish Emerson, more romantic than Mrs Stowe, was Henry David Thoreau, the most thoroughgoing of the New England Transcendentalists. Thoreau was really a Greek of the time of the god Pan, " with the delight in the simple round of the seasons and a responsiveness to natural beauty that belonged to the older civilization." [1] Indeed, with civilization in the ordinary (or modern) sense Thoreau would have nothing at all to do. He despised the cotton-mills of Lowell, and found even the village of Concord too urban. He withdrew to the woods and fields by Walden.

Most of the New England Transcendentalists were college men: Emerson and Thoreau were from Harvard; Longfellow and Hawthorne graduated from Bowdoin. Bronson Alcott, however, was not college-bred. They were all deeply impressed by classical culture, but Thoreau was the most Greek, both in spirit and in scholarship. He was Matthew Arnold's " Scholar Gipsy " in the flesh, and he earned his living like a gipsy, doing just as much work as was necessary to supplement the goods with which Nature provided him. He was a bachelor, and spent most of his time—four hours at least every day—walking in the woods, or just sitting by the waterside in the sunshine. An occasional essay or some odd-jobbing, making a fence or whitewashing a barn, supplied, with some gardening, the simple needs of his livelihood. Emerson when he wrote the poem *Waldeinsamkeit* (*Woodsolitariness*) understood and sympathized with Thoreau; nevertheless the serene and sociable Emerson would not have considered it quite

[1] V. L. Parrington, *The Romantic Revolution in America* (1927), p. 402.

sensible to go and live for years alone in a log cabin (made by himself) by a pond in a wood. Thoreau, on the other hand, thought that this was the only sensible way to live. It was on July 4, 1845, when he was twenty-eight, that Thoreau, the student son of a Concord farmer, and himself till then mostly a resident in Concord village, took up his abode on land belonging to Emerson by the pond of Walden, peaceful and secluded enough, though only one and a half miles from the village. He was at Walden two years. He wrote:

> Every morning was a cheerful invitation to make my life of equal simplicity, and, I may say, innocence, with Nature herself. I have been as sincere a worshipper of Aurora as the Greeks. I got up early and bathed in the pond; that was a religious exercise, and one of the best things which I did. . . . Morning brings back the heroic ages.[1]

This was Jean-Jacques Rousseau over again, living close to Nature on his happy little island in the Lac de Bienne.

Thoreau did not think that he was shunning life by adopting this Robinson Crusoe solitude of the woods. In the "Conclusion" to *Walden* he exhorts his readers: "However mean your life is, meet it and live it!" And in the chapter called "What I lived for," he says:

> I went to the woods because I wished to live deliberately, to front only the essential facts of life, and see if I could not learn what it had to teach, and not, when I came to die, discover that I had not lived.[2]

Many, if not most, of the pleasant things of society were, he held, just encumbrances:

> I never received more than one or two letters in my life that were worth the postage. . . . And I am sure that I never read any memorable news in a newspaper. . . . To a philosopher all *news*, as it is called, is gossip, and they who edit and read it are old women over their tea.[3]

[1] *Walden* (1886 edition), p. 86.
[2] *Ibid.*, p. 88.
[3] *Ibid.*, p. 92.

Give up hurry:

> Let us spend one day as deliberately as Nature, and not be thrown off the track by every nutshell and mosquito's wing that falls on the rails. Let us rise early and fast, or break fast gently and without perturbation; let company come and let company go; let the bells ring and the children cry—determined to make a day of it. Why should we knock under and go with the stream? Let us not be upset and overwhelmed in that terrible rapid and whirlpool called a dinner, situated in the meridian shallows. Weather this danger, and you are safe, for the rest of the way is downhill. With unrelaxed nerves, with morning vigour, sail by it, looking another way, tied to the mast like Ulysses. If the engine whistles, let it whistle, till it is hoarse for its pains. If the bell rings, why should we run? [1]

Of course, Thoreau desired something more than just not to hurry:

> Let us settle ourselves, and work and wedge our feet downwards through the mud and slush of opinion, and prejudice, and tradition, and delusion, and appearance, that alluvion which covers the globe, through Paris and London, through New York and Boston and Concord, through Church and State, through poetry and philosophy and religion, till we come to a hard bottom and rocks in place, which we can call *reality*, and say, This is, and no mistake.[2]

There is the Transcendentalist creed. And here is how Thoreau found it in reality:

> This is a delicious evening, when the whole body is one sense, and imbibes delight through every pore. I go and come with a strange liberty in Nature, a part of herself. As I walk along the stony shore of the pond in my shirt-sleeves, though it is cool as well as cloudy and windy, I see nothing special to attract me; all the elements are unusually congenial to me. The bullfrogs trump to usher in the night, and the note of the whippoorwill is borne on the rippling

[1] *Walden*, p. 95. [2] *Ibid.*, pp. 95–96.

> wind from over the water. Sympathy with the fluttering alder and poplar leaves almost takes away my breath; yet, like the lake, my serenity is rippled, but not ruffled.[1]

When he reached his cabin he found that there had been visitors: one had left a bunch of flowers, another a wreath of evergreens; another had pencilled his name on a yellow walnut-leaf or a chip of wood. Another had left a peeled willow-wand on the table. The odour of a pipe or cigar still lingered about the cabin. This was all pleasant enough. Thoreau did not wish to cut himself off altogether from society. He fairly often went into Concord village himself. On returning from a four-hour walk in the woods he was pleased with the signs of visitors, pleased with the social touch, the kindliness implied in all this. But he was not sorry to have missed the callers, though if they found him in he conversed with them, and shared his dinner, making a hasty pudding. So he was having the best of both the worlds—of society and of solitude. To some extent we can all have the means of doing this, if not quite so effectively as Thoreau.

This son of the woods at Concord was contemporary with another great figure of Concord—Nathaniel Hawthorne, a native and for long a resident of Salem, but resident also at Concord in 1842–45, 1852–53, and 1860–64. It is a remarkable fact that in the middle of the nineteenth century the best English prose was being written in New England, and mainly at Concord. Hawthorne's English is classic Greek in its simplicity, purity, and harmony. He conveys his thought almost, it seems, without effort, yet with impressiveness and emphasis. *The Scarlet Letter*, the novel of Puritan New England, was published in 1850. It is the epic of Salem, the town of the witch-burners, the home of stern Calvinist colonists who felt life to be one long, fierce contest with stormy sea and stony land, and with Satan, the power of darkness. Seventeenth-century

[1] *Walden*, p. 127.

Calvinism, with its doctrines of original sin, predestination, Hell, damnation, had by Hawthorne's time become the gentler, if mistier, faith of Unitarianism. Hawthorne's seventeenth-century heroine, Hester Prynne, submits to the stern Puritan code of morality, accepts its judgments, lives meekly under its chastisements, yet ends all her reflection on this with a query. The moral code remains, the judgment is just, and yet? . . . God is a loving God, but as such was scarcely known in Salem. Hawthorne felt that the answer to Hester Prynne's problem was not just the genial optimism of Emerson; so he too, like Hester, remains at heart a sceptic, baffled by the mystery of life.

The Transcendentalists, particularly the Concord group, are the most vigorous example, the authentic expression, of the New England Renaissance. In Boston and Cambridge it took a more eclectic, a more stylistic form, which has been called by Professor Parrington " The Reign of the Genteel " :

> It was the romanticism of Brahmin culture, with all Falstaffian vulgarity deleted, and every smutch of the natural man bleached out in the pure sunshine of manners. It was Victorianism of a more maidenly purity than the English strain, so carefully filtered by passing through the close Puritan mesh that the smallest impurities were removed. The first of literary commandments was the commandment of reticence.[1]

The tone of this criticism is ironical, satirical, a little patronizing. Boston and Cambridge were devoted to culture, to the library, the study, the lecture-room; and life was viewed by scholars through books and through their study windows. Brahmins, whether in the Orient or in the Occident, are a fortunate and sheltered class. Luckily only a small proportion of mankind wants to be, or has the capacity for being, Brahmins. But the Boston and Cambridge men of letters and scholars of the middle

[1] *The Romantic Revolution in America*, p. 336.

nineteenth century have an assured place in the history of culture—that is, in civilization. Prescott's *History of the Conquest of Mexico* (1843), Parkman's *Conspiracy of Pontiac* (1851), Motley's *Rise of the Dutch Republic* (1856), are works of research, of literature—cantos of the epics of mankind.

Longfellow's poetry has stood the test of time, in the sense that it has had continuous popularity, and is still read probably as much as any other poetry in an age when poetry-reading has gone out of vogue. It is easy enough, of course, as George Saintsbury has pointed out, to see defects in Longfellow's poetry. The poem called *Excelsior*, translated into literal prose—its deplorable title is quite untranslatable—is simply fatuous; and yet we would not have *Excelsior* unwritten. *The Psalm of Life* is, in George Saintsbury's phrase, " one of the most mixed and dangerous of Longfellow's pieces "; yet it was inspiring to the wholesome youth of the Victorian Age, and it will inspire any wholesome, not too sophisticated youth who reads it now. *Evangeline* is " a pretty poem; it lends itself admirably to illustration for drawing-room table books; it was a clever revival of an old, though hopeless, experiment in metre; its sentiment is not false; it has some beautiful passages." [1] *Hiawatha* is a " triumphal achievement." It does exactly what the poet wanted it to do: presents " an entirely strange civilization, or half-civilization, with imagery, diction, metre, and all, adapted in strangeness." [2]

The poet's journal and letters show a singularly happy and well-lived life. From 1836 to 1854 he was Professor of Modern Languages at Harvard, and wrote some volumes of poetry and two novels (*Hyperion* and *Kavanagh*) which at any rate are worth reading. By 1854 his published works were bringing him in enough income to enable him to retire from academic work. In a letter dated May 3, 1854, to Freiligrath, the German poet, he explains: " Household

[1] George Saintsbury, *Prefaces and Essays* (1933), p. 333.
[2] *Ibid.*, p. 336.

occupations, children, relatives, friends, strangers, and college lectures so completely fill up my days that I have no time for poetry." He was happily married, and had two sons and two daughters. No doubt he could have spent the Harvard professorial stipend conveniently; but he was now forty-seven, and, having sufficient money to maintain his household at Cambridge and to live as an independent scholar, he had sufficient strength of mind to make the decision, and never to regret it. In this year, 1854, he began *Hiawatha*. Every day gave him scope for interesting reading, and many, if not most, days inspired him to write something. He frequently read aloud to his family and friends, and not only his own works. He was sociable too, and he liked walking. In his Journal he notes (October 18, 1854): "My morning walk at sunrise is delightful in this weather. Met Mr Worcester, the lexicographer, jogging along on his black horse. He says, with a jolt after every word, 'Why—don't you—get a—horse and—ride as—I do?'" The next entry in the Journal is: "Hiawatha occupies and delights me. Have I no misgivings about it? Yes, sometimes. Then the theme seizes me and hurries me away, and they vanish." He felt that he was writing well; and the public on both sides of the Atlantic appreciated him. Nathaniel Hawthorne, now American Consul at Liverpool, wrote to him (May 11, 1855): "Did you hear how the Harrow schoolboys, a few months ago, decided by a formal vote (as I understood) that you are the first poet of the age?"

Even the great Civil War (1861–65) made no breach in the even tenor of life at Craigie House, Cambridge—for Longfellow at any rate. His tranquil work continued; his quiet social engagements were filled; he wrote his letters and gave innumerable autograph signatures. He died at Cambridge in 1882, and his bust was placed in Poets' Corner, Westminster Abbey.

The New England Renaissance was rounded off with

two writers, not geniuses, indeed, but perfect examples of their time and place—Oliver Wendell Holmes and James Russell Lowell. One was the quintessence of Boston wit, the other of Cambridge culture. Holmes was the chief contributor—that is, he contributed most material—to *The Atlantic Monthly*. *The Autocrat of the Breakfast-table* (1858) is a collection of these early articles. He was, like Longfellow and like Lowell (who was Longfellow's successor in the chair of modern languages), a professor at Harvard, though not in the faculty of liberal arts, but of medicine. Holmes lived at Boston. He was the perfect diner-out. If something sprightly in verse was wanted for an occasion nobody could write a more felicitous set of verses than Dr Holmes. His prose and verse is all good; and as he did not write a great deal of either, and collected his prose and verse in handy book form, he had, and still has, an appreciative audience. The secret of his charm is that he makes direct personal contact with his readers. Holmes is the *talking author*; he wrote most of his works in the first person, and this first person is himself.

Lowell lived at Cambridge, lectured in literature, wrote essays, poems. The essays are seldom read now, the serious poems only occasionally. But *The Biglow Papers* (1848) is a minor classic, known by name to the public, sometimes read, quoted in speeches and leading articles. Scholar, man of letters, straightforward, sensible gentleman, he worthily represented his country as Minister to the Court of St James from 1880 to 1885, thoroughly happy in London and in the politically congenial atmosphere of Gladstonian Liberalism.

Chapter IX

THE BIRTH OF A PARTY

NEXT to a great state the most powerful thing that mankind has produced is a great political party. It is not as permanent a thing as a state. Parties wax and wane, like the great Liberal Party of Great Britain. The Republican Party of the United States, almost supreme for about sixty years, has had catastrophic defeats, lean days; and the question has been asked whether it will not disappear altogether. But no sooner was the question asked than the Republicans began to gain constituencies.[1]

The Republican Party rose in an age of great expansion of the United States. The westward movement was in full course. Gold had been discovered in California in 1848. Everywhere, except in the Southern states, there was marked development: in the East, among its growing industries; in the Middle West, to which a fine class of German immigrants went after the failure of the German Liberal movement of 1848; in the Far West, the lure—and by no means a disappointing lure—of so many young men. Only the old, settled South seemed to have reached a (relatively) stationary condition. The planter aristocracy and the white farmers could make a living—in the case of the planters a very good living—but expansion of wealth and fresh economic opportunity were to be looked for only outside the old states, in the territories beyond the Mississippi which *might* be opened to slave-holding. This question of the territorial extension of slave-holding and the cognate questions were to split the American Union for a

[1] In the Congressional Elections of 1938.

time, and to put an end for ever to the old-style culture and comfort of the South.

The planter aristocracy was distinguished not only for its society—hospitable, cultured, chivalrous among themselves, paternal towards their slaves—but also for its political capacity. It might almost be said that it governed the United States from 1782 to the middle of the nineteenth century. Of the first thirteen Presidents ten were Southerners. There was no organized system of party politics, though the leading people called themselves either Democrats or Whigs. The Democrats were inclined to emphasize state rights; the Whigs were more Federalist; but the difference was not great, and they can scarcely be said to have been divided on any clear principle. The anti-slavery people, the Abolitionists, tended to be Whigs (Federalists) if anything, as state rights were a bulwark of slavery. The situation, however, became confused when Southern influence had the Fugitive Slave Bill of 1850 passed, putting the power of the Federal Government behind the right of individuals to apprehend fugitive slaves in any state. This act, which may be regarded as the efficient cause of the shattering of the Union eleven years later, was merely an amendment to a law of 1793 about fugitives from service or labour. "The important thing about the new law was that it provided Federal jurisdiction for these cases instead of utilizing the existing state judicial establishments."[1] Federal commissioners were set up and given power to enforce the Act within any state of the Union. The resentment, the agitation, the riots, caused by the insistence of Southern slave-owners or their agents upon the arrest of alleged fugitive slaves in free states like Massachusetts or Ohio, were the best possible advertisement of the evils of slavery. *Uncle Tom's Cabin*, published in 1852, really rose on the crest of the wave of the Fugitive Slave Bill.

[1] Channing, *History of the United States*, vi, 98.

The Whig Party—so far as it was a party—expired in trying " to swallow the Fugitive Slave Bill." As Federalists the Whigs could not object in principle to the use of Federal agencies to enforce the law. So far as they were " Free Soilers," or anti-slavery men—only *some* of them were such—they could not relish the pro-slavery intention of the Bill. The Whig Party, or interest or tradition, accordingly dissolved. The Democrats remained Democrats, and some ' Whigs ' may have joined them. A genuine political party, disciplined, organized, took the place of the Whigs.

There had, naturally, always been some rudimentary form of organization for nominating a Presidential candidate. The influential friends of some possible candidate formed a group for promoting his interest. They might be members of state legislatures or of Congress. They may have represented the views of constituents of their own way of thinking, but they had no express mandate. For the 1835· Presidential contest somebody thought of the device of holding a national convention to nominate a candidate. The first convention of this kind, consisting of Democrats from most constituencies, met at Baltimore in May 1835, and nominated by a two-thirds vote Martin van Buren. After this national Presidential conventions, Democrat and Whig, became the regular means for nominating candidates by vote of two-thirds of the deputies. Naturally the business of appointing deputies, arranging for a convention, adopting and ' running ' a Presidential candidate, required a permanent party organization, as soon as the people as a whole became aroused to the great issues at stake. This occurred in 1854–56.

It is clear, however, that party organization would begin in a state, or in a few states, before it extended over the whole nation. The origin of the Republican organization is claimed to be a convention held at Jackson, Michigan, on July 6, 1854. Soon every state had a Republican organization, and these state organizations convened the national convention for nominating a Presidential candidate.

The passage of the Kansas-Nebraska Bill into law was the cause of the controversy in which the Republican Party took form. No wonder the passage of the Bill brought the Free Soilers into the open, united. The Free Soilers were not necessarily Abolitionists, though, of course, all Abolitionists were Free Soilers. These, many of whom did not object to slavery going on in its old-established states, were determined that it should not be brought into new states or territories. The Missouri Compromise of 1820 (an Act of Congress) had satisfied the Free Soilers. It enacted that slavery should not be introduced in the land west of the state of Missouri (admitted as a slave state) and north of parallel 36° 30′. The Southerners objected to this, for as new territory was opened up to the west of the Mississippi or Missouri they wished to be able, if occasion arose, to settle there and to take their slaves with them. In 1850 the Missouri Compromise line was amended by another Compromise. By this New Mexico, taken into the Union as a territory, could have slaves; on the other hand, California, which was admitted as a state, was to have no slavery, although much of it was south of 36° 30′, and therefore was within the Slave Belt as defined by the Missouri Compromise. The Compromise of 1850 was a fair deal. The slavery interest and the Free Soilers gained an equal share of ground, but the *principle* of the Missouri Compromise—a fixed territorial line between free states and slavery—had been given up; the Free Soilers felt this to be a blow, and they reacted by further organizing and consolidating themselves. When, in 1854, it was found necessary to make two new territories—Kansas and Nebraska—a sharp political struggle took place which helped further to define and consolidate the two political parties.

Beyond the frontiers of the Thirteen States which originally comprised the American Union the Middle West as far as the Missouri-Mississippi line, and the Far West beyond the Rocky Mountains, had been settled and organized by the year 1854. There remained the broad area of land between the Missouri-Mississippi and the Rockies, where Americans were beginning to settle in considerable numbers, but where there was no government at all. In 1854 Stephen A. Douglas, a Democrat and senator from Illinois, promoted a Bill in Congress for constituting two territories in the unorganized area, to be called Kansas and Nebraska, with the proviso that whenever they became states their citizens should decide whether slavery was to exist there or not. The Kansas-Nebraska Act, in effect, made the Missouri Compromise void.

There ensued in the territory of Kansas some five years of controversy between the slavery interest and Free Soilers. There was much disorder, and blood was frequently shed; the ferocious John Brown, of Osawatomie, murdered five pro-slavery men for the cause of freedom. In the end the Free Soilers, when it came to voting a constitution, proved by far the more numerous: the constitution of the state of Kansas (adopted 1859) prohibited slavery.

By this time the Republican Party had been explicitly organized on a national basis in a convention at Pittsburg in February 1856. The Presidential election (or rather the election of electors for electing a President) fell within this year. The Pittsburg Republican Convention of February did no more than organize the party. Nomination was made in a subsequent Republican convention held at Philadelphia in June. John C. Frémont, of California, was chosen as Republican candidate, William L. Dayton, of Ohio, as candidate for the Vice-Presidency, but Abraham Lincoln, a lawyer of Springfield, Illinois, received 110 votes. The Democrats, meeting in convention at Cincinnati in the same month, voted in favour of maintaining the Kansas-Nebraska Act " as the only sound and safe solution of the slavery question," and nominated James Buchanan as candidate for the Presidency. When the people voted in November 1856 Buchanan headed the poll, the last Democrat to be elected President until another thirty-two years should pass. It has been suggested that Buchanan's election saved the Union. For if Frémont, a purely Northern, or 'sectional,' nominee, had been elected the Southern states would have seceded, " and public opinion of the North in 1856 was not in favour of coercing their fellow-countrymen back into the Union fold." [1] Indeed, it is a remarkable fact that many of those people who would count as Republicans—namely, the Abolitionist wing—were actively in favour of *disunion*. They advocated repeal of the Union, took " No Union with Slave-holders " as a kind of motto, and called the United States Constitution " a covenant with death " because it recognized the existence of slavery. This was the view of William Lloyd Garrison and his friends.

In 1857 two events occurred which further helped to define the two political parties and to strengthen the Republican Party. The first event was the decision of the Supreme Court in the Dred Scott case. Dred Scott, his wife, and two children were slaves belonging to a certain Dr Emerson, an Army surgeon, and after his death were held in trust for the benefit of Dr Emerson's widow. In Dr Emerson's lifetime Dred Scott had lived with his master in the free states of Illinois and Wisconsin. Later he was in the slave state of Missouri with Mrs Emerson. In 1846 he brought a suit against Mrs Emerson in the Court of Missouri in order to establish his freedom, on the ground that he had lived in free states. The Missouri State Circuit Court ruled that Dred Scott was a free man. Six years

[1] Channing, *op. cit.*, vi, 146.

later the state Supreme Court ruled that although he might have been free while living in free states, he had resumed his condition of slavery by returning to a slave state. In the end the case went to the United States Supreme Court, which decided in 1857 by five to four that Dred Scott was not, and could not be, a citizen in the meaning of the United States Constitution, and that no power had been given in the Constitution to Congress to confer citizenship on negroes. This decision was not merely adverse to the Dred Scott family (which, as a matter of fact, was emancipated soon afterwards by its owners), but in effect invalidated the Missouri Compromise of 1820, an Act of Congress. A great victory for the slave-owners, it stirred the Republicans to the depths. In 1857 a financial panic occurred, caused by over-speculation and perhaps by the disturbance of the money market in consequence of the discovery (1848) and mining of gold in California. The Ohio Life Insurance Trust Company failed, and many banks had to close their doors. It is one of the maxims of American politics that "the party in power is responsible for any financial reverse that may happen, and for the hard times and lack of employment that follow and severely affect the working classes."[1] Now the party in power (1857) was the Democrats. President Buchanan was a Democrat.

The raid of John Brown from Maryland and Virginia in 1859, his seizure of Harper's Ferry, as a rallying-point for fugitive slaves, with about twenty men on October 16, his desperate defence, his trial at Charlestown, Virginia, and his execution on December 2 had no direct effect upon the early history of the Republican Party. Abraham Lincoln called it an absurd effort, "which ends in little else than his own execution."[2]

The decisive year in the history of political parties in

[1] Channing, *op. cit.*, vi, 200.

[2] Quoted by O. G. Villard in *John Brown* (1910), p. 564.

America was 1860. The Whigs had disappeared. The Democrat Party was almost in disintegration. They were not of one mind upon the Slave Question. Stephen A. Douglas, of Illinois, was their most prominent man at this time, the only one who would have any chance at the approaching Presidential election; but, though he was the author of the Kansas-Nebraska Bill, he was not an out-and-out slavery man; he advocated "Squatter Sovereignty"—that each state should decide for itself to have slavery or not. His political opponent, Abraham Lincoln, of Illinois, in a series of public debates with Douglas, by shrewd questioning brought out the ambiguities of, at any rate, the Northern Democrats' position on the Slavery Question. On the other hand, the Republicans, though they had taken fairly definite form as a political party in 1856, were only 'sectional.' They represented Northern interests and views; they had no programme, no consciously held ideal, for the whole Union. Edmund Burke had long ago pointed out that no grouping of men is a genuine political party if it represents only sectional or class interest, if it is not prepared to stand for the interest of the whole people and to promote the common good. Abraham Lincoln declared the same thing in other words when he set forth to contest the Illinois senatorship in 1858: "A house divided against itself cannot stand. I believe this government [that is, the Union] cannot endure permanently half slave and half free."

The fateful conventions of 1860 were held, in Chicago by the Republicans, in Baltimore by the Democrats. The national convention of the Republican Party, comprising Abolitionists, Free Soilers, industrial protectionists, and place-hunters, nominated Lincoln for their candidate, at first by a bare majority, ultimately by a unanimous vote.

The Democrat national convention, meeting at Baltimore in June, soon split into two bodies. One of these nominated Douglas as the Democrat candidate; the other nominated John C. Breckinridge, of Kentucky. A third convention, the remnants of the old Whigs, also met at Baltimore, and nominated John Ball, of Tennessee. At the elections in November Lincoln was returned at the head of the poll, although his three opponents together received a larger number of votes. South Carolina and six other states—Louisiana, Texas, Georgia, Alabama, Mississippi, and Florida—at once seceded from the Union. Virginia (all except the West Virginians) seceded later, in April 1861, after hostilities had opened at Fort Sumter. Arkansas, Tennessee, and North Carolina followed Virginia with the " Confederate States of the South."

Secession brought clean-cut definition into the Republican Party. The Republicans could not help now believing in union, in the Federal principle, whether they were prepared to fight for it or not. The Secessionists, who were all Democrats (though not all Democrats were Secessionist), naturally emphasized state rights. The Republicans saved the Union and became " the Grand Old Party." They continued to emphasize—not very strongly—Federal power, though without disregarding state rights; and they continued—quite wholeheartedly—to emphasize industrial protectionism, free labour, and free land made possible through a Homestead Act. The Democrats, after the war and reconstruction were over, continued to emphasize—moderately—state rights, and to be at any rate less rigorously protectionist than the Republicans. The main strength of the Republicans continued to be in the Eastern states and in the Middle West and, less markedly, in the West. The Democrat Party had undivided allegiance in the ' solid South.' Representing what James Bryce called " the centripetal and centrifugal tendencies," [1] the two parties remained fairly well defined and powerfully organized against each other until the fourth decade of the twentieth century, when party issues

[1] *The American Commonwealth* (1907 edition), ii, 5.

again became confused, when the Democrats, borne into office on the wave of the great economic depression in 1933, adopted policies of Federal action, and when the Republican Party reacted by standing up for state rights. It was then that people began to ask whether the Grand Old Party was going to disappear altogether.

The Secession and the Civil War ruined the South. When troops of the Confederacy in South Carolina on April 13, 1861, attacked Fort Sumter, which had a Federal (Union) garrison, the South sacrificed the culture and comfort of a social system over two hundred years old. Lincoln acknowledged that slavery was legal under the United States Constitution in the states where it existed in 1861, and he was willing to leave it there without making any attempt to secure an amendment of the Constitution. Some later Republican President, however, commanding the support of a large majority, would be likely to solve the Slavery Question by having an amendment to the United States Constitution passed into law. The Southern slave-holders and their sympathizers would not wait for this, and so seceded from the Union. By this time the Republican and Democratic Parties were clearly defined, and they have divided American politics ever since. They have made the United States the most perfect example of a genuine two-party system.

Chapter X

THE LAST AGE OF PAPAL ROME

PIUS IX had fled from Rome to Gaeta, in the kingdom of Naples, in consequence of the revolution of November 1848. He did not at once return when French troops sent by Louis Napoleon, President of the Second French Republic, drove back the forces of the Roman Republic of Garibaldi, Armellini, and Saffi, and forced their way into the Eternal City on July 3, 1849. The Papal power was restored, but Pius IX and his court of cardinals remained at Gaeta until the spring of 1850. Escorted by King Ferdinand II of Naples, he crossed the frontier of the Papal State at Epitaffio on April 6, 1850, and entered Rome by the Porta San Giovanni at 4 P.M. on Friday, April 12. The old administrative system had been already restored; and until September 4, 1870, the Papal State remained under the government of priests. This at least was the theory of Roman administration, though Cardinal Antonelli, the all-powerful Secretary of State, was only in minor orders. He retained the position of Secretary of State down to his death in 1876.

The Papal State (or States of the Church) extended in 1850 from Terracina, sixty miles south-east of Rome, to Ferrara, on the river Po, a distance of 381 miles. It contained eighteen provinces, and had a population of something over three million. Supposed to be a guarantee of Papal independence, it was the weakest state in the world, and depended for its security upon a French garrison of about twenty thousand men. These were stationed at Rome and at Civita Vecchia. There were also the Swiss Guards of the Pope, and in addition there was a regular

Pontifical army of some seven to ten thousand men, recruited by the voluntary system, very slovenly and inefficient. *Gendarmes* or *sbirri* were very numerous. Passports were required by natives as well as by foreigners who moved from one province to another. There were large numbers of administrative and legal officials; and as nearly all the higher posts were held by clergy there was no incentive for the lay officials to be efficient and keen. The Pope was an absolute sovereign, assisted by advice from the resident Cardinalate. The city of Rome had a municipal council called the Senate, but the Pope nominated the members.

The administration of the Papal State was more than paternal: it tried to regulate everything. The economic system was highly protective; prohibitive duties barred legitimate trade, but smuggling went on incessantly. The customs officials at Civita Vecchia and the other ports made comfortable incomes by conniving at smuggling. The influx of foreign commodities combined with the native produce of a fertile countryside kept the cost of living low. Everything produced in the Papal State, even the food of the people, paid tax to a Treasury which always needed money; but these numerous small indirect taxes, though they employed a vast number of petty officials, did not greatly raise the cost of living. Most of the people lived by agriculture, in the towns by shopkeeping, except in Rome, where large numbers lived on doles from the charitable foundations. About half the Roman population of 200,000 had no regular occupation.

Pius IX, a month short of fifty-eight years old at the restoration in 1850, was then a high-spirited, physically active man. He went about Rome freely, usually in a carriage, and he greatly enjoyed paying surprise visits to monasteries or nunneries, to artists' studios, or even to the houses of quite homely people. Frequently he would drive in his carriage outside the walls; dismounting, he would then go for a long walk in the country. He often took a holiday at Castel Gandolfo, the summer-house on the shore of Lake Albano which Urban VIII had built. Here Pius IX enjoyed country life, picnics, walks, hill-climbing. On these expeditions he was conversational and jolly, and not too insistent on his dignity, though he never forgot it. Cheerful, benign, approachable, he was naturally popular with the Romans; and they do not seem to have greatly regretted his abandonment of his youthful Liberalism. He now no longer thought of making any political concessions. His views seemed perfectly medieval. He was prepared to see miracles in daily life; and when the opportunity occurred to display and magnify his power by decreeing (December 8, 1854) the dogma of the Immaculate Conception of the Virgin he seized it with avidity. Politically unprogressive though he was, he was not averse from employing the inventions of science. The Papal Government was the first Italian Government to use adhesive postage-stamps. In 1853 gas-lamps were installed in the streets of Rome. In 1854 the telegraph was inaugurated in the Papal State. Pius IX was willing, almost anxious, to have railways. In 1856 he granted a concession to a company for the construction of a railway from Rome to Civita Vecchia, 50 miles; and in 1858 a concession was given for a line from Rome to Frascati, 15 miles. Not until 1860, however, was there any railway open to traffic in the Papal State. There was no great commerce for which railways could be needed. Living was cheap in the Papal State. The inhabitants did not move about much. Foreign visitors—and there were very many of these—were still on the whole of the unhurrying type, and were pleased enough to travel by carriage or postchaise. They came to enjoy the scenes and sights of Rome in the mellow light of the decline, the sunset, of the Papal State. Mr Gladstone, after visiting Italy in 1850, wrote to Manning (January 26, 1851), who was still a cleric of the Church of England:

Some things I have learned in Italy that I did not know before—one in particular. The temporal power of the Pope, that great, wonderful, and ancient erection, is *gone*. The problem has been worked out; the ground is mined; the train is laid; a foreign force, in its nature transitory, alone stays the hand of those who would complete the process of applying the match.

Gladstone was not absolutely wrong; but the temporal power lasted, though decreasing, for another twenty years.

Nor, in its own way, should life in the Papal State during those years be reckoned a bad thing, though the people were not living on a plane of lofty idealism or of exalted national tension. The State was an anachronism; the way of life was an anachronism. Yet there were some good things about both. It is true that there were no political liberties, nor in theory guarantees of personal liberty. Provided, however, that people paid their taxes, which were numerous enough, though petty, they were not likely to have much to do with the police. There was no conscription, no compulsory education. In fact, the people were not compelled to do anything, although they were expected to go to church, and did do so, without appearing to be very spiritually inclined. They were poor; the standard of life was low, and there was no great industry or commerce to raise the standard. Nevertheless that the people were not without a margin above their necessities is indicated by the existence of savings banks, which were numerous and were favoured by the Pontifical Government. This statement does not apply to Rome itself, where, as we have seen, more than half the population of about 200,000 people lived on casual jobs and the endowed charities. Most of the rest of the Roman population, even the aristocracy, took in boarders or let apartments. There were no good hotels or inns in Papal Rome, though there were innumerable taverns where a good though homely meal could be had.

Under Papal rule society in Rome had always been cosmopolitan, and it remained so to the end. The Roman aristocratic families, all extremely old, except the banking Torlonia, had ancient foreign connexions. Living in their decayed palaces on the proceeds of country estates, they could not—except the Duke of Sermoneta and Prince Torlonia—afford to hold a splendid *salon*; nevertheless they managed to mix freely with the Diplomatic Corps and with the many distinguished people who came to Rome for long or short periods. The splendour of the Roman Catholic Church, the gorgeous pageantry, the pervasive religious, if not precisely spiritual, atmosphere, the numerous and eminent *personnel* of the Papal Court, not secluded, but on the contrary moving freely in society, contributed to the charm and cosmopolitanism of social life. In Lord Beaconsfield's *Lothair* the Cardinal (who is, of course, the great Wiseman), advising the hero of the novel about travelling, says:

> If my advice were asked by a young man who contemplated travelling on a proper scale I should say begin with Rome. Almost all that Europe contains is derived from Rome. It is always best to go to the fountain-head, to study the original. The society too, there, is delightful. I know none equal to it. That, if you please, is civilization, pious and refined. And the people, all so gifted, and so good, so kind, so orderly, so charitable, so truly virtuous. I believe the Roman people to be the best people that ever lived, and this too while the secret societies have their foreign agents in every quarter, trying to corrupt them, but always in vain. If an act of political violence occurs you may be sure it is confined entirely to foreigners.[1]

Lothair is convinced. To Theodora, the passionate Italian secularist patriot, he says, "Rome is the country of the world, and even the doting priest you talk of boasts of two hundred millions of subjects." Yet the term of the

[1] *Lothair*, Chapter XLVIII, *ad fin.*

temporal power was approaching, and Lothair himself goes to take part in the work of 'liberation.' He views the City from one of its hills in the twilight of the Papal rule. The Monseignore, who is with him, says:

> " 'Tis well that we came, is it not? And now we will seat ourselves." Below and before them, on an undulating site, a city of palaces and churches spread out its august form, enclosing within its ample walls sometimes a wilderness of classic ruins, column and arch and theatre, sometimes the umbrageous spread of princely gardens. A winding and turbid river divided the city in unequal parts, in one of which there rose a vast and glorious temple, crowned with a dome of almost superhuman size and skill, on which the favourite sign of heaven flashed with triumphant truth.
>
> The expression of relief which, for a moment, had reposed on the face of Lothair, left it when he said in an agitated voice, " I at length behold Rome! "[1]

The end of the temporal power could not be far off. That life was peaceful and comfortable in the Papal State was not sufficient justification, at any rate in the eyes of Italian nationalists and European Liberals. A progressive policy in constitutional matters would not have saved Rome. In any case Pius IX would not hear of liberalism or constitutionalism. In 1857 he had made a four months' journey through the State, listening to complaints on local matters; magistrates had been instructed not to allow constitutional questions to be opened. Besides the French garrison in Rome and Civita Vecchia, there were Austrian garrisons in the Legations—Bologna, Forli, Ferrara, Ravenna. Such protection did not add to the dignity of the temporal power. In 1859 Victor Emmanuel II of Sardinia and Napoleon III, Emperor of the French, made war upon the Austrians, and after the battles of Magenta and Solferino annexed Lombardy to Sardinia. In 1860

[1] *Lothair*, Chapter LXI, *ad fin.*

Victor Emmanuel, after revolutions in Central Italy and plebiscites, was able to annex the Grand Duchy of Tuscany, the Duchies of Parma and Modena, the Papal Legations. Later in the year, after Garibaldi had conquered the kingdom of Naples, Victor Emmanuel invaded the Papal territories of Umbria and the Marches. The Papal army—not the French garrisons, but the regular Papal troops—met the Sardinians in battle at Castelfidardo (September 18, 1860) and were completely defeated. Plebiscites were held in Umbria and the Marches by the Sardinian Government, and these territories were annexed to Sardinia, called the kingdom of Italy from the year 1861. The temporal power was reduced to Rome and the districts of Civita Vecchia, Viterbo, Velletri, and Frosinone. The French garrison was still in Rome.

The Papal army had fought with courage at Castelfidardo. To be effective, however, better organization and equipment were needed. Monseigneur de Mérode, Papal Minister of War from 1860 to 1864, worked with tremendous enthusiasm at making an army out of the usual elements who go to make up any military force open to foreigners. Soldiers of fortune came from all over Europe, some of them being already experienced soldiers, others serious 'Crusaders,' others scapegraces and tatterdemalions seeking pay and food and licence. In 1864 the French Government negotiated with the Italian Government the Convention of September 15. The Italian Government undertook not to attack the Papal territories; the Emperor of the French undertook to withdraw his garrison from Rome. The French troops were actually withdrawn in the years 1865–66; the last left in December 1866. The Papal Government was not sorry to see them go. They were a heavy expense, and they quarrelled continually with the Papal troops.

The makers of the Convention of September 15—at least, the French makers—had reckoned without Garibaldi. In 1867 he had arranged for a private invasion of the Papal State, like his expedition to Sicily in 1860. On October 23, 1867, coming from Florence, he crossed the frontier of the Papal State with his Redshirts. Napoleon III, however, was not going to be bamboozled in this way. He sent General Failly and an expeditionary corps by sea to Civita Vecchia. They arrived on October 29, went to Rome, and joined the Papal army, which was commanded by General Kanzler. The victory over the Garibaldians at Mentana on November 3 was won mainly by the Papal troops, though French troops entered into action too, and, of course, fought well. Outnumbered, outmanœuvred, and outgunned, Garibaldi's army had no chance, and the French would have made a better political impression all round if they had left the Papal army to repel the invasion alone, confining themselves to garrisoning Rome. Napoleon III, not unreasonably, regarded himself as released from the Convention of September 15, and the restored French garrison now stayed on in Rome. He paid dearly in 1870 for his interest in the Roman question, for as long as French troops were in Rome King Victor Emmanuel, in spite of his former obligations to the Emperor, would not raise a finger to help him. To maintain the temporal power was a curious policy of the French Emperor, who had done so much towards making a United Italy by his military assistance to Victor Emmanuel in 1859 and his diplomatic assistance in 1860. This guarantee of the Papal State has been called the only consistent element in his foreign policy. It began, in the way many durable things do, with what was meant to be a purely temporary measure in 1849, when Louis Napoleon was President of the Second French Republic and wanted to make sure of the clerical vote in France. He had tried to release himself by the Convention of September 15, 1864; and now Garibaldi's raid and the battle of Mentana of November 3, 1867, had brought the incubus of the occupation of Rome back upon the Emperor's failing shoulders.

Pius IX would make no compromise with the kingdom of Italy. His temporal power might be declining, but he asserted his spiritual power in ways that would have astonished Hildebrand or Innocent III. There was his Decree of the Immaculate Conception in 1854, the Syllabus condemning "progress, liberalism, and modern civilization" in 1864, and in 1870 (July 18) there was the astonishing assertion, agreed to by a General Council of the Church, with two dissentient votes, of the Infallibility of the Pope. The old gentleman simply basked in the warm rays of spiritual power which amply compensated for the loss of temporal power.

Benjamin Disraeli, having experienced one crowded hour of glorious Prime Ministership (actually it was ten months) in 1868—the year after Mentana—was living between Hughenden and the House of Commons, working and waiting until the irrepressible Gladstone should give him another chance of holding the supreme office in the State. Politics in opposition did not now take up all Disraeli's time: he went back to his old taste for novel-writing, not indulged since 1847, and composed *Lothair*, surveying Rome and the temporal power, "the Italian Mission in England," Cardinals and English Dukes, from the library window at Hughenden. He sees in his mind's eye Theodora, Roman, passionate for the union of Italy, nationally mystic, resistant to priestly power. It is 1867; the French garrison has for the time being withdrawn. Lothair, who is later drawn into the Garibaldian raid and fights at Mentana, says to her, "You speak of Rome?" She replies:

> "Yes, of the only thought I have ever had. I speak of that country which first impressed upon the world a general and enduring form of masculine virtue; the land of liberty and law, and eloquence and military genius, now garrisoned by monks and governed by a doting priest."

"Everybody must be interested about Rome," said Lothair. "Rome is the country of the world, and even the doting priest you talk of boasts of two hundred millions of subjects."

"If he were at Avignon again I should not care for his boasts," said Theodora. "I do not grudge him his spiritual subjects; I am content to leave his superstition to Time. Time is no longer slow; his scythe mows quickly in this age."

Some of the Cardinalate may have felt the approach of the scythe. Antonelli seems to have done so. Far too intelligent to be unaware of the inexorable forces arrayed against the temporal power, he was content to carry on the existing system, to maintain it as long as he could by subtlety and inertia, but not to worry too much if the end were coming. There was an 'Old Guard,' however, that never surrendered. Like Monseignore Berwick in *Lothair*, they said to themselves, "So long as we never relinquish our title to the Eternal City we shall be eternal." To a friend the Monseignore remarked, "If Rome fall, not an existing dynasty in Europe will survive five years." Disraeli, when he wrote this sentence, may have believed it in regard to the Continental dynasties, not the British. Then, with one of his astonishing flights of imagination, he makes one of his characters suggest a plan for saving a vestige of the temporal power, for securing a 'token' state to the Pope, as has actually been done by the Lateran Treaty of 1929. Monseignore Berwick's mysterious visitor in London says:

"I wish we could devise some plan which, humanly speaking, would secure to his Holiness the possession of his earthly home for ever. I wish I could induce you to consider more favourably that suggestion that his Holiness should content himself with the ancient city, and, in possession of St Peter's and the Vatican, leave the rest of Rome to the vulgar cares and the mundane anxieties of the transient generation." [1]

[1] *Lothair*, Chapter L.

Monseignore Berwick's answer was: *non possumus*. So it would soon come to the decision at the hands of Italian invaders or insurrectionists within. "Whatever then happens," said the General in *Lothair*, "we shall at least get rid of the great imposture."

Pius IX, who believed in miraculous protection (especially in regard to himself), accepted the French intervention and the victory of Mentana as a miracle; and he may have thought that another miracle would save the temporal power in the next crisis. So 1870 found Eternal Rome unchanged and unmoved, except for the moderate excitement caused by the presence of some eight hundred prelates at the Vatican Council.

A theocracy could last only in Tibet. In Western Europe of the late nineteenth century its persistence was inconceivable. Everybody knew this. Yet as nobody knew when the moment of dissolution would come everybody in Rome accepted the situation as it was, and enjoyed it while it lasted. The word 'everybody' is relative: there were some exceptions—members of secret societies who would like to have made an insurrection. There was no insurrection, however; the last years of Papal power were a mellow sunset. The people of Rome were not impatient for their freedom. Living remained cheap. The magnificent pageantry of the Church, the numerous holidays, the frequent appearance of the Pope and Cardinals outside the Vatican City, the concourse of interested visitors—royalty, aristocracy, men of letters and artists, pilgrims—the absence of politics, all made Rome one of the most refreshing places in the world. The kind, witty, talkative old Pope, growing more and more hale every day as he also grew more set in his mind, was one of the pleasantest public figures in Europe, far more approachable than any other royalty, serene, unselfconscious, gentle, garrulous, yet supremely dignified in person and in office.

Of course, the temporal power in Rome could not go

on, though one sometimes wonders why not. It was the "stationary state" which John Stuart Mill explains in his *Political Economy* as perhaps the only happy one; but society is seldom for long stationary. And so the visitors came and went; the artists painted their pictures; the shrewd Diplomatic Corps attended parties and clubs and wrote their routine reports and wondered how long it would last; and the Roman people bought and sold and chattered in the streets and *cafés*.

On July 18, 1870, war broke out, after a brief, tense crisis, between the Germans and the French. The inexorable demands of the military machine immediately affected the garrison in Rome, which took ship from Civita Vecchia on August 5. There was a fair-sized Papal army left—about thirteen thousand—but there was no use in trying to defend the city. It had not been because of the size of the French garrison that Victor Emmanuel kept from attacking Rome: it was because of the French flag which the regiments bore. A dozen French privates and a corporal would have been an insuperable bar to the entry of Italian troops. On September 2, however, the Emperor of the French and his best army were captured at Sedan; and on September 4 the Imperial Government in Paris fell. The Provisional 'Government of National Defence' was not going to insist upon the observance of the Convention of September 15, 1864, if, indeed, the convention existed then.

In order to demonstrate to the world that he was the victim of violence Pius IX ordered the gates to be locked and guarded; but to avoid bloodshed the defence was not to be prolonged. The Italian army was now in the Papal State, and not far from Rome. It was waiting for a popular insurrection in Rome which never occurred.

On September 19, 1870, the Pope left the Vatican for the last time, and climbed the Scala Sancta. At 5.15 A.M. on September 20 Italian guns opened fire on the Porta

Pia and upon other parts of the wall. The Pope remained calm and celebrated Mass in his private chapel; many of the Diplomatic Corps were present. For some reason the defence was prolonged, contrary to the Pope's original instruction. At last, when the bombardment had continued for over four hours, inflicting a number of casualties, the Pope sent peremptory orders to General Kanzler to raise the white flag over the dome of St Peter's. Firing ceased a few minutes after 10 A.M. The Italian troops, under General Cadorna, began to file through the Porta Pia at midday. Generals Kanzler and Cadorna signed articles of capitulation. Pius IX took no part in the proceedings, nor did he recognize the annexation of Rome by the kingdom of Italy. He remained in the Vatican; the Italian authorities carefully kept outside the precincts. A plebiscite was held in Rome, and the annexation was completed.

Chapter XI

"L'EMPIRE, C'EST LA PAIX"

IT is probable that Louis Napoleon was sincere when he declared, on October 9, 1852, at Bordeaux, that the Empire was peace. Most people are sincere when they are in a condition of exaltation; and it may be that this cool and calculating man was for the moment uplifted by the prospect of Napoleonic revival. He was still only President of the Second French Republic, but the *coup d'état* of December 2, 1851, had made him a kind of dictator-president; and a complaisant Senate was soon to invite him to be Emperor.

Louis Napoleon, or the Emperor Napoleon III, as he became on December 2, 1852, appreciated peace. In certain respects he was in advance of his time. He knew that peace was something far richer than just the absence of war. It was work and art and letters, the fruitful advance of science, social life, and the culture of mind and spirit. In his mind's eye he saw muddy, narrow streets and dark, noisome alleys of Paris made into spacious, clean avenues and squares and gardens, with flowers and fountains and playgrounds for children; French steamships crossing the oceans in friendly rivalry with the English Cunarders and other liners; the great world assembling in Paris to assist at 'Universal Exhibitions' of the best and most interesting of the products of mankind; and the common man and woman, active, cheerful, contented, decently paid, well housed, cared for in sickness and old age, protected by the law, comforted by religion.

This was the best side to Napoleon III's character—his sympathy with the common people. While still an exile from his native land, before he seemed to have the slightest prospect of a throne, he had written pamphlets and papers on social questions, and had expounded policies for the good of the working man. As Emperor, inclined to be phlegmatic, physically tired, and bored with business, he would brighten up and become alert when his Ministers mentioned some social project or charitable endeavour. In his conspiratorial days he had had occasion to flee to the United States for a few months; always inquisitive, observant, studious, he could not fail to notice in American politics and society the persistent fundamental policy of giving a fair chance in life to the common man. Among his first acts was the foundation of two 'public utility' companies—the Crédit Foncier in 1852, the Crédit Mobilier in 1853—to provide cheap credit for the small man in farming and industry.

Having this dream of an empire, peaceful, enlightened, humane, Napoleon III was not unmindful of the heavenly vision. Paris, after the improvements, the town-planning, carried out by Georges-Eugène Haussmann, Prefect of the Seine, became more beautiful than ever. As a centre of art and intellectual culture it was second to no other city, though London rivalled it in this age. The Universal Exhibitions of 1855 and 1867—especially the latter—were magnificent successes. Although the great English poets and novelists of the Victorian Age were unsurpassed anywhere, their works had not the European currency that the literature of the Second Empire had. It was as if the intellectual ascendancy of the *ancien régime*, of France in the eighteenth century, was revived in the nineteenth. The French language was the current coin of the intellectuals as well as of the diplomatists of Europe; and the latest work of the Dumas, father and son, of the brothers Goncourt, of Daudet, of Hugo (an exile), were on every *salon* table. All Europe hummed the melodies from Offenbach's operas. The Emperor advocated reduction of armament and promoted peace conferences; the last to be held during his reign took place at Geneva in 1869. He believed in effecting "peaceful change" by diplomacy and plebiscites, and benefited through these means by the acquisition of Nice and Savoy for France in 1860. He would have achieved the transference of Venetia from Austria to the kingdom of Italy by purchase in 1866 if Francis Joseph at the last moment had not given way to bad advice. Any historian who concentrated his attention on the humanitarian efforts of Napoleon III would find much to support the claim, *l'Empire, c'est la paix.*

On the other hand, the old-school historians, who regarded history as a chronicle of wars, would find the reign of Napoleon III to fit beautifully into their scheme. There was scarcely a year of the reign without a war. In 1849, while he was still only President of the Second Republic, Louis Napoleon had a brief Italian war, when he sent General Oudinot with an expeditionary force to reduce the Roman Republic of Mazzini and to restore the temporal power of Pius IX. The President became Emperor Napoleon III on December 2, 1852. There followed a whole series of wars, big and little: Crimean War, 1854–56; Franco-Austro-Sardinian War (France and Sardinia in alliance), 1859; Chinese War (France and Great Britain in co-operation), 1860–61; campaign in the Lebanon, 1861; Mexican War, 1863–67; Roman Relief Expedition (battle of Mentana against Garibaldi), 1867; Franco-German War, 1870. Every one of these wars could have been avoided with honour and advantage. On no single occasion was the French Empire defending itself or any 'vital' interest from attack. Every war except the last was made by Napoleon III to further a national or dynastic policy. The final, the Franco-German War of 1870, was incurred because the Emperor (or the Empress) insisted upon demanding an absurd guarantee after the diplomatic question—the Hohenzollern candidature for the Spanish throne—had been settled by a complete German withdrawal. In fact, the reign of Napoleon III has more distinct wars against civilized peoples than any other reign in history, not excepting that of Napoleon I. And yet Napoleon III was, beyond any other ruler of his age, considerate for the welfare and happiness of the common people, who have to bear the chief burden of every war. He hated to see human suffering; and the agonizing scene of the battlefield of Solferino in 1859, which was a victory for French arms, was one of the things that turned him to making a premature peace treaty. On the other hand, when a vital French interest really was at stake, when the call of honour and the prospect of advantage imperatively demanded intervention on the side of the public law of Europe, in the war of Prussia against the Germanic Confederation in 1866, Napoleon III did nothing—except to ask Bismarck for a *pourboire*.[1]

Of the many ill-conceived military enterprises of Napoleon III the Mexican Expedition was the worst. Like all the schemes of his Imperial years, it had its roots in his dreams as a young man. Imprisoned at Ham from 1840 to 1846 for an attempt to provoke an insurrection at Boulogne, he had reflected, collected statistics, written pamphlets, among them one on Central America and the prospect of an Isthmian Canal. Doubtless this was the germ of the Mexican Expedition. That the prisoner of Ham should one day restore the altars and found an Imperial throne in Mexico would be no more astonishing than that he should resurrect the Napoleonic Empire in France. Indeed, the Mexican adventure, when it started, seemed to have far better prospects than the aim of the proscribed, exiled Bonaparte of 1848 to win the throne of France.

In 1861 Mexico was a kind of no man's land. There had

[1] *Pourboire* is Bismarck's word. Napoleon III called it 'compensation.' One of the suggested French items of compensation was Belgium!

really been no settled government there since the fall of the Spanish monarchy in 1821. In the next forty years Mexico had fifty presidents and dictators, not one of whom ever completely controlled the whole people, and most of whom came to a bad end.[1] The country was a happy hunting-ground for adventurers, for there was land and silver to be won, and perhaps even supreme power for a season. Louis Napoleon was one of the greatest adventurers of the nineteenth century. Mexico offered opportunities which he could scarcely ignore.

Civil war is expensive. Mexico, being in chronic civil war, had chronic deficit in its finances. The Government had, of course, borrowed, chiefly from foreign sources. The bonds fell into default, and the bond-holders, in pressing their claims, naturally expected support from their Governments. The British, French, and Spanish Governments had negotiated certain conventions for liquidation of the foreign debt of Mexico, but revolutions and a certain lack of zeal, but chiefly a lack of means, had interfered with the execution of the conventions. In the nineteenth century the Governments of creditor Great Powers acknowledged a certain responsibility for the financial claims of their nationals, and were prepared, in the last resort, to support these claims by force, by landing military detachments at a port of the debtor state and taking over the customs duties in pledge. Action of this kind with regard to defaulted Turkish, Greek, and Chinese bonds had been taken at various times, and was considered to be in accord with the law of nations; the practice was followed in the twentieth century by the British and German Governments (in 1902) in regard to Venezuela bonds, and by the ' Allied Governments ' in 1921–23 on account of the German reparations. There has always been a fear on the part

[1] An exception was Antonio Lopez de Santa-Anna, who, after fifty-five years of almost incessant fighting, plotting, flight, restoration, died in his bed in Mexico City on June 21, 1876, at the age of eighty-one.

of the debtor Governments that this kind of debt enforcement against them might lead to the loss of territorial sovereignty. As a matter of fact, however, this has never happened. No creditor Power has ever gained territory as the result of the debt-collecting process, nor, indeed, as a rule, has there been any intention of gaining territory. The Mexican expedition was exceptional.

On October 31, 1861, the French, British, and Italian Governments signed a convention engaging themselves to send sufficient naval and military forces for the seizure of fortresses on the Mexican coast. The objects stated in the Convention of London were to secure the safety of European residents and the execution of Mexico's financial engagements. In addition to seizing the coast fortresses, the commanders of the expeditionary forces were authorized to carry out *such other operations as they should deem necessary for achieving the specified aim*. The historian of the Second Empire [1] believes that this clause concealed a vast aim of vague design of Napoleon III, and another on the part of the Spanish Government. It was their lost provinces that the Madrid Government were thinking of. Nevertheless the original expeditionary force or forces did not pass the measure of a coastal debt-collecting enterprise. If the naval units were powerful (particularly in view of the fact that Mexico had no navy) the potential land forces were not too big—700 marines from Great Britain, 2500 soldiers from France, 6000 from Spain. The contribution of the Spanish Government, in view of its small stake in the Mexican debt, was rather extravagant, and its appointment of General Prim to command its forces rather grandiose. The expedition, however, was still only a reply—a normal reply—of creditor Powers to a defaulting Government; but, besides the dreams of Napoleon III and the schemes of General Prim, there were involved the ambitions and grievances of Mexican exiles in Madrid and

[1] P. de la Gorce, *Histoire du Second Empire* (1911), iv, 27.

Paris. These men wanted to have their estates back; and if they had any definite political point of view it was monarchist and clerical.

In the middle of December 1861 the Spanish expeditionary force descended upon Vera Cruz, which was forthwith abandoned by the Mexican authorities. At the beginning of 1862 the British and French forces arrived. Thus Vera Cruz passed under joint occupation of the three Powers.

From the first the British authorities had no great enthusiasm for the expedition; and the enthusiasm of the Spanish Government soon waned before the realities of Mexican affairs. An unpleasant impression was made on its associates by the French Government's adoption of the claim of the banker Jecker. This man, a Swiss established in Mexico, had become owner for some seventy-five million francs of depreciated Mexican bonds, which, of course, were in default in 1861. The French included Jecker's bonds in the claim which, along with British and Spanish claims, was presented to the Mexican Government after the landing at Vera Cruz. It is now known, and was probably suspected then, that the Duc de Morny, half-brother of Napoleon III and President of the Corps Législatif, was financially interested in the Jecker bonds. In his correspondence Jecker called Morny his partner (*associé*), and disclosed the fact that this partner was to have 30 per cent. of the profits on the bonds—profits which, naturally, could be realized only if the Mexican Government resumed, or, rather, began, payment of the defaulted bonds. Napoleon III had no part in the unsavoury Stock Exchange gambles which poisoned the atmosphere of his Court, though it is difficult to believe that he never suspected their existence.

After the landings at Vera Cruz in December–January 1861–62 the next step was for the associated Powers—in effect, their diplomatic agents acting together—to present the financial claims of their Governments in the form of an ultimatum. This was done. Then, on account of the heat on the coast and of the yellow fever which began to appear among the troops, the French and Spanish commanders moved their men up-country to the plateau, on the road to Mexico City, and stationed them at Tehuacan, Orizaba, and Cordova. This movement, however, was not a further exercise of military pressure against the existing (Juarez) Government of Mexico, for the British force was kept resolutely to its ships, and the Spanish and French troops, even when reinforced by 4000 fresh soldiers under General Lorencez, were quite inadequate for a march to the capital. The occupation of Tehuacan, Orizaba, and Cordova was, in fact, made by agreement between the Franco-Spanish commanders and President Juarez in the Convention of Soledad (February 19, 1862). Oddly enough, by negotiating the Convention of Soledad the French and Spanish acknowledged the legality of the Juarez Government, and promised to respect "the independence, sovereignty, and territorial integrity of the Republic." Nevertheless the same ships which brought General Lorencez and 4000 French reinforcements to Vera Cruz on March 5, 1862, brought General Almonte, the leader of the exiled conservative Mexican notabilities from Europe. This man was believed to be a son of the priest Morellos, one of the leaders of the first Mexican revolution —the war of liberation from Spain. Almonte's arrival at Vera Cruz was expected by the French Government to be the preliminary to a movement among the conservative—that is, the clerical, anti-Juarez—Mexican gentry, who were still in the country. No such movement took place. Nevertheless Almonte was in the French expedition, and Napoleon III had now somehow slipped into a great Mexican political adventure. The British, however, were now thoroughly averse from the whole enterprise, which was just costing large sums of money to the British Treasury, and was not showing any prospect of debt collection. General Prim, too, saw the Spanish force, originally the largest in the expedition, completely overshadowed by French troops and by French prestige and French political aims. After a last conference at Orizaba on April 9, 1862, among the associated commanders and diplomatic agents, in which the British and Spaniards demanded that General Almonte be sent back to Europe, the debt-collecting expedition came to an end. The British and Spanish commanders on their own authority withdrew their troops—naturally their instructions must have allowed them discretion—and sailed from Vera Cruz, receiving, when they came in touch with the telegraph, full approval from their Governments. The French troops, and General Almonte, remained. On April 17, 1862, Almonte proclaimed a Provisional Government. On May 5 General Lorencez, having marched his 6000 troops from Cordova through Orizaba, attacked Puebla de los Angeles, held by troops of the Juarist Government, with whom the Convention of Soledad had only a few weeks previously been signed. The French attack was repulsed with heavy loss. Lorencez made a difficult but successful retreat to Orizaba, and there stopped, still well up on the Mexican plateau.

When the news of the French repulse before Puebla reached the Tuileries Napoleon III had the choice of abandoning the enterprise or of engaging in a limitless adventure. To abandon the enterprise involved writing off a considerable financial loss and incurring a loss of military prestige. To go onward offered a prospect of large and increasing expenditures, with, possibly, a brilliant gain of prestige, nothing more; in the meantime large numbers of the French Army—a small force would not be of any use—would be locked up in Mexico, five thousand miles from home. Napoleon III seems not to have hesitated. With an unwonted display of energy he pushed forward preparations for large reinforcements, and asked for and received the necessary credits from the Corps Législatif. Towards the end of July 1862 a complete army of 23,000 troops under General Forey sailed for Vera Cruz.

Forey was a good professional soldier, without any very great distinction. He was successful in Mexico, for he had excellent troops, was prudent yet vigorous, and had good luck. It is true that he might have shown still more vigour, for after taking over the command from General Lorencez at Orizaba in November 1862 he stayed there for five months at heavy financial cost, and some military wastage too. When, however, he did start to advance with two divisions (about 25,000 troops) from Orizaba in March 1863 his success was undeniable. He captured Puebla after sixty days' siege, of which the hero was one of his generals of division, François Bazaine, then fifty-two years old. It was Bazaine's division which on May 8, 1863, defeated a Juarist relieving army at San Lorenzo. This victory brought about the surrender of the garrison of Puebla on May 17. Forey now displayed exemplary energy. He pushed onward at once to Mexico City, sixty-eight miles from Puebla. President Juarez hastily left the capital, transferring his Government to San Luis Potosi. Bazaine's division arrived first, entering Mexico City on June 7. Forey made a solemn entry four days later. He set up a Provisional Government, or Junta, in which the chief man was General Almonte. The Junta convened a body of notables, or 'Constituent Assembly,' which proclaimed their decision (July 11, 1863) to offer the Imperial crown of Mexico to the Archduke Maximilian of Austria. Failing Maximilian, the choice of ruler was to be left to the Emperor Napoleon. This decree of the Constituent Assembly was published to all the world. Thus the fatal die was cast—not so much for Maximilian, who could have refused the offer, but for the French Empire, which was now involved in a hopeless adventure. General Forey seems to have had no instructions to adopt the Archduke

Maximilian as candidate for the Mexican throne, nor, indeed, did he do so. The Constituent Assembly, however, was acting under Forey's protection and with his approval. Napoleon III at once withdrew Forey, at the same time raising him to the rank of Marshal (August 1863). Bazaine became Commander-in-Chief of the French army in Mexico, now increased to the number of 34,000. He did not belie his reputation for energy. On January 5, 1864, he occupied Guadalajara, the second city of Mexico. Juarez had to leave San Luis Potosi and transfer the seat of his Government to Monterey.

On May 28, 1864, the Archduke Maximilian and his wife, the Archduchess Charlotte, landed from the Austrian cruiser *Novara* at Vera Cruz. This was one of the strangest Odysseys in the annals of royalty, as strange as any that later Victorian novelists were to imagine for their heroes of Balkan principalities or African adventure. Maximilian, younger brother of the Emperor Francis Joseph, was aged thirty-one years ten months when he landed at Vera Cruz. Like many of the Habsburg princes, he was a man of adventurous spirit, physical energy, personal honour, intelligence, and culture, without, however, any originality. He had been a keen naval officer, and, through his zeal and interest, might almost be called the creator of the modern Austrian Navy. As Viceroy of Lombardy-Venetia in 1857–59 he had conducted himself with dignity and enlightenment. The Franco-Austro-Sardinian War had cost the Austrian Empire the province of Lombardy and control of the Central Italian duchies. Since then Maximilian and Charlotte had been living in the splendid palace Miramar, which he had built on a beautiful site on the Adriatic coast, near to Trieste. Already in 1859 his name had been mentioned in diplomatic circles as that of a possible choice for a Mexican throne. The Emperor Napoleon III, who was a silent schemer, and the Empress Eugénie, who was a Spaniard and clerical, seem to have been, in some way not yet elucidated, connected with a group of 'conservative' Mexican exiles at Paris. As the Mexican Expedition developed in 1862–63 the monarchist scheme developed too; and after the French forces had occupied and established themselves in Mexico City, and Forey's Constituent Assembly had voted for Maximilian, a deputation of the Paris group arrived at Miramar (October 3, 1863). Maximilian, for whom the visit and offer were no surprise, was probably in the depth of his mind determined to accept, though he held off for a time and asked for a vote of the Mexican people. The French military authorities obtained some sort of vote of approval of the Habsburg prince in the half-dozen Mexican towns which they occupied. This was sufficient for Maximilian, who forthwith embarked at Miramar (April 14, 1864), after concluding with Napoleon III a convention agreeing to pay off the French bondholders and to recoup the French Government for the expenses of the Mexican expedition.[1]

When the Emperor, with his Empress, arrived at Vera Cruz on May 28, 1864, things were not going altogether badly for his cause. Bazaine was making the most of his army of 34,000 men, was driving the Juarists from town to town, finally took Monterey, and believed that President Juarez would flee for refuge to the United States. The obstinate President, it is true, found refuge still somewhere in Mexico, but the French occupied, and for a time held, most of the urban centres of population. Maximilian, who with the Empress made his entry into Mexico City on June 12, 1864, was given a good reception by the populace.

The bulk of the Mexicans undoubtedly wanted only peace, and they would gladly accept any Government which would ensure them that blessing. Maximilian desired only to give them peace and good law, and in the string of towns which the French troops occupied for him

[1] Convention of Miramar, April 10, 1864.

peace and order prevailed. There was, however, an implacable minority who could never submit to Maximilian: they were committed far too deeply by hostile acts against his, the 'conservative,' party, and his resources were wholly inadequate to the task of overcoming them and policing the whole land. Mexico extends over 750,000 square miles of land, much of which, before the days of motor-cars and aeroplanés, was almost impenetrable. It was perfect for guerrilla warfare. This kind of warfare, which is accompanied almost inevitably by murders and by massacres of prisoners, practically excludes the possibility of compromise. Maximilian, though a merciful, tolerant man, recognized this fact by his decree of October 3, 1865, treating all who were in arms against him as rebels liable to the death penalty.

Three things made Maximilian's position really hopeless. First, that he relied on French bayonets, and those only of a temporary nature; for in the existing condition of French finances and of the political affairs of Europe it was impossible for Napoleon to maintain the expedition beyond 1867. Second, President Juarez and his guerrillas, adapting themselves to the peculiar social and geographical conditions of Mexico, nullified the Imperial organization. Third, the Government and people of the United States were invincibly opposed to *any* extension of a European 'system' on the American continent. They were just as resolved in 1865 to maintain this attitude as they had been in 1823, when President Monroe enunciated his celebrated 'doctrine' against the suspected reimposition of a Bourbon prince upon South American territory.

From April 1861 to April 1865 the United States was torn in two by civil war. The secessionist Southern states, the 'Confederate States of America,' might gain a useful ally if Maximilian's Empire was established; but the North, the Federal Government, was on this account only all the more implacably opposed to the French and to

Maximilian. On April 9, 1865, the American Civil War came to an end with the surrender of General Lee at Appomattox Court House.

The end of the American Civil War really involved the end of the Mexican Empire. Maximilian's only chance was to establish his throne before the United States Government could seriously address itself to the Mexican question. A conceivable alternative was that Napoleon III should go on backing Maximilian and face a war with the United States. At the end of the Civil War the United States had excellent generals used to large-scale operations and half a million trained men under arms. The idea of Napoleon III fighting such a power in Mexico when he could not even overcome the Juarist guerrillas was fantastic. He had gone into the Mexican adventure largely to 'contain' the somewhat aggressive Anglo-Saxon Northern states, and he had failed; but there was a much more aggressive people whom, so long as he had Mexico on his hands, he could not 'contain' in Europe. The dispute between the Prussian and Austrian Governments over the question of the reform of the Germanic Confederation was working up to a struggle for supremacy in Germany. The Austro-Prussian War, the battle of Sadowa-Königgrätz, the dissolution of the Germanic Confederation, and the rise of Prussia to supremacy all took place in the summer of 1866. Napoleon III, who had just succeeded (as he thought) in freeing himself from the incubus of the Roman occupation (see p. 126), had also been desperately trying to extricate himself from the Mexican imbroglio.

Maximilian's party in Mexico, never very numerous nor very powerful, were now afflicted by the lassitude of prolonged and fruitless civil war. The Corps Législatif in France was showing increasing reluctance to vote credits for the Mexican Expedition. Maximilian's bonds were falling on the Paris Bourse, and no more Mexican bonds could be placed. Napoleon III made his decision, and announced at the opening of the legislature (January 22, 1866) that the French troops would be withdrawn—one-third of the Expeditionary Force in the autumn of that year, the remaining two-thirds in the spring and autumn of 1867. The Convention of Miramar of April 10, 1864, had stipulated for the maintenance of 20,000 French troops until the year 1867.

The idea of leaving Maximilian alone in Mexico was, of course, hateful to every Frenchman. The best solution for everybody would have been if Maximilian had abdicated. He decided not to do so. His wife set forth for Europe to seek help. She embarked at Vera Cruz on July 8, 1866 (five days after the defeat of the Austrians by the Prussians at Sadowa), and landed at Saint-Nazaire on August 8. Neither Napoleon III nor the Emperor Francis Joseph could do anything for her cause. At the end of September, on a visit to the Vatican, she had a mental breakdown, and never recovered. The Empress Charlotte died at Brussels in 1927.

Bazaine, who had his headquarters at San Luis Potosi, was withdrawing the garrisons, while there was still opportunity to do so, from the outlying towns. Maximilian was trying to sort out his Mexican friends, resolved to stay on in the country, relying on such native party as he could form and retain. The French did not actually withdraw at the dates originally announced. They remained in Mexico throughout the year 1866, but were withdrawn in February and March 1867. Their losses were never officially announced, though privately a high military authority informed a British statesman that 28,000 men died on the expedition.

Bazaine and the French diplomatic agent did their best to induce Maximilian to abdicate and to leave Mexico along with the French troops. Maximilian refused, apparently hoping to snatch a victory by means of his partisans and then to be able to abdicate 'voluntarily' and with honour. He still had some troops—about one thousand friends or mercenaries from Europe, the rest native Mexicans. His desperate finances were occasionally helped from the customs duties of Vera Cruz. His officers could make levies of troops and supplies in places under their control; but such levies were detrimental to his popularity. Deserters were common in his forces.

The last French companies, with Bazaine, left in the transports on March 12. By this time Maximilian had left Mexico City, which was still held for him by a Mexican, General Marquez, and established himself at Queretaro, about a hundred and fifty miles north-west from the capital. By taking this bold step Maximilian burned his boats, for he had gone away from the life-line, the road from Mexico to Vera Cruz. He entered Queretaro on February 19, and was well received by the inhabitants, who numbered, perhaps, twenty thousand. He was soon besieged by the Juarists, but held out successfully for two months. The defences were then delivered to the enemy by the treachery of one of his officers, Colonel Lopez. Maximilian and two faithful Generals, Miramon and Mejia, were tried by court-martial, and were shot on June 19, 1867, at Queretaro. The European diplomatic agents used all their personal and official influence to obtain remission of the sentence from President Juarez, who remained impassive and inflexible. Maximilian's last days are known from the description of his friend and physician, Samuel Siegfried Carl von Basch. The Emperor cast aside his restlessness and pride; he was calm, conversational, solicitous for the interests of his companions. Dr Basch embalmed the body, which President Juarez permitted to be taken off for Europe in the Austrian cruiser *Novara*; it is buried in the Capucin church at Vienna.

Forty-seven years after the shooting of the Archduke

Maximilian at Queretaro another Austrian Archduke, Francis Ferdinand, was shot at Sarajevo. This last tragedy in the ill-starred family of the Emperor Francis Joseph led directly and swiftly to the fall of the Empire of Austria. The shooting at Queretaro in 1867 did not precipitate a crisis, but was itself part of a crisis which the Emperor Napoleon created for himself when he undertook the Mexican Expedition. This crisis was one, and not the least, of the factors in the decline and fall of the Second Empire.

Chapter XII

HUMOUR

PHILOSOPHERS and scientists have speculated on the qualities which differentiate man from animals; and it has been suggested that one of the distinguishing qualities is laughter. This statement might be challenged or criticized. No one, however, will deny that the ability to see humour in a situation or idea and to laugh at it is a distinctively human faculty. It is not shared equally by all peoples; nor is it a monopoly of the most civilized. The American negro has had it since the early plantation period, and apparently did not derive his sense of humour from his white master. Some white peoples are deficient in humour. At some periods of the world's history it has almost disappeared.

Humour, four or five hundred years ago, would have been called "a mental disposition or temperament, as determined by the proportion of bodily humours or fluids." The Elizabethans, according to Ben Jonson, regarded it as something freakish, capricious, whimsical: *Every Man in his own Humour*. The grand and abiding meaning, however, established before the beginning of the eighteenth century, was: "The faculty of appreciating what is humorous and amusing, or of expressing it." The *Oxford Dictionary* explains further that it is less purely intellectual than wit, and is often allied to pathos.[1] It is different from merriment. The humorous man is not certain to be merry. Jaques in *As You Like It* was not merry or mirthful. 'Merrie England' did not mean humorous

[1] W. Little, *The Shorter Oxford English Dictionary on Historical Principles*, s.v. "Humour."

England; and the French, who have never been called merry, have a strong faculty of humour. No people has a monopoly of this faculty, which, however, is far stronger in some than in others. 'Receptive humour,' the faculty of *perceiving* what is ludicrous or amusing, is fairly common, though some individuals lack even this; the faculty of expressing it is comparatively rare. In the nineteenth century it was perhaps found most commonly among the English and Americans, and next to them in the French people.

The Romantic Age of thought and literature may be considered to extend from about 1790 to 1840. As a whole, though there were exceptions, the 'Romantics' took themselves too seriously to be humorous. In the next forty or fifty years the humorists entered into their own. It is the great age of *Punch*; of Dickens, Thackeray, Trollope; of Mark Twain; of Edmond About and Alphonse Daudet; of *Simplicissimus*; of Fritz Reuter. When they died humour did not vanish with them, but was less common, less developed, and less appreciated. In an age not so tolerant as the late nineteenth century humour tends to disappear.

Humour is the enemy of humbug and sham. With kindly but irresistible touch it strips away the sheath of make-believe with which men delude and mislead themselves and one another. Fanaticism, vanity, and greed are laid bare; their excesses, subterfuges, and lies are exposed. In the clear light of common sense, of the wisdom of the people, hypocrisy, legend, 'ideology,' are exposed for what they are; and sanity, tolerance, judgment, assert their influence. Humour is the critic and the guide of society—a critic without malice, without offence, a guide without harshness or constraint. Matthew Arnold said that the effect of culture was sweetness and light; such, too, is the effect of humour.

The seventeenth and eighteenth centuries were not rich

in humorists, though Molière, Swift, Addison, Fielding, and Sterne are among the greatest. Thackeray delivered a very interesting set of lectures on "The English Humourists of the Eighteenth Century," but the title might almost as well have been "English Literary Life in the Eighteenth Century," for he did not confine himself wholly, or even mainly, to the theme of humour.

In the early nineteenth century Miss Austen wrote six 'domestic' novels of faultless artistry and delicate humour, four published in her lifetime (*Sense and Sensibility*, 1811; *Pride and Prejudice*, 1813; *Mansfield Park*, 1814; *Emma*, 1816) and two after her death (*Northanger Abbey* and *Persuasion*, 1818). Scott, with *Waverley* (1814) inaugurated his great human comedy. Here society—particularly that of eighteenth-century Scotland—is described with understanding and affection, which evokes smile or laugh where it does not call for tears. It was *Pickwick* (1837), however, that established the standard of English humour, and exposed the possibilities of English life and language as material for a master-humorist. *Pickwick* has breadth and boisterousness like Fielding's, wit like Miss Austen's, 'pawkiness' like Scott's. It is clean, candid, comic, and wise—a description of life and a commentary which engenders in the reader knowledge, love, and understanding of his fellows. It was no accident that 1841 (July 1) is the year of the first number of *Punch*. For though Dickens himself had nothing directly to do with the inauguration of London's famous weekly, *Punch* is the weekly *Pickwick*, clean, candid, comic, and wise, continuing the tradition, maintaining the standard, of this masterpiece of the human comedy.

English humour of the middle and later nineteenth century, in general kindly and sensible, had one persistent aberration, now fortunately extinct and forgotten—the practical joke. If the practical joke is at all humorous it is a low form of humour. If it excites mirth by its surprise and its ridiculousness it is cruel mirth, laughter at an unfortunate person's discomfiture; it is one of the milder kinds of sadism. Its chief exponent—and for a time he enjoyed considerable popularity—was one Henry Cockton (1807–53), author of *Valentine Vox, the Ventriloquist* (1840). Nobody reads this work now, or if he did would laugh at it.

Pickwick, which, though published in book form in 1837, had begun to run as a serial in 1836, falls outside the middle period of the nineteenth century, but it is the base and the standard of the grand development that followed upon Dickens' triumph. Though he went on writing until 1870, he never repeated the success of *Pickwick*; indeed, he was wise enough not to try. *Pickwick* is not a novel, but a charming, rollicking comedy; it is the comedy of manners in England at the end of the Romantic Age. Dickens' subsequent work was done mainly in the novel, properly so called, a serious tale, an imaginative history where wit and humour have their place, but are not the predominant motive. Nevertheless *Nicholas Nickleby* (1839), *American Notes* (1842), *Martin Chuzzlewit* (1843), and to a less extent *David Copperfield* (1850), contained something of the ' Pickwickian ' tradition. There is much less of it in those fine romances *Bleak House* (1853), *A Tale of Two Cities* (1859), *Great Expectations* (1861).

The burlesque and satirical aspects which exist, though they are not very pronounced, in *Pickwick* are accentuated in a contemporary work, Gogol's *Dead Souls* (1837), which has been called the Russian *Pickwick*. It is a story of genial, high-spirited fraud, a man who ' buys ' from landowners serfs actually dead within ten years, but alive in the eyes of the taxing authorities until the next ten years' assessment should be made. These " dead souls," though taxable, could also be offered as security for mortgages. Thus Chichikov, the buyer-up of dead souls, is able to raise large sums of money by loan on their security, and to lead a remarkable life in one part of Russia after another. It is not impossible that Gogol was influenced by *Pickwick*. Gogol in 1836 left Russia, then under the somewhat heavy hand of Nicholas I, and went to Rome, where he wrote the first part of *Dead Souls*. *Pickwick* is kindly, humane; *Dead Souls*, comic and rollicking though it is, has bitter and deadly satire in it. They are each an instance of a type of story, very popular after 1837—the travel story. Neither Dickens nor Gogol invented this type. The *Odyssey* is the first and the supreme instance. Cervantes, Fielding, Scott, all used the travel theme; but it was Dickens and Gogol who constructed their whole book as a journey. In the eyes of these two great 'humanists,' as in the main view of the ancient Greeks, life was not a psychological state, but a journey—a varied, sometimes pathetic, often comic, always interesting, journey, full of incidents, rich in characters. *Huckleberry Finn* (1884), America's richest work of humour, is another Odyssey, the tale of a voyage on a raft down the Mississippi.

French humour, which grew with great strength in the middle and late nineteenth century, was partly expressed in the travel form in the work of Daudet. Balzac, who died in 1850, had given or increased a psychological bias in the French novel, a bias which was not favourable to humour. The themes of human passion—love of power, love of money, love of self, fear, sex—so predominant in Balzac's novels, are scarcely susceptible of humorous treatment. Balzac is very occasionally humorous, as in *Le Curé de Tours*. The *curé*, succeeding to his dead friend's choice *appartement*, sincerely mourned him: "He would not, perhaps, have resuscitated him, but he mourned him." This remark is sardonic; as with all humour, there is an element of truth as well as of surprise in it; but it represents a low view of human nature. Alexandre Dumas, the elder, who probably was not a better character than Balzac, took a more wholesome view of life. *Les Trois*

Mousquetaires (1844) has the same exuberance, the *abandon*, the zest for life, for movement, the optimism, which were the redeeming qualities of Rabelais. Humour, however, is not prominent in Dumas' novels, though the character of Porthos has something truly Falstaffian about it. Dumas' many *Travels*, containing as they do a Rabelaisian Frenchman's descriptions of foreign society in many lands, have more humour in them. They are, however, not read now, and their popularity in his own day was not such as to give them a commanding place in the history of humour. Edmond About's *Roi des Montagnes* (1856) from this point of view is more important. This story of a journey in Greece, of Greek bandits, and, finally, of the brigand chief turned Minister of Justice, is a delicate farce which has amused generation after generation. Yet it is not primarily a travel novel: travel is an incident in it; the burlesque of brigandry is the chief motive. In the three *Tartarin* books we find the genuine travel humour. Cervantes and Dickens were Daudet's masters. Tartarin is specifically described as a kind of combined Quixote and Sancho Panza. And there is much of the Pickwickian flavour in *Tartarin of Tarascon* (1872), the first of the trilogy: there is the burlesque journey to Algiers; the stranger, a charlatan, casually met at the outset and turning up opportunely later in the story; the ludicrous misfortunes of the hero; his surprising and triumphant return home.

Besides his Tarasconais style, Daudet had a less exuberant but equally diverting style of wit in which he wrote the stories and sketches of Provence called *Lettres de mon Moulin* and his reminiscences called *Trente Ans de Paris*. The *Lettres de mon Moulin* were composed, partly at any rate, while Daudet was staying at Champrosay with Eugène Delacroix, the painter, and they appeared in the journal *Figaro*. Published in book form in 1869, they had no immediate popularity, but gradually established themselves in the hearts of the French. The *Thirty Years of Paris*, published in 1888, has the quiet humour, the wit, but scarcely a breath of the gentle satire which the French of the Second Empire so prized. The last page of the book, which concludes a description of Daudet's meetings with Turgeniev at Flaubert's house, has just a trace of bitterness: " *Mon Dieu*, what a queer thing is life, and how fine is that fine word of the Greek language, *Eironeia*! "

The *Tartarin* books have the surprising, the ludicrous, the ironical, elements which in very varying proportions are found in every work of humour. In general the French writers or speakers tend to emphasize the ironical element. The kindly Daudet, however, tended to emphasize the surprising and ludicrous. In *Port Tarascon* the good citizens are wrecked on a desert island in the Pacific. After they have sojourned there some time, and managed to live together somehow, a French gunboat visits the island. An officer lands, advances over the beach, and accosts the strange white inhabitants (for whom, of course, their home town, Tarascon, is the hub of the universe):

QUESTION. " What nationality are you ? "
ANSWER. " Tarasconais! "

The satire is powerful, yet gentle, kindly, delicate. Later, with Anatole France, satire and irony become almost the chief motives. These are the basis too of the humorous drama of the Second Empire, the amusing satire on official life. Satire directly exposes human folly or weakness in a way which calls forth laughter or smiles. This is the method of the comedy about rather insipid High Society under the Second Empire, Pailleron's *Le Monde où l'on s'ennuie*, first produced at the Comédie Française in 1881. Irony indirectly attacks folly or weakness by appearing to adopt or defend them. This was, for instance, the method of Henri Rochefort in his weekly review *La Lanterne* (1868), perhaps the most dangerous literary attack on the Second Empire. Direct, overt attack the Imperial authorities could meet in the law-court, but irony which appeared only anxious to support and defend them was more difficult to deal with. Napoleon III could not, for instance, express disapproval of a panegyric upon Napoleon II; and yet the following from *La Lanterne* was obviously not meant to advance the prestige of the Empire: " What a reign, my friends, what a reign! No contributions, no war, no Civil List! " Napoleon II, it should be borne in mind, if he reigned at all, reigned for four days after Waterloo at the age of two years.

The influence of Dickens is seen in mid-century German humour, in Freytag's *Soll und Haben*, for instance, published in 1855. It is a story of domestic life, business, and money-lending, with more of the atmosphere of *David Copperfield* than of *Pickwick*. The life of the German people seems to proceed according to a peculiar rhythm. Depressions of an intellectual and moral kind alternate with periods of zest and exaltation. When Freytag was writing *Soll und Haben*, about 1855, one of these depressions had spread over all Germany. The inspiring political and intellectual movement culminating in the Revolution of 1848 had ended in disillusion, in the failure of Liberal hopes, in the re-establishing of bureaucracy and censorship. In the preface to *Soll und Haben* Freytag tells how he stood with Duke Ernst II of Sachsen-Coburg in the spring of 1853 on the terrace of the Kallenberg, looking down and out upon the magnificent landscape of Thuringia. The Duke, leaning on the stone balustrade, regarding the peaceful, harmonious scene below, spoke of the confusion of spirit, the relaxed intellectual and moral condition of the people. Since then " a frightful war "—the Crimean—had flamed out and burned away, " and with darkling anxiety the German people regard the future of the Fatherland." *Soll und Haben* was received with joy; it was a great escape novel. Its kindly humour, its genial atmosphere of the domestic hearth, its cheerful acceptance of the world's business of making and spending, of buying and selling, helped to restore peace of mind to the German *bourgeoisie.*

The authentic tradition of German humour, however, was not after the manner of Dickens, but of Sterne. Jean-Paul Richter was the master of this quaint, impish style. After his death in 1825 there was no one to continue the tradition until the Mecklenburger Fritz Reuter started to write. A Jena student, and, like all the Jena students of the Romantic Age, given to high jinks and politics, Fritz Reuter was imprisoned by the Prussian Government from 1833 to 1840. This dreadful experience did not sour his nature, though it spoiled his health and drove him to drink. About 1850 he took to writing in the quaint Platt-deutsch, the Low German, of the Mecklenburgers. *Ut de Franzosentid* (*From the French Time*), 1860, and *Ut mine Stromtid* (*From My Storm Time*), 1864, are masterpieces of German humour. The ancient wisdom of the little town and of the farm are here displayed in the kindliest setting, in a world of common sense and smiles. Reuter is a sunny Puck, playing tricks all the time with the mankind that he describes, but innocent, good-natured tricks, all love, no malice. There is, as in most humorous works, at any rate a flavour of social criticism. Fritz Reuter founded no ' school '; German humorous writers are not very common. Nevertheless there was started in his time one of the most pungent of humorous works, independent and critical, *Fliegende Blätter*, which began at Munich in 1844.

The richest vein of all was found in America in the middle and later nineteenth century. American humour is largely the product of the frontier. The conditions of frontier life, the quaint characters, the eccentricities, the reality and common sense, the jollity and camaraderie, and the lively ' backchat ' of camp life—all this tended to develop a unique humorous outlook and liveliness of speech. The American frontier was not always in the West. It began in the Eastern states, and kept shifting westward as settlement advanced into the wilderness. Many families shifted their abode three or four times in the same generation. Taking up fresh land, they would clear the ground and build a log house, engage in adventure with Nature and their fellow-men, make quaint experiments in religion, as in other matters, and after some years of relative stability would sell or abandon their lot and move off with the moving frontier. In their wake remained small towns and villages, little centres of more or less stable society, but still with many of the frontier characteristics. Amid such conditions Abraham Lincoln grew up and developed the humorous outlook with which he viewed life even in its direst time. One of his biographers has described this early environment:

> However scant might be cash and houses, each town had its grocery, and these famous ' stores ' were by far the chief influence in shaping the ideas of the Westerner. There all congregated, the idlers all day long, the busy men in the evening; and there, stimulated by the whisky of the proprietor, they gossiped about everybody's affairs, talked about business and the prospects of the neighbourhood, and argued about the politics of the country, the state, and even the nation. Jokes and stories, often most uncouth and gross, whiled away the time. It was in these groceries and in the rough crucible of such talk, wherein grotesque imagery and extravagant phrases were used to ridicule pretension and to keep every man in his place, sometimes also to escape taking a fact too hardly, that what we now call ' American humour,' with its peculiar native flavour, was born.[1]

The English at once recognized their affinity with this new manifestation. Doubtless the common English tongue had much to do with the appreciation of Dickens in

[1] J. T. Morse, *Abraham Lincoln* (1893), i, 28.

America and Mark Twain in England. Besides this, however, besides the language, there is a common, or at any rate similar, attitude in the English and Americans towards life: they are naturally inclined to look at the 'funny side' of things. The frontier flavour in American humour was an added charm which the English on their island had never discovered for themselves. They appreciated, too, another element in American humour—its curious Puritan background. "Much of the quaintness observable in American humour," writes the editor of Artemus Ward's works, "has come down from the old Puritans, whose sober treatment of comic things and comic treatment of sober matters gave their talk a very different effect at the present time to what they intended."[1] The camp meeting and the village preacher, for instance, furnish much of the humorous material of *Huckleberry Finn*. The incongruities of word and of thought, in which American humorous writing is so rich, are an inheritance from New England Puritanism.

Mark Twain was the greatest of this new school of 'frontier' humorists, but he was not the first. Artemus Ward, whose real name was Charles Farrar Browne, discovered the humorous possibilities of the travelling show, the small town, the camp meeting, the overland stage. His work never really rose above buffoonery, even in his best sayings, like that about the Mormons, "whose religion is singular, but their wives are plural." He overloads his work with misspellings, and sometimes forces the incongruities of religious fundamentalism just beyond the boundary of good taste. It may be, however, that Artemus Ward never reached the maturity of his powers, for he was only thirty-three in 1867 when he died.

The greatest contribution to the humour of the latter half of the nineteenth century was made by Mark Twain. The incongruities of Puritanism and the naïveties of

[1] J. C. Hotten, *The Complete Works of Artemus Ward* (1865), Introduction.

frontier life are the material of his humorous books. Mark Twain, whose real name was Samuel Langhorne Clemens, was born at Florida, Missouri, in 1835. His life, which lasted until 1910, was spent mainly in the Mississippi Valley, in Nevada during the mining boom, and latterly in the Eastern states. In 1869 he published *The Innocents Abroad*. " Probably no other book in American literature," writes Carl von Doren, " has ever been more representative than the *Innocents* was of the age which produced it." [1] It is a travel book, and, like the Prologue to the *Canterbury Tales*, it keeps alive for ever the company on the road. In *The Innocents Abroad* the company is the comfortable *bourgeoisie* of the Victorian Age, good-natured, companionable, tolerant, open-minded; not highly cultured, but desiring to learn and interested in things of the mind and spirit; naïve and unselfconscious, and thus furnishing material for anecdotes to a humorous, quizzical observer. The observer, of course, is Mark Twain.

Roughing It, which came out in 1872, describes a journey by stage-coach from St Louis into Nevada, and the life of a miner and journalist at Carson City, Nevada. In this book, along with some exaggeration and burlesque, the irrepressible outcome of the Rabelaisian element of Mark Twain's genius, there is enshrined the life of the gold-digging or silver-mining frontier society of the fifties and sixties. After *Roughing It* came the Mississippi ' epics '— *Tom Sawyer* in 1876, *Life on the Mississippi* in 1883, and *Huckleberry Finn* in 1884. The last is the great river romance of America, of the world. In its magic pages are boyhood and age, innocence and guile, the open road, life in the woods, life on a raft, in a small town, farm, and opulent planter's home. Rollicking humour and high spirits carry the narrative along from incident to incident amid sunshine of smiles and laughter that no amount of repetition can dim. Huck is the eternal boy who cheers

[1] *Dictionary of American Biography*, s.v. S. L. Clemens.

mankind with his simple graces. His unspoiled mind and clear eyes are receptive of the comic element in human affairs. His naïve comments, spontaneous laughter, resourcefulness, chivalry, gaiety, sense of fun, are the essential spirit of youth, the wisdom that comes not with age.

The sense of humour was strongly developed in the middle decades of the nineteenth century. Between *Pickwick* (1837) and Jerome's *Three Men in a Boat* (1889) every ten years may be said to have produced some outstanding achievement in this kind: *Punch* began in 1841; Trollope's *Barchester Towers* appeared in 1857; *The Innocents Abroad* in 1869; *Tartarin of Tarascon* in 1872; *Huckleberry Finn* in 1884. Anatole France and George Bernard Shaw continued the tradition in the early twentieth century, but in an Iron Age it tends to disappear.

Chapter XIII

QUEEN VICTORIA AS A LETTER-WRITER

THE most gracious of the literary activities scarcely survived into the second and third decades of the twentieth century. Its greatest age was in the eighteenth century. Probably no other correspondents have combined the conscientiousness and the interesting quality of Voltaire, Catherine the Great, and Rousseau. In the nineteenth century the art still flourished, and among some of the most notable people. Sir Walter Scott, Carlyle, Emerson, Bismarck, Cavour, Queen Victoria, Disraeli, Randall Davidson, Henry James, Woodrow Wilson, the Emperor William II, were incessant correspondents, and wrote admirable letters. The causes of the decay of the art are obscure, but seem to be connected with the habit of dictating to a typist.

To be a good letter-writer a person must have a sense of duty, industry, sympathy, sociableness, liveliness of mind. Without sense of duty the letter is not begun; without industry it becomes no more than a note; without sympathy it makes no appeal to the recipient; without sociableness its composition is a burden; without liveliness of mind it is ruined by dullness. Queen Victoria excelled as letter-writer because of her strong sense of duty, unflagging industry, wide sympathy, essential sociableness, and, perhaps surprisingly, indubitable mental liveliness. She had not every good quality. For instance, she had little sense of humour—in fact, so far as the letters indicate, none at all. She was not particularly generous in her estimates of character. She was a little too conscious of her dignity, and there is more than a hint of pomposity in her correspondence. Nevertheless there shines through it all the spirit of a good woman, widely experienced, thoughtful, sagacious, firm-minded, and understanding. The collected *Letters* are one of the worthiest, the most characteristic, memorials of a great reign. The editors of the first series aver that " the collected papers form what is probably the most extraordinary series of State documents in the world." Including the copies of the Queen's letters, the answers, and relevant documents, the series only down to the year 1861 numbered between five hundred and six hundred volumes.

Letter-writing, if a person can settle down and take time over it, is a means of self-expression—indeed, of self-realization. The writer brings out his or her own ideas and, by putting them on paper, defines them. The Princess Victoria, like all girls in the nineteenth century, was carefully disciplined. She had, they all had, what would now be called a ' repressed ' youth. " I was brought up very simply," she wrote in a memoir,

> never had a room to myself till I was nearly grown-up; always slept in my mother's room till I came to the throne. At Claremont and in the small houses at the bathing-places I sat and took my lessons in my governess's bedroom.

The crowd of dignified German royalties and the solemn bishops with their great wigs made an oppressive atmosphere for the self-willed child. As she grew up writing letters or keeping a journal was a relief to her, a release of her personality. She preferred then, and continued all through life to prefer, a sympathetic man as her correspondent. At first this was her uncle, King Leopold I of Belgium; thirty years afterwards it was Lord Beaconsfield. She could say things in her letters to men that she could not have put on paper to any woman—for instance, that Louis XIV, *le grand roi*, was her " great admiration." [1]

[1] To the King of the Belgians, February 2, 1835.

Nothing like this ever crept in among the banalities of the Queen's feminine correspondents.

Sovereigns tend to be lonely—woman sovereigns particularly. Queen Victoria found companionship by correspondence. The perpetual formal audiences, the unceasing notes from Prime Minister to Queen, and from Queen to Prime Minister, all expressed in the third person, kept the world at a respectful distance and chilled the surrounding atmosphere. The Queen's letters to her Prime Ministers, in spite of their *oratio obliqua*, are human enough, but never intimate. She turned with genuine pleasure and affection to write in the first person singular to Uncle Leopold.

After her marriage with Prince Albert in 1840 the need for companionship through correspondence ceased for twenty years. The letters of this period are mainly State papers—not all, of course. The correspondence with Uncle Leopold of Belgium continued with undiminished affection, and sometimes attained a magnificent level. For instance, perhaps the best description of Nicholas I is given in a letter of the Queen to Leopold written from Buckingham Palace on June 11, 1844, during the Tsar's visit. Even the official letters are good reading, and have much of human interest, particularly those dealing with ecclesiastical patronage. In 1845 (March 24) the Queen, who had sound, Broad Church views, wrote to Sir Robert Peel about a stall (or canonry) of Winchester "which she would like to see filled by a person decidedly adverse to Puseyism." With regard to appointments to what she calls "church sinecures," she admitted that it was reasonable for the Prime Minister "to recommend to such places persons of political connections." She added, however, very sensibly: "It would be of great use both to the Church and the country to give these places of emolument to Churchmen distinguished for their *scientific attainments* who have neither the means nor the time to prosecute their researches."[1] Writing to Melbourne in 1845 (April 3) about the estate which she was going to purchase at Osborne, the Queen becomes lyrical:

> She thinks it is impossible to imagine a prettier spot—valleys and woods which would be beautiful anywhere; but all this near the sea (the woods grow into the sea) is quite perfection; we have a charming beach quite to ourselves. The sea was so blue and calm that the Prince said it was like Naples.

To Earl Grey, Colonial Secretary (October 26, 1848), about the battle of Boomplatz, in which Sir Harry Smith defeated some South African Dutch, she writes:

> The Queen has received Lord Grey's letter, and is glad to hear that Sir H. Smith's wound was not of a serious nature. The loss of so many officers, the Queen is certain, proceeds from wearing a blue coat whilst the men are in scarlet; the Austrians lost a great proportion of officers in Italy from a similar difference in dress.

As a matter of fact, the Queen was mistaken: all the officers but one at Boomplatz wore the uniform of the Cape Mounted Rifles, like the men. This fact, however, does not detract from the interest of the Queen's comment. Perhaps the most celebrated State paper of the whole series, that in which (doubtless with the help of the Prince Consort) she drafted a rule concerning Foreign Office dispatches, is charged with feeling and thought. Its date is August 12, 1850. It was written to the Prime Minister, and refers to the high-handed conduct of the irrepressible Secretary of State for Foreign Affairs, Lord Palmerston:

> With reference to the conversation about Lord Palmerston which the Queen had with Lord John Russell the other day, and Lord Palmerston's disavowal that he ever intended any disrespect to her by the various neglects of which she has had

[1] To Lord John Russell, March 25, 1847.

so long and so often to complain, she thinks it right, in order to *prevent any mistake* for the *future*, shortly to explain *what it is she expects from her Foreign Secretary.* She requires: (1) That he will distinctly state what he proposes in a given case, in order that the Queen may know as distinctly to *what* she has given her Royal sanction; (2) Having *once given* her sanction to a measure, that it be not arbitrarily altered or modified by the Minister; such an act she must consider as failing in sincerity towards the Crown, and justly to be visited by the exercise of her Constitutional right of dismissing that Minister. She expects to be kept informed of what passes between him and the Foreign Ministers before important decisions are taken, based upon that intercourse; to receive the Foreign Dispatches in good time, and to have the drafts for her approval sent to her in sufficient time to make herself acquainted with their contents before they must be sent off. The Queen thinks it best that Lord John Russell should show this letter to Lord Palmerston.[1]

Lord Palmerston followed this rule for a time, but in December 1851 sent off an important dispatch to the French Government without first submitting it to the Queen, and was promptly dismissed. Who dismissed him? The official letters correctly enough place the constitutional responsibility on the Prime Minister, but it is pretty clear who moved the Prime Minister.

December 19, 1851

Lord John Russell has now to advise your Majesty that Lord Palmerston should be informed that your Majesty is ready to accept the Seals of Office, and to place them in other hands. . . .

December 20, 1851

[First answer.] The Queen has now to express to Lord John Russell her readiness to follow his advice, and her acceptance of the resignation of Lord Palmerston.

[Second answer, same day.] With respect to a successor to Lord Palmerston, the Queen must state that after the sad

[1] *The Letters of Queen Victoria* (1907), ii, 315.

experience which she has just had of the difficulties, annoyances, and dangers to which the Sovereign may be exposed by the personal character and qualities of the Secretary for Foreign Affairs, she must reserve to herself the unfettered right to approve or disapprove the choice of a Minister for this office.

Apart from the letters to Leopold of Belgium, the Queen's letters to foreign sovereigns have something of the nature both of State papers and private correspondence. Letters to Napoleon III are in French, to King William of Prussia in English. The Crimean War and French alliance naturally necessitated a certain amount of association of the Queen and the Emperor of the French. The Queen and Prince Consort were guests at Saint-Cloud in August 1855. The first great Paris Exposition Universelle was being held then, although the Crimean War was going on and the siege of Sebastopol was being pressed. The Queen had been thrilled by the London Exhibition of 1851—Albert's great personal triumph—described enthusiastically in the Queen's correspondence. She scarcely mentions, however, the Paris Exposition, and in her letter addressed to Napoleon III after the visit she does not allude to it at all.

There is a strong *personal* element, and practically always a very sensible one, in the Queen's official correspondence. For instance, the following extract from a letter written (November 5, 1853) to Lord Aberdeen, Prime Minister, is illuminating in regard to the character and intelligence of the Queen and of Stratford Canning (Lord Stratford de Redcliffe), and in regard to the kind of correspondence maintained by the Queen with her Prime Ministers:

Although the Queen will have the pleasure of seeing Lord Aberdeen this evening, she wishes to make some observations on the subject of Lord Stratford's last private letters communicated to her yesterday by Lord Clarendon. They exhibit clearly on his part a *desire* for war and to drag us into it. When he speaks of the sword which will not only have to be drawn, but the scabbard thrown away, and says the war to be successful must be a " *very comprehensive one* " on the part of England and France, the intention is unmistakable, and it becomes a serious question whether we are justified in allowing Lord Stratford any longer to remain in a situation which gives him the means of frustrating all our efforts for peace. The question becomes still graver when it is considered that General Baraguay d'Hilliers seems from Lord Cowley's account of his conversation with him equally anxious for extreme measures.

The Queen must express her surprise that Lord Stratford should have coolly sent on so preposterous a proposal as Redschid Pasha's note asking for a Treaty of Alliance, the amalgamation of our Fleets with the Turkish one, and the sending of our surplus ships to the " *White* " sea (!) without any hesitation or remark on his part. As the note ends, however, by saying that the Porte desires *que les points ci dessus émenés* (*sic*) *soient appreciés par les Cours d'Angleterre et de France, et que ces Cours veuillent bien déclarer leur intention d'agir en conséquence*, this appears to the Queen to afford an admirable opportunity for stating plainly and strongly to the Turkish Government that we have *no intention* of being used by them for their own purposes. This time such a declaration might be *handed in* to the Turkish Government, so that there can be no mistake about the matter for the future.

The Queen encloses the letter and note, and wishes Lord Aberdeen to show her letter to Lord Clarendon.[1]

The Government did not see fit, or at any rate the Ministers could not make up their minds, to recall Lord Stratford from Constantinople.

In an official letter (October 2, 1854) addressed to Lord Dalhousie, Governor-General of India, the Queen's sense of justice and humanity impel her to speak on behalf of the young Sikh Prince whose country had been

[1] *The Letters of Queen Victoria* (1907), ii, 560–561.

conquered by British arms and had been annexed in 1849:

> This young Prince has the *strongest* claims upon our generosity and sympathy; deposed, for *no* fault of his, when a little boy of ten years old, he is as innocent as any private individual of the mistakes which compelled us to depose him and take possession of his territories.

This intervention was successful, in so far as ample financial provision was made for Prince Dhuleep Singh's future. The Queen's humanity and common sense also appear in her letters to Lord Panmure, War Secretary in the last year of the Crimean War. After visiting a military hospital the Queen does more than express sympathy for the wounded soldiers to her Minister: she makes highly practical suggestions for improving the hospital conditions (March 5, 1855). A covering note (March 14, 1855) sent to the Foreign Secretary with returned dispatches calls attention to one of the rules of diplomacy—namely, to make matters as easy as possible for the opposite party from whom you are demanding concessions:

> The Queen returns the letter and dispatches from Vienna. They don't alter her opinion as to our demands. Every concession in form and wording ought to be made which could save Russian *amour-propre*, but this ought in no way to trench upon the *substance* of our demands.

Even what would be expected to be formal confirmation of an Honours List (November 9, 1856) becomes a terse piece of criticism:

> With respect to the list for the Bath, the Queen is somewhat startled by the large number. Before sanctioning it she thinks it right to ask for an explanation of the services of the officers, and the reasons for which they are selected for the honour. She returns the list for that purpose to Lord Panmure, who will, perhaps, cause the statement to be attached to each name. This, of course, does not apply to the foreigners.

In regard to the Victoria Cross, instituted during the Crimean War, the Queen did not have her own way, though she expressed her view convincingly. She agreed that those who have gained the honour should be allowed to have some letters after their name; not V.C., however.

> V.C. would not do. K.G. means a *Knight* of the Garter, C.B. a *Companion* of the Bath, M.P. a *Member* of Parliament, M.D. a *Doctor* of Medicine, etc., etc., in all cases designating a person. No one could be called a Victoria Cross. V.C., moreover, means a Vice-Chancellor at present.[1]

In fact, every line of her official letters shows her determination not to be reduced (as she wrote to Lord Derby, Prime Minister) " to a mere signing-machine."

After the death of Prince Albert (December 14, 1861) the course of the Queen's life changed. She retired into private life, as much as a sovereign possibly could, and nursed her grief. To the remonstrances of her Ministers she replied with tragic cries of distress. Nevertheless, though she avoided ceremonial functions as much as possible, she did not neglect her other duties of State, but continued to work harder than ever, and found consolation in this. Letter-writing was a relief to her overcharged mind and spirit. We can imagine her sitting down with positive pleasure to write a long letter to Disraeli or to Dean Wellesley of Windsor or to one of her many relatives abroad. She had always been a good letter-writer, and she became one of the best in English literature. Her official letters to her Prime Ministers continue to be, as before, really personal letters containing good advice. It is remarkable that these experienced Ministers required to have offensive or irritating passages of their dispatches reworded by the Queen. Prince Albert had prevented a war with the United States by suggesting a bland, considerate paragraph in place of a brusque one during the '*Trent* Affair' in 1861. The Prince's paragraph was no

[1] Undated. ? June 1857.

less firm than Lord John Russell's: it was only differently expressed. In the first year of the Civil War an American (Northern) cruiser had stopped an English mail-steamer, *Trent*, and had taken from it two passengers who were agents of the rebel Confederation. The British Government demanded an apology and the restitution of the two prisoners. The Prince Consort suggested, in place of the paragraph making these demands, one asking for much the same thing in inoffensive language. The Prince Consort's paragraph was:

> Her Majesty's Government, bearing in mind the friendly relations which have long subsisted between Great Britain and the United States, are willing to believe that the United States naval officer who committed this aggression was not acting in compliance with any authority from his Government, or that if he conceived himself to be so authorized he greatly misunderstood the instructions which he had received.

A note in the Queen's handwriting (December 1, 1861) reads: "This draft was the last the beloved Prince ever wrote; he was very unwell at the time, and when he brought it in to the Queen he said, 'I could hardly hold my pen.'" Lord John Russell, who was Secretary of State for Foreign Affairs at the time, accepted the new paragraph; and the American Government acceded to the demands so tactfully expressed. The Southern deputies were released, and the *Trent* crisis was solved. The example of all this was not lost on Queen Victoria, though her Ministers seem not to have profited by it as much as they might. She frequently drew their attention, when draft dispatches were submitted to her, to "passages which she considered might have an irritating effect." A passage in her *Journal* (July 2, 1864) shows that the Queen could be even more explicitly critical, as when she and Lord Clarendon (in a conversation about the Schleswig-Holstein affair) spoke about "the deplorable tone of bullying" in Lord Palmerston's diplomacy, and "we both agreed in hoping this tone would die with him."

Lord Palmerston, who was still very much alive—he was nearly eighty years old and died next year—complained on July 5, 1864, to the Queen about her use of "irresponsible advisers." The specific ground of complaint on this occasion was in reference not to foreign policy, but to ecclesiastical appointments. The Queen, who after the Prince Consort's death often dictated official letters to her secretary and let him sign them, in her answer to this complaint of Lord Palmerston wrote herself (July 7, 1864):

> The Queen acknowledges Lord Palmerston's letter of the 5th. . . . She is much surprised at the tone of Lord Palmerston's remarks, for he can never pretend that the Sovereign has not the right, as every one else has, to ask anyone she chooses about any person who is recommended for an appointment to her.

That the Queen was able to follow a firm line in dealing with her Ministers, and to give them good advice on matters of high policy, is all the more remarkable inasmuch as she was suffering severely from grief. She could not lay bare her heart to the blustering Palmerston ('Pilgerstein,' as she and King Leopold used to Germanize the name), but she could do this to a fine aristocrat like Lord Derby. It is impossible to mistake the cry of anguish in the following eloquent passage:

> To express *what* the Queen's desolation and utter misery is is almost impossible; every feeling seems swallowed up in that *one* of unbounded *grief*! She feels as though *her life* had ended on *that* dreadful day when she lost that bright Angel who was her idol, the life of her life; and time seems to have passed like *one long, dark day*!
>
> *She* sees the trees budding, the days lengthen, the primroses coming out, but *she thinks* herself *still* in the month of December! The Queen toils away from morning till night,

goes out twice a day, does all she is desired to do by her physician, but she wastes and pines, and there is that within her *inmost soul* which seems to be undermining her existence! And *how can* it be otherwise? The happiness and comfort of twenty-two years crushed *for ever*; and the Queen, who did nothing, thought of nothing, without her beloved and gracious husband, who was her support, her constant companion, her guide, who helped her in *everything*, great and small, stands *alone* in her trying and difficult position, struggling to do her duty, as she will do to her last hour, with a broken, bleeding heart, and with but *one* consolation—to *rejoin him* again—*never* to *part*! [1]

While in this mood, which persisted for a very long time, the Queen remained more secluded than the British people could sympathize with. She explained—it can scarcely be said that she defended—her seclusion in words of genuine agony:

The Queen was *always* terribly nervous on all public occasions, but *especially* at the opening of Parliament, which she *dreaded for days* before, and hardly ever went through without suffering from headache before or after the ceremony; but *then* she had the *support* of her dear husband, whose presence alone seemed a tower of strength, and by whose dear side she *felt safe* and *supported* under *every* trial. *Now* this is *gone*, and no child can feel more shrinking and nervous than the poor Queen does, when she has to *do* anything which approaches to representation. She dreads a council *even*.

Her nerves are *so* shattered that *any* emotion, *any* discussion, *any* exertion, causes much disturbance and suffering to her whole frame. The constant anxieties inseparable from her difficult and unenviable position as Queen and as mother of a large family (and that a *Royal family*) without a husband to guide, assist, soothe, comfort, and cheer her, are *so* great that her nervous system has no power of recovery, but on the contrary becomes weaker and weaker.

[1] *The Letters of Queen Victoria,* Second Series (1926), i, 20.

This being the case, Lord Russell (whose kind consideration she fully appreciated) will at once see that any great exertion which would entail a succession of *moral shocks*, as well as very great fatigue, which the Queen must avoid as much as possible, would be *totally out of the question.*

She has no wish to shut herself up from her loyal people, and has and will at any time seize any occasion which might offer to appear amongst them (painful as it ever is now), provided she could do so without fatigue or exertion of any *State* ceremony entailing full dress, etc.[1]

A little later she was protesting to Lord Russell (January 22, 1866) against having to go to open Parliament:

That the public should wish to see her she fully understands, and has *no* wish to prevent—quite the contrary; but why this wish should be of so *unreasonable* and unfeeling a nature as to *long* to *witness* the spectacle of a poor, broken-hearted widow, nervous and shrinking, dragged in *deep mourning ALONE* in *STATE* as a *Show*, where she used to go supported by her husband, to be gazed at, without delicacy of feeling, is a thing *she cannot* understand, and she never could wish her bitterest foe to be exposed to.

Slowly but steadily the Queen's mood of distress disappeared, and she attained to something like serenity. Her correspondence was quite friendly with Lord Russell, who after Palmerston's death in 1865 became Prime Minister until 1867. She was more at her ease with Lord Derby, Prime Minister in 1867–68. It was Disraeli, however, the next Prime Minister, who succeeded in making official correspondence a pleasure to her. Even before his Prime Ministership, when he was Chancellor of the Exchequer, and occasionally had to communicate with the sovereign, he had been able to introduce some Attic salt into the communications. Referring to an attack on the Reform Bill which was being debated in the House

[1] *The Letters of Queen Victoria,* Second Series, i, 244–245.

of Commons, he wrote to the Queen (June 17, 1867): " It was a *conspiration des salons*, but powerfully equipped. When all was ripe *The Times* thundered." His first letter (February 26, 1868) as Prime Minister to the Queen must be unique of its kind:

> Mr Disraeli with his humble duty to your Majesty.
>
> He ventures to express his sense of your Majesty's most gracious kindness to him, and of the high honour which your Majesty has been graciously pleased to confer on him.
>
> He can only offer devotion.
>
> It will be his delight and duty to render the transaction of affairs as easy to your Majesty as possible, and in smaller matters he hopes he may succeed in this; but he ventures to trust that in the great affairs of State your Majesty will deign not to withhold from him the benefit of your Majesty's guidance.
>
> Your Majesty's life has been passed in constant communion with great men, and the knowledge and management of important transactions. Even if your Majesty were not gifted with those great abilities which all now acknowledge, this rare and choice experience must give your Majesty an advantage in judgment which few living persons, and probably no living Prince, can rival.
>
> He, whom your Majesty has so highly preferred, presumes to trust to your Majesty's condescension in this behalf.[1]

After this missive of respectful devotion there came another, dated on the same day, containing recommendations for appointments to office. He proposed Ward Hunt as Chancellor of the Exchequer:

> Mr Ward Hunt's appearance is rather remarkable, but anything but displeasing. He is more than six feet four inches in stature, but does not look so tall from his proportionate breadth; like St Peter's, no one is at first aware of his dimensions. But he has the sagacity of the elephant as well as the form.

[1] *The Letters of Queen Victoria*, Second Series, i, 505.

The Queen relished this salt, and if she did not reply with equal humour—it is doubtful if she could—she at any rate took some pleasure in her replies. Disraeli's first Prime Ministership, however, lasted for only ten months, and for five years (1869–74) she had to correspond with Mr Gladstone as Prime Minister. Her letters to Gladstone were never better than rather chilly.

With Disraeli (Lord Beaconsfield from 1876) as Prime Minister for the second time (1874–80) she had the happiest relations, maintained by an incessant correspondence. Their only difference was over ecclesiastical appointments. Disraeli's recommendations on these appointments were good, but were always made with a view to the interest of the Conservative Party. The Queen, who was averse from extremes of all kinds, and was distressed at the growth of ritualism, was determined that the Prime Minister should look beyond party interest. "There are *far larger* questions *at stake*," she wrote to Disraeli (November 9, 1875).

> It must be *remembered* that the appointments in the Church are *all* important for *good* or *evil*, being wide-reaching and of *long* duration in their results, far exceeding the stability of the best of Governments.

In the last fifteen years of the Queen's life she appears to have written rather fewer, and also considerably shorter, letters than in previous years. The three concluding volumes of published *Letters of Queen Victoria* have a large proportion of letters addressed to her, and also copious extracts from her Journal. Old people tend to find letter-writing onerous and arduous, and accordingly to write, if not less frequently, at any rate at less length. It cannot be said, however, that the Queen's industry ever flagged. The extracts printed from her Journal indicate how full and exact it was. Her letters addressed to her Prime Ministers, if not so expansive as in the time of Melbourne,

Peel, Derby, or Disraeli, show no lack of knowledge, interest, or trenchancy. Her dislike of Gladstone, of his policy and his party, is made clear in nearly every line of her numerous letters to him. Nor did she make any effort to conceal this from her other Ministers. To G. J. Goschen, who was a Member of Parliament, but not in the Cabinet, she wrote, referring to a debate on the Irish question: "Mr Gladstone's speech was very unsatisfactory." When Lord Salisbury's Government was defeated in the House of Commons she wrote to Goschen: "You will not be surprised if I am startled at the unfortunate vote of last night, which has come like a thunderbolt. . . . I hope and think that Mr Gladstone could not form a Government." To Lord Salisbury she wrote of her trust "that a very short time (if any) will elapse before she sees him again in office." When Gladstone entered into office her letters became perfectly glacial:

> The Queen, in thanking Mr Gladstone for his report of what took place last night in the House of Commons, must say that she read it with deep and unfeigned regret. Mr Gladstone's speech appeared to support that wretched Mr Labouchere's views, while opposing his outrageous resolution. . . .

And: "The Queen is sorry that Mr Gladstone repeats the cry against the wealthy and educated classes of the country, which does not appear to rest on any foundation."

When Mr Gladstone resigned, after failing to carry the first Home Rule Bill, the Queen accepted the resignation without a word of thanks for services rendered, in four lines: "The Queen will accept this resignation, and has at once sent to Lord Salisbury; but, as he is abroad, there may be a little delay before any arrangement can be finally decided." [1]

[1] The letters here quoted to or about Gladstone are from *The Letters of Queen Victoria*, Third Series (1930), i, 16, 22–23, 31, 73, 154, and 163. The

The Queen's grasp of foreign affairs remained as firm as ever, and she continued to express herself as forcefully. When Alexander of Battenburg, Prince of Bulgaria, was kidnapped, she wrote to Salisbury: "We are horrified at these news from Bulgaria. On what ground can this have been done? It is these Russian fiends. . . ." Evidently her attitude did not escape other people, for later she is writing to Salisbury: "The Queen is *quite* furious at anyone daring or presuming to say *she* wanted to make war on Russia to replace Prince Alexander." She thought that the Ambassador, Sir Robert Morier, was mismanaging affairs at St Petersburg: "He is *not safe there.* He should be given leave of absence at once." This to Lord Salisbury, and in another letter, still referring to Morier: "He does awful mischief." She took to telegraphing, not, apparently, because speed was essential, but perhaps because a telegram had a more forceful air than a letter. To Lord Salisbury she wires: "You told me when you left office in February that I should impress on Lord Rosebery the importance of bringing as few subjects on *foreign affairs* before the *Cabinet* as possible. Trust you will follow this course now." When it was proposed to give Heligoland to Germany, in exchange for African territory, she wired to Salisbury: "It is a very *serious question*, which I do not like." [1] She added that Gibraltar might be asked for next.

She remained equally trenchant regarding ecclesiastical affairs: "The Queen has taken pains to enquire into some of the people who [*sic*] Lord Salisbury mentioned as candidates for bishoprics. . . . The Queen fears the Dean of York would not do. He is a High Churchman. . . ." Later (to Sir Henry Ponsonby): "The Dean of York (a

dates are January 24, January 27, January 29, March 5, July 4, and July 20, 1886.

[1] *The Letters of Queen Victoria*, Third Series, i, 179, 181, 203, 211, and 612. The dates are August 22, August 23, September 8, and September 21, 1886, and June 9, 1890.

Cust) is said to be quite unfit for a bishopric. . . . Canon Fleming is said not to be quite a gentleman. . . ." [1]

A careful and complete study of the letters throughout the reign of sixty-three years would yield interesting results, and might lead to surprising and controversial conclusions about the Queen's statesmanship, her attitude towards party government, her views on society and economics. There can, however, be no controversy over her position as one of the great letter-writers of her age. The *Letters* express the age as it was—its political affairs, interesting, important, exciting, but not, in retrospect, for the most part of supreme significance. They express too the age's domesticity. The Queen was interested in the marriages, births, and deaths of all the people whom she met, in the families of her Ministers, the aristocracy, the princes and crowned heads of Europe, and particularly, of course, her own numerous kindred. Royal society is seen in the *Letters* as a thing in itself. The royalties are a world of their own, a European clan or caste. They have mundane cares and contacts with their Governments and subjects, but they swim above these, like planets in the heavens. When, however, a mere citizen takes the opportunity—such as the Queen's *Letters* offer him—of ascending into this rarer air, this royal empyrean, he finds people united by warm domestic affection, enjoying their family parties, their visits and travels, their christenings and marriages, their reading, churchgoing, sport. Queen Victoria's letters show all this, although she had no inclination and no time for sport; but she had a large heart, kindly sympathy, charity (but not for *all* men), experience, memories. She had the great merit of being interested in people, endlessly interested in people, not consciously interested in herself. She was, except in her grief-stricken period, wholesome in mind, spirit, outlook; not an egoist;

[1] *The Letters of Queen Victoria*, Third Series, i, 536 and 541; December 21 and 24, 1889.

never bored with people or with her duties. The mother of a large family, the centre of a large and increasing line, she spread her interest outward, and genuinely felt herself to be the mother of all her people. The *Letters* are the monument, the expression, and the proof of this unique position.

Chapter XIV

THE TASTE FOR LONG POEMS

THE characteristic enjoyments of cultured people were the long poem, the long novel, the ample oil-painting, the theological essay; to a less extent the drama. Most surprising of these tastes seems now that for the long poem. Few people in the second quarter of the twentieth century read long poems—perhaps few read poetry at all—although for a year or two Bridges' long poem *The Testament of Beauty* and Benet's *John Brown's Body* attracted attention.

Nevertheless almost every previous age since 'Biblical' or classical times had its long poem: the tenth century before Christ had *The Song of Songs* (*Song of Solomon*) and the Sanskrit *Vedas*; the ancient Greeks had the *Iliad* and *Odyssey*; the Roman Empire had the *Æneid.* The minstrels of the Dark Ages sang *Beowulf* and the *Chanson de Roland*; the twelfth century had the *Heimskringla* and other sagas; Dante gave the *Divina Commedia* to the fourteenth century and all ages. The gentry and ladies of the sixteenth century, the Renaissance, received with avidity, as intellectual treats, Ariosto's *Orlando Furioso* (1532), Camoens' *Lusiads* (1572), Tasso's *Gerusalemme Liberata* (1576), Spenser's *Faerie Queene* (1596), and read them like novels. The seventeenth century had *Paradise Lost*; the eighteenth was rather poor in long poems, though Klopstock's *Messiah* (1748) found many readers. The early nineteenth century had Scott's *Lady of the Lake*, Byron's *Childe Harold*, and Pushkin's *Evgeny Onegin.* The second forty years of the nineteenth century did equally well, or better, in respect of long poems: it had Tennyson's *In*

Memoriam (1850), Elizabeth Barrett Browning's *Aurora Leigh* (1856), Robert Browning's *Ring and the Book* (1868). In the class of long novels *Vanity Fair* began to come out in 1847, *David Copperfield* in 1849; Mrs Craik's *John Halifax, Gentleman,* was published in 1857, *Barchester Towers* also in 1857, and *Adam Bede* in 1859; Shorthouse's *John Inglesant* circulated privately years before it was published in 1881. Theological books which created a great stir were *Essays and Reviews* (1860), Newman's *Apologia* (1864), Seeley's *Ecce Homo* (1865). William Holman Hunt's picture *The Light of the World* was completed in 1854.

Of the three long poems of the 1840–80 period—*In Memoriam, Aurora Leigh, The Ring and the Book*—the most surprising at the time of publication was *Aurora Leigh.* It was the first really long poem written by a woman. Mrs Browning had produced some remarkable poems, sensational and humanitarian; many people had read or heard of *The Cry of the Children,* published in 1843. She was known to be an invalid, and when Robert Browning married her in 1846 she had been, if not bedridden, at any rate couch-ridden, for years. Her father lived " emotionally and æsthetically, like some detestable, decadent poet, upon his daughter's decline." She was led to believe herself to be dying; " but she was a high-spirited woman, full of that silent and quite unfathomable kind of courage which is only found in women, and she took a much more cheerful view of death than her father did of life." After she eloped in 1846 to Italy with Robert Browning she lived for fifteen years " in infinitely better health than she had ever known before." [1] She was fifty years old when *Aurora Leigh* was published in 1856, and though at the time of publication the Brownings were in London, they had been living for ten years in Florence. Except in the opening verses, however, there is little about Italy in the book

[1] The quotations above are from G. K. Chesterton's *Robert Browning* (1903), pp. 60, 61, and 72.

—for *Aurora Leigh* was a whole book, a novel in verse, of more than eleven thousand lines, a total of over ninety thousand words. For a poem this is long, though it cannot compare for length with the giant novels of the period, like *Vanity Fair*, which has over three hundred thousand words. Swinburne, who was nineteen years old when *Aurora Leigh* came out, wrote forty years later that its publication was quite an event: " The advent of *Aurora Leigh* can never be forgotten by any lover of poetry who was old enough at the time to read it." [1] He further says that her devout and undevout imaginings caught hold on her passionate fancy and sensitive conscience, and then flew into utterance, all air and fire. This is true; but he is badly amiss when he concludes:

> The career of Aurora in London is rather too eccentric a vision to impose itself upon the most juvenile credulity: a young woman of family who lodges by herself in Grub Street, preserves her reputation, lives on her pen, and dines out in Mayfair is hardly a figure for serious fiction.

This kind of life is common enough now. What Swinburne could not conceive as credible in 1898 Mrs Browning, with only a very limited experience of life, and none at all of " Grub Street," foresaw in 1856.

Although few or no people read long poems now, anyone who could be induced patiently to start on *Aurora Leigh* would fairly soon find that it gripped him. This beautiful, if rather terrible, tale in blank verse has an effect something like that of *Jane Eyre*, which was published nine years earlier (1847). Aurora Leigh was born in Italy, soon lost her Florentine mother, and at thirteen lost her English father. Her father's sister then came out to Italy and took her to England. Aurora grew up in her aunt's country-house, and finds it all very prim and dull, though she conscientiously enough learns her history and geography and the sewing and crocheting that the aunt

[1] Note to the edition of 1898.

prescribes as being ladylike. All the time, however, she has an inner life, fostered by reading of the poets:

> The only teachers who instruct mankind
> From just a shadow on a charnel-wall
> To find man's veritable stature out
> Erect, sublime—the measure of a man,
> And that's the measure of an angel, says
> The apostle. Aye, and while your common men
> Lay telegraphs, gauge railroads, reign, reap, dine,
> And dust the flaunty carpets of the world
> For kings to walk on, or our president,
> The poet suddenly will catch them up
> With his voice like a thunder—" This is soul,
> This is life, this word is being said in heaven,
> Here's God down on us! what are you about? "
> How all those workers start amid their work,
> Look round, look up, and feel, a moment's space,
> That carpet-dusting, though a pretty trade,
> Is not the imperative labour after all.

Aurora's cousin, Romney Leigh, who owns a big house near the aunt's, proposes marriage to her. She rejects him. Romney is entirely devoted to good work—orphanages and Factory Acts—and Aurora believes that those things are his only real love. The aunt dies suddenly, and her estate passes to Romney, who endeavours chivalrously to induce Aurora to accept all the personal property—the rest being entailed—but she refuses and goes up to London. There she earns a living by writing for cyclopædias and popular journals; and in the leisure-time that she thus earns she writes poetry: " In England no one lives by verse that lives."

She lives and works for three years in a chamber up three flights of stairs " in a certain house in Kensington." She keeps in a drawer an ivy-wreath that she was wearing when Romney Leigh had found her out in the fields and had proposed marriage to her. In the three years in London she had some literary successes, crowns about as satisfying as the faded ivy-wreath:

> Those Olympian crowns
> We run for, till we lose sight of the sun
> In the dust of the racing chariots!

One day a lady climbed the stairs and called on Aurora:

> A lady called on me on such a day.
> She had the low voice of your English dames,
> Unused, it seems, to need rise half a note
> To catch attention. . . .
> "Lady Waldemar."
> She said her name quite simply, as if it meant
> Not much indeed, but something. . . .

Lady Waldemar, who is not an attractive character, wants to marry Romney Leigh; but Romney has become attached to a poor girl, Marian Erle, whom he has been helping. Lady Waldemar wants Aurora to break off this attachment or engagement. Aurora, however, at once declares that she will do everything to help Romney to his happiness; and she goes to visit Marian in a slum which Mrs Browning describes with disquieting realism. The marriage is arranged to take place, and guests high and low are invited to the church. There is another realist description of the coarse, deformed, savage poor who come as guests, and the worldly, fashionable ladies and men who come too, converse, and display the different world in which they live. Mrs Browning has the "two nations" of rich and poor more sharply defined even than Disraeli has in *Sybil*. The bridegroom is present, but when the time comes for the bride to appear there is a terrible scene: no bride, only a letter brought to the church door by a slum boy from Marian saying that she has judged it best to disappear. The smooth-faced Lady Waldemar is at the bottom of this horrible plot.

Aurora later—a year or two later—finds Marian in Paris with an illegitimate child, a baby boy. Marian tells her dreadful story. Lady Waldemar had sent her off with a maidservant to go to Australia. The maidservant instead had taken her to France. To Aurora Marian said:

I was not ever, as you say, seduced,
But simply murdered.

Aurora takes the girl to her heart. Together with the baby they go off to Italy to some place near Florence where Aurora's father had lived. Here they are happy enough. Aurora writes no more poetry, but she and Marian talk and think much; and Aurora writes and receives letters, long letters, reproduced in the blank verse of the poem. One night Romney turns up. He has not married Lady Waldemar; he has come to ask Marian to marry him. Marian lets him make the offer, which she feels is characteristic of his nobility, and in a sense morally legitimizes her son; but though she falls at his feet and weeps on them, she will not marry him. Romney tells Aurora his sad story: the burning of his house by villagers, the ingratitude of the outcasts he had helped. Suddenly Aurora—they were speaking out of doors, in the Italian night—realizes that he is blind; a falling beam, probably directed his way by a man he was succouring, had destroyed the optic nerve, though his eyes still appeared as if normal. He turns to go, and then Aurora, who has been explaining why she has long ago refused to marry him, and why it is better so, breaks out that she does love him.

[ROMNEY.] "Farewell, Aurora."
[AURORA.] "But I love you, sir;
And when a woman says she loves a man,
The man must hear her. . . .
Now I know
I loved you always, Romney."
There were words
That broke in utterance . . . melted, in the fire,—
Embrace, that was convulsion, . . . then a kiss
As long and silent as the ecstatic night,
And deep, deep, shuddering breaths, which meant beyond
Whatever could be told by word or kiss.

Aurora Leigh is a regular novel in verse, a novel of

society, like Pushkin's *Evgeny Onegin.* Robert Browning's *Ring and the Book* is certainly not a novel. It is one of the longest poems in the language—indeed, in any language—having twenty-one thousand one hundred and sixteen lines. Together they comprise twelve books, each of which is a separate story. Yet each story has the same theme—the murder of Violante and Pietro, parents, and of Pompilia, their daughter (or alleged daughter), by Pompilia's husband, Count Guido Franchesini. Book I, which is introduction, after describing the making of an Etrurian-style Ring—which has absolutely nothing to do with the story—tells how Robert Browning found the Yellow Book:

I found this book,
Gave a *lira* for it, eightpence English just,
(Mark the predestination!) when a Hand,
Always above my shoulder, pushed me once,
One day still fierce 'mid many a day struck calm,
Across a Square in Florence, crammed with booths.

The purchase was a piece of luck, for the book looked just like hundreds of others which anyone can, or could, buy any day in Florence among the junk crammed on the open-air booths:

'Mongst odds and ends of ravage, picture-frames
White through the worn gilt, mirror-sconces chipped,
Bronze angel-heads once knobs attached to chests,
(Handled when ancient dames chose forth brocade)
Modern chalk drawings, studies from the nude,
Samples of stone, jet, breccia, porphyry
Polished and rough, sundry amazing busts
In baked earth (broken, Providence be praised!)
A wreck of tapestry, proudly-purposed web
When reds and blues were indeed red and blue,
Now offered as a mat to save bare feet
(Since carpets constitute a cruel cost)
Treading the chill scagliola bedward: then
A pile of brown-etched prints, two *crazie* each,
Stopped by a conch a-top from fluttering forth

—Sowing the Square with works of one and the same
Master, the imaginative Sienese
Great in the scenic backgrounds—(name and fame
None of you know, nor does he fare the worse:)
From these. . . . Oh, with a Lionard going cheap
If it should prove, as promised, that Joconde
Whereof a copy contents the Louvre!—these
I picked this book from.

Browning leaned on the railing by the fountain in the square—"June was the month, Lorenzo named the Square"—and dipped into the book. It was in Latin, with an Italian title; the contents were the pleadings in a Roman murder trial of the year 1698. As he began idly to read his attention was aroused, then riveted to the subject. He started walking homeward, still reading:

And on I read
Presently, though my path grew perilous
Between the outspread straw-work, piles of plait
Soon to be flapping, each o'er two black eyes
And swathe of Tuscan hair, on festas fine;
Through fire-irons, tribes of tongs, shovels in sheaves,
Skeleton bedsteads, wardrobe-drawers agape,
Rows of tall slim brass lamps with dangling gear—
And worse, cast clothes a-sweetening in the sun:
None of them took my eye from off my prize.

The Yellow Book (now in Balliol College Library), which has been reissued and may be read by the curious, is partly in print, partly manuscript. To Browning it was a return of the past—that is, history, life:

Pure crude fact
Secreted from man's life when hearts beat hard,
And brains, high-blooded, ticked two centuries since.
Give it me back! The thing's restorative
I' the touch and sight.

The historian must be a poet if he is to see the living past. Browning was primarily a poet—creative, imaginative, lyrical, but mostly directed towards creating or recreating, imagining, singing the past as he saw it. The greater part of his work is deliberately historical: *Balaustion's Adventure*, from the Peloponnesian War, in the fifth century B.C.; *Sordello*, named after the mysterious and solemn soldier described by Dante; *Paracelsus*, the life of a medieval scholar; *Strafford*, a study of the struggle of Crown and Parliament; *King Victor and King Charles*, an incident of the years 1731–32. Hosts of shorter poems all reproduce some aspect of the past: *The Bishop orders his Tomb at St Praxed's Church*; *How They Brought the Good News from Ghent to Aix*; *Cavalier Tunes*; *Incident of the French Camp*:

> You know, we French stormed Ratisbon;
> A mile or so away,
> On a little mound, Napoleon
> Stood on our storming-day.

The battle of Sedan and the fall of the Second Empire moved Browning in 1871 to review the history or autobiography of Louis Napoleon Bonaparte in a long reverie, *Prince Hohenstiel-Schwangau, Saviour of Society*, ending:

> My reverie concludes, as dreaming should,
> With daybreak: nothing done and over yet,
> Except cigars!

British India stirs the poet: he composes, "Comfort you, my great unhappy hero, Clive." *Home-thoughts from the Sea* are thoughts of the British Navy, Cape St Vincent, Trafalgar, Gibraltar:

> "Here and here did England help me: how can I help England?"—say,
> Whoso turns as I, this evening, turn to God to praise and pray,
> While Jove's planet rises yonder, silent over Africa.

Even an ecstatic lyric of love takes unerringly an historical direction—the American Civil War:

> In one year they sent a million fighters forth
> South and North,
> And they built their gods a brazen pillar high
> As the sky,
> Yet reserved a thousand chariots in full force—
> Gold, of course.

Oh, heart! oh, blood that freezes, blood that burns!
Earth's returns
For whole centuries of folly, noise and sin!
Shut them in,
With their triumphs and their glories and the rest.
Love is best!

With the eye of the historian, with the vivid imagination of the poet, Browning, reading the Yellow Book, saw the murder trial of 1698, the course of pride, deceit, and folly, leading to the tragedy, and the redeeming qualities and acts of one or two good people concerned in the whole affair. Burning to express it all, the poet tells the story over again, not once, but twelve times; in the introduction, to which he gives the name "The Ring and the Book"—

Now, as the ingot, ere the ring was forged
Lay gold (beseech you, hold that figure fast!)
So, in this book lay absolutely truth,

—in "Half-Rome" and "The Other Half-Rome," two sides of the popular version of the story; in "Tertium Quid," another popular version, supposed to be more balanced; in "Count Guido Franchesini," the clever defence by himself of the murderer; in "Giuseppe Caponsacchi," the version of the friar who helped the persecuted wife of Count Guido to escape from her husband's house, though this did not save her from the Count's vengeance; in "Pompilia," the seventeen-year-old murdered wife, who lived just long enough to tell her tale; in "Dominus Hyacinthus de Archangelis," sprightly "defender of the poor," who defends, ineffectively, Count Guido—

Burying nose deep down i' the briery bush,
Thus I defend Count Guido

—in "Juris Doctor Johannes-Baptista Bottinus," who delivers the verdict; in "The Pope," good old Innocent XII, infirm and on the brink of the grave, but still able to think clearly, and firm-willed enough to be able to confirm the judgment; in "Guido," who speaks again, before execution; and in "The Book and the Ring," spoken by Browning once more in the first person, which is the conclusion of the whole matter.

The publication of *The Ring and the Book* in 1868–69 was hailed as a literary event. It is characteristic Browning work on the grand scale. Although long, it is not verbose. Much of it is terse. It has tremendous vigour. The lines have energy, spirit, fire. Each one of the twelve books is somebody speaking; the introductory book and concluding book are Browning speaking directly. Each of the intervening ten books is a single speech, fifteen hundred lines long or more. Surely this is an effort that no one has ever before expected the public to make: to read ten consecutive speeches in verse, a total of nearly twenty thousand lines? And Browning's verse, though it flows like a rapid river, is not smooth, and its twists and turns are not easy to follow. Yet people did read it then, as they could, if they took the trouble, read it now, because they liked participating in the life and thought of the great joyous man who wrote it. They were serious-minded people who liked having problems of character and morality presented to them and worked out with the large tolerance—each character having its say—that was part of Browning's philosophy of life. They were historically minded too, and in particular they were interested in those days in Italian history, present and past. Browning's epic raised the curtain on a throbbing drama of seventeenth-century Italy which fascinated the English reader, just as, twelve years later, did Shorthouse's story of John Inglesant's long sojourn in Florence, Rome, Naples, and the Abruzzi.

As one long narrative follows another the story, far from palling, grows in intensity. The friar Giuseppe Caponsacchi's defence of Pompilia's good name is a magnificent piece of oratory, of passionate vindication of a beautiful character, contempt of the wretched creature who murdered her, justification of his own action as priest and man. He dreams for a moment how sweet life might have been had he been a layman and married to Pompilia:

> I do but play with an imagined life
> Of who, unfettered by a vow, unblessed
> By the higher call—since you will have it so—
> Leads it companioned by the woman there. . . .
>   All this, how far away!
> Mere delectation, meet for a minute's dream!
> Just as a drudging student trims his lamp,
> Opens his Plutarch, puts him in the place
> Of Roman, Grecian; draws the patched gown close,
> Dreams, " Thus should I fight, save or rule the world! "
> Then smilingly, contentedly, awakes
> To the old solitary nothingness;
> So I from such communion pass content. . . .

Content? He pauses, his heart full of the tragedy of the dying girl; finishes:

> O great, just, good God! Miserable me!

Pompilia, stabbed and hacked, lingered a day or two while the bodies of Pietro and Violante were being exposed in the church where hers would soon join them. She too speaks, has a whole book to herself. The story, which she tells quite simply, goes to the depths of pathos, like Marian's story in *Aurora Leigh*, and even more poignantly, for there is just a touch of theatricality about Marian's story, and none in Pompilia's.

Dominus Hyacinthus de Archangelis, the Procurator for the Poor, puts the case for Guido, and Doctor of Law Johannes-Baptista Bottinus, advocate of the Papal Fisc, for Pompilia and Caponsacchi, humorously and fairly convincingly: they would be more convincing if they appeared more in earnest. Then there follows the good old Pope Innocent XII, who has the power to confirm the sentence of death against Guido or to quash it:

In God's name! Once more on this earth of God's
While twilight lasts and time wherein to work,
I take His staff with my uncertain hand,
And stay my six and fourscore years, my due
Labour and sorrow, on His judgment-seat,
And forthwith think, speak, act, in place of Him—
The Pope for Christ. Once more appeal is made
From man's assize to mine: I sit and see
Another poor weak trembling human wretch
Pushed by his fellows, who pretend the right,
Up to the gulf which, where I gaze, begins
From this world to the next—gives way and way,
Just on the edge over the awful dark;
With nothing to arrest him but my feet. . . .
I have worn through this sombre wintry day,
With winter in my soul beyond the world's,
Over these dismalest of documents
Which drew night down on me ere eve befell. . . .
Therefore there is not any doubt to clear
When I shall write the brief word presently
And chink the hand-bell.

The Pope's long soliloquy is the least dramatic and the most obscure—indeed, the only obscure one—of the whole series; but at last, after many stimulating lines in a maze of syncopated trains of thought, it works out to its logical *dénouement*:

And how should I dare die, this man let live?
Carry this forthwith to the Governor!

The Ring and the Book was one of the most famous books of its time, widely known, if not widely read in its entirety. Browning, who had a friendly, exuberant personality, was very proud of this *tour de force* of blank verse. Though it lacks the sustained stream of narrative of an epic, it has at any rate the vividness of a historical drama. Yet he had been unable to interest genuine novelists in the theme and plot of the Yellow Book, so he felt compelled to re-write it himself. Some years after the publication of the poem two poetesses who wrote under the name of Michael

Field were visiting Browning, then seventy-nine years old, in his home in Warwick Crescent.

> The room where he lives as a poet is small, with red curtains and two plain bookcases filled with old books; over the mantelshelf is an Italian picture; there is a cast of Dante, some portraits, some vigorous studies of peasants. . . . Out of a drawer came the very book, bought for ninepence on a Florentine bookstall (white vellum, with a mixture of print and old letters) on which *The Ring and the Book* was founded. We held it in our hands; he translated to us here and there. He said how he had sent it to three novelists, but they could do nothing with it. So one fine morning he determined to work at it, and began his poem. " You could have done it," he said; when we protested he added, " Not in my way." [1]

In Memoriam was the most famous and most cherished long poem of the Victorian Age. It was published in 1850, when Tennyson was forty years old. The title is curious, for the friend to whose memory the poem was dedicated died seventeen years earlier. Arthur Henry Hallam was the son of the eminent Whig historian, Henry Hallam. He and Tennyson became friends at Trinity College, Cambridge. They travelled together in France and on the Rhine, and visited at each other's homes. Hallam became engaged to Tennyson's sister Emily. In 1833 the Hallams went for a tour on the Continent; at Vienna the son suddenly took ill and died of apoplexy on September 15. He was twenty-two years old. The body was brought from Trieste (which Tennyson in *In Memoriam* calls " the Italian shore ") to England, and was buried at Clevedon Court, on the Severn, near Bristol.

Tennyson had no profession except that of poet. He led a moody, innocent life with his widowed mother and sister in London, achieving great success with his

[1] *Works and Days from the Journal of Michael Field*, edited by T. and D. C. Sturge Moore (1933), p. 15.

occasional volumes of verse. Carlyle called the big, bearded, handsome man " a Guardsman spoiled." In 1850, on the death of Wordsworth, he was made Poet Laureate, and married Emily Sellwood, when, he subsequently said, the peace of God came into his life. In the same year *In Memoriam* was published. It is a long series of lyrics which he had been writing and polishing for sixteen or seventeen years.

Arthur Henry Hallam was a youth of rare beauty of character and promise of ability, perhaps of genius. He is referred to in a number of passages of *In Memoriam.* A few incidents are described, such as Hallam's visit to Tennyson's home, Somersby Rectory, in Lincolnshire, in 1831 (LXXXVII), but nowhere is there a picture in firm outline; Hallam is a spirit, present in the poem, but unseen, an essence rather than a form, a personality—a somewhat vague one—not a distinct figure. The core of the poem is the belief or apprehension that love is the base of the universe, and that human love is a counterpart of the Christian's relation to God.

Love is and was my Lord and King,
  And in his presence I attend
  To hear the tidings of my friend
Which every hour his couriers bring.

Love is and was my King and Lord,
  And will be though as yet I keep
  Within his court on earth, and sleep
Encompassed by his faithful guard,

And hear at times a sentinel
  Who moves about from place to place,
  And whispers to the worlds of space
In the deep night that all is well.

. . . .

Strange friend, past, present, and to be;
  Loved deeplier, darklier understood;
  Behold, I dream a dream of good,
And mingle all the world with thee.

. . . .

My love involves the love before;
My love is vaster passion now;
Tho' mix'd with God and Nature thou,
I seem to love thee more and more.

It is remarkable that a poem of such length and dealing with so solemn and so sad a theme attained its great popularity at once and for the rest of Queen Victoria's reign. Nine years after *In Memoriam* Darwin published *The Origin of Species*. The tranquil, firm faith of *In Memoriam* reassured people who were more than a little perturbed by the theory of evolution and natural selection, which at once assumed so great an ascendancy in science and philosophy.

The Victorians were sentimental, but not morbid; and there is just a touch of morbidity about *In Memoriam*; there is not exactly a cult of death in it, but there is just a trace of this. Tennyson himself was a good representation of the Victorian Age, with a wholesome, cheerful outlook on life, a firm faith in God, a belief in progress. The poem—or rather poems, for *In Memoriam* is really a collection—shows "the progress of sorrow"; and the final stage is assurance of immortality and continuation of communion with the departed friend. The haunting words of the prologue, beginning "Strong Son of God, immortal Love," which give the epitome of Tennyson's faith, and were echoed in the hearts of countless readers, were written in 1849, the last of the series, not the first. Sorrow has progressed to calmness and assurance of the future. Actually the most cheerful section of *In Memoriam*, the *nearest* to being joyous (for none of the great elegy is really joyous anywhere), is the last, the epilogue, and was written seven years earlier than the prologue. The epilogue celebrates the marriage in 1842 of Tennyson's youngest sister, Cecilia, to Edmund Lushington, Professor of Greek in the University of Glasgow. Tennyson apostrophizes Cecilia:

O true and tried, so well and long,
  Demand not thou a marriage lay;
  In that it is thy marriage day
Is music more than any song.

Then he refers to Hallam's engagement to Emily Tennyson, frustrated by death in 1833:

Nor have I felt so much of bliss
  Since first he told me that he loved
  A daughter of our house; nor proved
Since that dark day a day like this.

Tho' I since then have number'd o'er
  Some thrice three years; they went and came,
  Remade the blood and changed the frame,
And yet is love not less, but more;

. . . . .

Regret is dead, but love is more
  Than in the summers that are flown,
  For I myself with these have grown
To something greater than before.

The last stanza of the poem, last of the epilogue written in 1842, already expresses Tennyson's complete conviction, in a last allusion to Hallam, his " friend in God ":

That friend of mine who lives in God,

That God, which ever lives and loves,
  One God, one law, one element,
  And one far-off divine event;
To which the whole creation moves.

Comparing *In Memoriam* with two other great elegies, Milton's *Lycidas* and Shelley's *Adonais*, a commentator has pointed out that " in each case the grief of the opening has passed at the close into triumph." In the two earlier elegies, however, the transition from grief to triumph or spiritual assurance is rapid; it " is felt by the reader to occupy but a few hours of concentrated experience."[1] In Tennyson's elegy, however, the experience occupies some

[1] A. C. Bradley, *A Commentary on Tennyson's "In Memoriam"* (1901), p. 21.

years. There are three Christmastide songs in *In Memoriam.* The first is in section XXX:

With trembling fingers did we weave
  The holly round the Christmas hearth. . . .

  We sung, tho' every eye was dim,
  A merry song we sang with him
Last year: impetuously we sang.

"Last year" was the year of Hallam's death; so the first Christmastide was 1834. The second song is in section LXXVI:

Again at Christmas did we weave
  The holly round the Christmas hearth;
  The silent snow possess'd the earth,
And calmly fell our Christmas-eve.

The poet's grief is calmer too. The third and last (along with New Year's Day) is in sections CII–CIV, after the Prologue probably the most famous songs of the whole poem, the dearest to the Victorians. This third Christmastide is approached quietly:

The time draws near the birth of Christ;
  The moon is hid, the night is still;
  A single church below the hill
Is pealing, folded in the mist. . . .

It closes in the triumphant 'ringing-in' of all things beautiful and good, and of the Redeemer Himself:

Ring out the old, ring in the new,
  Ring, happy bells, across the snow:
  The year is going, let him go;
Ring out the false, ring in the true.

Ring out the grief that saps the mind,
  For those that here we see no more;
  Ring out the feud of rich and poor
Ring in redress to all mankind.

. . . .

Ring in the valiant man and free,
  The larger heart, the kindlier hand,
  Ring out the darkness of the land,
Ring in the Christ that is to be.

The following spring (1837) is chronicled in sections CXIII and CXIV, and fifteen more short lyrics conclude the poem, except for the epilogue composed on the occasion of the marriage of Edmund Lushington and Cecilia in 1842. Accordingly, discounting the epilogue (1842) and the magnificent, assured prayer which is the prologue (1849), the main poem or collection known as *In Memoriam* portrays a spiritual progress from gloom to triumph in something over three years. Readers obtained more than poetic appreciation and spiritual comfort from the poem: they were confirmed in their faith in the good, the beautiful, progress and immortality.

Perhaps it was their belief in progress which chiefly distinguished the Victorians from those of other ages. They did not hold (as many people of the eighteenth century believed of themselves) that they were at the apex of civilization, though perhaps they actually were. They were pleased with their achievements, their rich literature, their scientific discoveries and inventions, their missionary and philanthropic efforts; but they also thought that they could do better, and that subsequent generations would do better still. They took it for granted that there would be 'progress,' not just in this or that direction, but generally throughout society. 'Progress' was not a conception of particular improvements, though these were worked for and welcomed, but of an ever further advance towards the divine perfection.

Victorian literature, accordingly, was optimistic. Many of its popular novels had pathetic themes, like some of Dickens', or satirical, like some of Thackeray's, but they were all hopeful. Theological works had wide circulation. Poetry was probably more widely read than at any other epoch in history. Milton's poetry had an excellent market down to the end of the nineteenth century. Long poems were regarded somewhat in the same way as the very long novel is to-day—as something companionable that would last. Thus *Aurora Leigh* circulated as a good sentimental story. *The Ring and the Book* was a bright, vigorously written historical novel in verse. *In Memoriam* was the expression of the human heart, of the ideal of human friendship, and of the progress of the soul in communion with the Eternal.

Chapter XV

EMINENT VICTORIANS

THE eighteenth century was, on the whole, something of a cosmopolitan age; the nineteenth century was not. Peoples were becoming politically-minded and nationalist; and though Mazzini preached that once they had become free they would recognize their common brotherhood, they did not do so. The English people in this respect were like the rest. "The French wars made England insular, and conscious of its insularity, as it had not been since the Conquest."[1] 'High society' and 'middle-class' society were serious, even earnest, under the Evangelical impulse; never ridiculous—except when abroad. The travelling Englishman in the middle of the nineteenth century, with his broad-check suit, his mutton-chop whiskers, his vacant expression, was a favourite caricature in foreign journals; but so was "Mounseer" or "Meinherr" in English drama and fiction. The English and Continentals were not understanding one another very well, in spite of what Carlyle was doing in England for the Germans and of what Taine was doing in France for the English.

It is clear that in some respects development on the Continent was separate from development in Great Britain; in other respects it was similar, though the rhythms were different. Painting, architecture, and literature had each a development of its own in Great Britain, different from the contemporary developments on the Continent. On the other hand, industry, science, education, and politics had

[1] G. M. Young, "Portrait of an Age," in *Early Victorian England*, ii, 416.

each much the same trend on the Continent and in Great Britain, though the rate of progress and the stages of progress were different on one side of the Channel from the other. This fact is particularly obvious in what has been called the Industrial Revolution.

In Great Britain an industrial economy based—so far as it was industrial at all—upon handicraft, water-power, and horse transport, was gradually transformed into an economy based upon the factory system, steam-power, and railway transport, in a period from about 1750 to 1850. For various reasons the British people had the start of the Continental peoples. The Napoleonic wars, which diminished the available capital on the Continent more rapidly than in Great Britain, resulted in the British lead being increased. Most, though not all, of the great names in the industrial history of the mid-nineteenth century are British. The greatest men of the steam-engine and railway were George Stephenson, "the father of the locomotive," who lived until 1848; Robert Stephenson, the assistant and worthy successor of his father, almost as active on the Continent as in England until his death in 1859; and Isambard Kingdom Brunel, the engineer and practically the constructor of the Great Western Railway from 1833 to 1859. The history of Isambard Kingdom Brunel is typical of a process fairly common in his time, and perhaps becoming fairly common again to-day. This was the process by which Great Britain, owing to its free institutions, attracted to itself a good deal of Continental ability. I. K. Brunel's father was a Frenchman, born in Normandy, who began his career in the French Navy. As his opinions were not agreeable to the French Revolution, he went to the United States, and eventually to England, where he obtained employment as an engineer in the Government dockyards, married, and settled down. The son, I. K. Brunel, was born an Englishman, and was trained for work in England, though he was sent to school for a couple of years in Paris before entering his father's office.

The Continent contributed many people distinguished in English industry and finance. George Joachim Goschen, the leading authority on foreign exchange in the sixties—his *Theory of the Foreign Exchanges* was first published in 1861—was the grandson of a Leipsig business-man who settled in London and educated his family for English careers. It was G. J. Goschen who, as Chancellor of the Exchequer under Lord Salisbury, carried out the great conversion of the National Debt to a 2½ per cent. basis in 1888.

In the iron and steel industry the greatest name in the middle decades of the century was undoubtedly that of Bessemer, a Hertfordshire man, largely self-taught, whose process for making steel was brought to complete success by the year 1856. Andrew Carnegie, of Pittsburg, who may, however, be considered biased in favour of steel, called Bessemer one of the greatest benefactors of mankind. Steel, which before his time cost the almost prohibitive sum of £50 to make a ton, was produced by Bessemer's process at about £10 a ton.

The huge public works carried out by Governments or by 'public utility' companies in the middle nineteenth century and subsequently were taken in hand by a comparatively new kind of business man, called a contractor. It is true that there are few really new things in business management, and something like the modern contractor existed in Roman times; but he was unknown in the Middle Ages, and in the eighteenth century he was chiefly a financier. The great contractor who can undertake the construction of almost any kind of public works—railways, roads, bridges, housing estates, waterworks—and carry it through by means of a vast army of technicians, executives, skilled and unskilled labourers, is really a mid-nineteenth-century creation. The greatest of all contractors was Thomas Brassey. Between 1834, when he obtained a contract for the construction of a viaduct on the Grand Junction Canal, and his death in 1870 he was leaving his mark deep upon England, France, Italy, Canada, Australia, India. Brassey was the railway contractor *par excellence*.

In all industrial development the Continental people, though behindhand, were not slow in following. Alfred Krupp, of Essen, took over a small iron forge in 1848, with, he said later, only three workmen. Three years later, in the first of the great International Exhibitions, so characteristic of nineteenth-century optimism and energy, he exhibited at London the somewhat sinister achievement of a six-pounder steel gun. At the Paris International Exhibition of 1867—that magnificent display made in the fading glory of the Second Empire—Krupp exhibited a single steel block of fifty-two tons.

In one sphere of industry the Continental peoples were rather in advance of the British. If the British had bigger factories the Continental had better ' welfare ' conditions. The British Government's *General Report on the Sanitary Conditions of the Labouring Population* (1842) noted that the Continental factory-workers as a whole had more sanitary conditions than had British workers. In Great Britain Robert Owen (1771–1858) and Richard Oastler (1789–1861) worked nobly to raise the standard of conditions both in factories and in housing of the ' working class.' It took a considerable time, however, to achieve general improvement in British factories. This, probably, can be dated from Disraeli's second Ministry (1874–80). The dreamer, who so poignantly described the dreadful living and working conditions of the factory hands in his novel *Sybil* in 1845, was able as Prime Minister thirty years later to effect—unfortunately rather late in time—a series of much-needed reforms. On the Continent factories throughout the nineteenth century were, in general, smaller than in England, and were more under the control of the families which owned them. These two features—relatively small factories and ownership in the hands of the family which founded the business—tended to have a beneficial effect upon social conditions inside the factories, and even outside.

In view of the pre-eminence of British industry, of the solid and, indeed, magnificent results achieved by industry, integrity, thrift, and ability, and also of the benediction given to these qualities by Protestant Evangelicalism, it is not surprising to learn that one of the most popular writers of the period was Samuel Smiles. This excellent man, one of eleven fatherless children, rose by his industry, integrity, and intelligence to the position of Secretary of the South-Eastern Railway. His best-known and most prized book, *Self-Help*, was the result of discussions among a group of like-minded young men, a ' mutual improvement society,' who met with him at Leeds in the eighteen-forties. It was published in 1859, though mostly written some years before this. Twenty thousand copies of the book were purchased in its first year. It is full of homely, practical wisdom, strong common sense, richly illustrated and enforced by examples of men who triumphed over circumstances by self-help—by industry, integrity, thrift, foresight, caution, courage, and ability. His advice, arguments, examples, exactly suited an age of expanding industries and markets, an age when men and business throve by competition, when *laissez-faire* was in the ascendant, and when progress towards even greater and, it was believed, even more widely diffused prosperity was being achieved through the unfettered exercise of individual talent and energy. Samuel Smiles' *Lives of the Engineers*, told in a notable series of books between 1857 and 1884, are a contribution to economic history. Along with *Self-Help*, they might almost be called the epic or saga of nineteenth-century industry in the spacious days of *laissez-faire* and the expanding international market.

The great iron steamship lines—the Cunard, the Peninsular and Oriental, the Messageries Maritimes, and others, with the splendid, fast freighter and passenger ships which sprang into fame in the eighteen-fifties—were carrying the goods to supply this international market. The sign of this international market, its glory, its blazon, its evidence, its temple, was the International Exhibition, instituted by the Prince Consort in 1851, and reproduced every decade in the great capitals of Europe.

John Stuart Mill's *Principles of Political Economy* was published in 1848, two years after the triumph of Cobdenism, when Sir Robert Peel carried the Repeal of the Corn-importation Restriction Laws. More comprehensive and systematic than David Ricardo's *Principles of Political Economy and Taxation*, published in 1817, it explained, amplified, and confirmed the Ricardian view: that all men knew what was their economic interest, and that the general good would be best attained through leaving them free to pursue it. After all, this was what Adam Smith, in a less theoretical manner, with copious practical illustrations drawn from the 'Mercantilist' State action of his day, had advocated in his *Wealth of Nations* (1776). State action was, as viewed by these economists, not only in itself cumbrous and expensive, and therefore directly wasteful, but also indirectly more wasteful still because it diverted trade and industry into artificial channels, instead of leaving it to flow unchecked in the channels of individual utility. The individual's economic good was the same as the general economic good—that is, to buy in the cheapest and to sell in the dearest market. In an unfree market such a principle would be dangerous to the common good: it might result in artificial cheapness, artificial dearness. In a free market, however, national and international, free competition would ensure the best bargain in every case, and therefore the maximum of advantage to the seller and to the buyer. It would ensure that each individual, each country, should concentrate on making or selling the things they were best suited to produce or sell. Thus would be secured the perfect division of labour, between individuals, between countries, therefore the maximum of production at the minimum cost, and therefore, under a system of free exchange, the maximum of distribution and general prosperity. State intervention was necessary for the protection of women and children, but it should be reduced to a minimum, for all State action was a restraint upon trade. The test of the utility of any system was whether, on balance, it made people happier or not, or rather, for there must always be 'hard cases,' whether it made more people happy or not. To put the matter another way, the test of utility was the promotion of "the greatest good of the greatest number." John Stuart Mill was the greatest of the Utilitarians, with an unrivalled power of lucid argument from general to particular that brought philosophy, if not into every British home, at any rate into the mind of every thoughtful man of the rising middle class.

Mill was quite convinced that the Continental peoples were too prone to accept Government regulation, but he thought that the British people were too prone to suspect it and to oppose it. He concluded his great chapter "Of the Grounds and Limits of the *Laissez-faire* or Non-interference Principle," and with that his *Political Economy*:

> I have not thought it necessary here to insist on that part of the functions of government which all admit to be indispensable—the function of prohibiting and punishing such conduct on the part of individuals, in the exercise of their freedom, as is clearly injurious to other persons, whether the case be one of force, fraud, or negligence. Even in the best state which society has yet reached it is lamentable to think how great a proportion of all the efforts and talents in the world are employed in merely neutralizing one another. It is the proper end of government to reduce this wretched waste

to the smallest possible amount, by taking such measures as shall cause the energies now spent by mankind in injuring one another, or in protecting themselves against injury, to be turned to the legitimate employment of the human faculties—that of compelling the powers of nature to be more and more subservient to physical and moral good.

Mill thought that on the whole there was not quite enough Government intervention in Britain, and that for humanitarian reasons the application of the principle of *laissez-faire* should be modified. As it happened, there was a whole school of philanthropists—most of them Evangelical English Churchmen—to check the extreme tendencies of *laissez-faire*. The type, it might be said the perfect type, of the English philanthropist was the seventh Earl of Shaftesbury, noble by birth and by nature, rich, serious, responsible, unselfish, and Puritan. "To mention all the religious and benevolent societies in which he was interested," says a writer of the eighties, "would be to name the most prominent and useful agencies for good of the present day." He was Chairman of the Lunacy Commission for fifty-seven years. He was largely responsible for the Act of Parliament of 1840 prohibiting the employment of boy chimney-sweeps; for the Factory Act of 1844, limiting the working hours of women to twelve a day, and of children under thirteen to six and a half hours a day; of the Regulation of Lunatic Asylums Act of 1845; of the Ten Hours Act of 1847; of the Workshop Regulation Act of 1867. He was an energetic supporter of the Ragged School movement and the Sunday School movement. His example of wide charity, of earnest, sustained personal effort, impressed itself upon all the upper classes of the British Isles, and left a permanent impress on British society.

Humanitarianism had its romantic writers, powerful in creating a general sentiment. Dickens' most directly propagandist novel, *Oliver Twist*, was published in 1838,

Mrs Gaskell's *North and South*, on balance a not unpleasing picture of mill life, in 1855; but the most persistent novelist of social questions was Charles Kingsley. This vigorous personality was typical of the Church of England of his time, when the excitement of the Oxford Movement had passed away, leaving as a permanent achievement its earnestness and historical sense. Kingsley was a preacher, an energetic pastoral worker, and he also had time, plenty of time, to be a scholar, lecturer, pamphleteer, hymn-writer, novelist. Three of his novels were about social questions—*Yeast* (1848), describing the life of the agricultural labourer; *Alton Locke* (1850), the life of poor tailors; and *The Water Babies* (1863), a charming myth inspired by child labour. Most of Kingsley's literary work was done while he was rector of Eversley, in Hampshire. Two comrades of his in religious and social activity among the 'working-classes,' particularly in London, were Frederick Denison Maurice, a clergyman of the Church of England and Professor of Theology in King's College, London, from 1846 to 1853, and Thomas Hughes, a practising barrister with a vigorous style of writing, seen at its best in *Tom Brown's Schooldays* (1857). Maurice founded the Working Men's College and Queen's College for Women, both in London, with the help of Kingsley and Hughes. Their ideals were expressed by themselves in two phrases which became famous—"Christian Socialism" and, less happily, "muscular Christianity." Besides Maurice and Hughes, Kingsley found a great practical helper in George Peabody, of South Danvers, Massachusetts, an American merchant who settled in London in 1837, and lived there until his death in 1869. Besides nobly endowing philanthropic and educational institutions in the United States, Peabody gave various sums amounting to £500,000 towards building working-class houses in London. The work was carried on after his lifetime by Peabody Trustees, whose rented houses in the eighteen-eighties were the homes of some twenty thousand Londoners. Responsibility for riches, the application of great sums to carefully selected and investigated objects, was characteristic of Miss Burdett-Coutts, who succeeded to the wealth of Coutts' banking-house in the same year as Queen Victoria, her friend and admirer, succeeded to the throne. The Baroness Burdett-Coutts (as she became in 1871) made broad-minded charity and munificent giving almost a fashion among the wealthy 'upper middle' class and the aristocracy of Great Britain. Nevertheless personal service of well-to-do and delicately nurtured young women was not fashionable, indeed, was practically unknown, until Sidney Herbert, Secretary-at-War during the Crimean War, asked Miss Florence Nightingale in 1854 to go out to the military hospital at Scutari. "The Lady of the Lamp" became for a time the most famous woman in England, and still perhaps attracts more attention in school text-books than any Englishwoman outside the throne.

Before the Oxford Movement started in 1833 there was a period when the Church of England seemed to a great extent to have lost its moral earnestness and historic tradition. The great field of the Industrial Revolution, of the rapidly increasing working-class population, had been entered and almost monopolized by the Wesleyans. The Oxford Movement, the sermons, discussions, tracts, and books, the personalities of its exponents—Newman, Keble, Hurrell Froude, Pusey, Manning, Ward—restored to the Church of England earnestness, eager spiritual endeavour, the sense of tradition and continuity, the dignity of historic ritual, appreciation of architecture. The movement overshot its aim, however, when it carried some of its most prominent exponents from the catholicity of historic Anglicanism to the Roman Catholicism of the Ultramontane Revival. On February 2, 1843, Newman preached his last university sermon in St Mary's, Oxford, on "Development in Christian Doctrine"—perhaps his best sermon. He was received into the Roman Catholic Church on October 9, 1845. Henry Edward Manning, sometime Fellow of Merton College, Oxford, and Archdeacon of Chichester, after years of study, perplexity, and agonized thinking, was received into the Roman communion on April 6, 1851. Ward was received on September 5, 1845. The Roman Catholic Revival was so strong that Pius IX felt able to restore the Roman Catholic hierarchy in England in 1850, dividing the country into dioceses, and appointing Dr Wiseman to be Archbishop of Westminster. When the admirable Wiseman—good-natured, tactful, endlessly industrious as student, writer, speaker, and ecclesiastical politician—died in 1865 Manning became Archbishop of Westminster. Gradually he established for himself a position surely unique in modern English life. No priest had made so great a figure there since Cardinal Wolsey. He was not only the unchallenged leader and promoter of his own community:

> He gradually came to play an important part in public affairs, upon questions of labour, poverty, and education. He sat on Royal Commissions, and corresponded with Cabinet Ministers. At last no philanthropic meeting at the Guildhall was considered complete without the presence of Cardinal Manning. A special degree of precedence was accorded to him; though the rank of Cardinal-Archbishop is officially unknown in England, his name appeared in public documents—as a token, it must be supposed, of personal consideration—above the names of peers and bishops, and immediately below that of the Prince of Wales.[1]

Lord Beaconsfield, who had both high artistry and unfailing social insight, naturally brought His Eminence into the brilliant society of *Lothair*.

It might almost be called a religious age. The Oxford Movement, Evangelicalism, the Roman Catholic Revival, are evidences of this. So too is the missionary spirit, ex-

[1] Lytton Strachey, *Eminent Victorians* (1926 edition), pp. 97–98.

pressed so strongly in the career of David Livingstone, a giant, but not alone, for the great British and American missionary societies were at work among every non-Christian people, and were equalled in energy and earnestness by the Roman Catholic missionary orders. David Livingstone, cotton-mill hand of Blantyre, Lanarkshire, went out under the London Missionary Society to Kuruman, in Bechuanaland, South Africa, in 1841. It is doubtful whether any one man by his own unaided efforts ever in a lifetime achieved more good. Whether it was preaching and teaching the Gospel, bringing hygiene and medical aid to the sick, uncovering the evils of the slave trade, his labour was unceasing. Moreover, it was widespread. He probably travelled more miles even than John Wesley, and mainly on foot. His journeys back and forth across Africa, his amazing explorations of the Zambesi and the great lakes of Central Africa, caught the imagination of all the English-speaking peoples, and attracted emulation in missionary and exploring enterprise. His influence over the native tribes among whom he worked was unique. His native attendants served him, amid terrible hardships, with unswerving fidelity; and when, by Lake Bangweolo, on May 1, 1873, they found him, on his knees, dead, they embalmed the body and carried it, with amazing perseverance and courage, through the forests and swamps down to the coast for transport to England.

David Livingstone may be said almost to have had his peer in General Gordon, the soldier whose conduct was unswervingly dictated by conscience, whose constant study was the Bible, whose continual effort outside his military duties was social work among the poor. Gordon's courage and fortitude, his military achievements, his religious spirit, his hatred of evil, cant, and hypocrisy, his knowledge of the Bible, his travels in China, Africa, India, Eastern Europe, made him the boys' hero of the Victorian Age, at any rate of the millions of boys who passed through

Sunday school. How many of them read the thrilling romance of that life—the life of the daring subaltern in the Crimean War; the invincible leader of a band of Chinese 'Ironsides' against the Tai-ping rebels; the hammer of slave-traders in Central Africa; the worker in London slums; the explorer in the Holy Land! No one could help admiring the man who, when made Governor-General of the Sudan, reduced his salary from £10,000 to £2000; who, when private secretary to the Viceroy of India, resigned his post because he could not write, "The Viceroy has read your memorandum with interest." "You know perfectly," he said to the Viceroy's *aide-de-camp*, "that Lord Ripon has never read it." Two days later he was off to Pekin.[1] And just as the missionary field had many lesser Livingstones, so the British Army had a considerable number of lesser Gordons—officers who read their Bible, laboured to make their men God-fearing, and gave their military service in the spirit of the seventeenth-century Puritans. It was, of course, a small army, and for forty years after the Crimea it had no big war. There was no idea that it would have to fight in Europe. Its duty was to keep the peace throughout the British Empire, and its 'active' service was in a surprising number of 'little wars,' in which the expeditionary force numbered a few hundreds, or at most a few thousands. The officers were expert enough. The little wars were usually conducted efficiently; but they could always be conducted as gentlemen's wars. There was no General Staff, no plan for invasion of neighbouring states, or for the mass slaughter of dense populations. The issues at stake were not the existence of the country nor the fate of future generations. The military profession was not, normally, exacting, scientific, grim, and soulless; and the officers had plenty of time and plenty of energy left for other interests besides soldiering. Some were explorers or hunters; many retired early

[1] Strachey, *Eminent Victorians*, p. 231.

and took to politics or literature; some preached or wrote hymns. In the old British Army an officer could be known "from China to Peru"; after Gordon probably the most familiar contemporary military name was that of Captain Fred Burnaby, whose *Ride to Khiva* was published in 1876. There may have been Gordons and Burnabys in the Royal Navy, but they are not known to history. The Navy had plenty to do in its incessant patrol of all the seas, but few incidents brought it into public light. Its most gifted writer, Captain Marryat, retired from service in 1830 at the age of thirty-eight. *Mr Midshipman Easy* was published (1836) before the reign of Queen Victoria, but *Masterman Ready* in 1841, *The Settlers in Canada* in 1844, and *The Children of the New Forest* in 1847 fall within the period.

Those first forty or fifty years of Queen Victoria's reign were not a materialist period in Great Britain, nor on the Continent. The Italian Risorgimento can be claimed as a spiritual movement. The movement for German unity had a spiritual aspect too, until Bismarck, who became Minister-President of Prussia in 1862, took the movement in hand, and conducted it with blood and iron. The Russian upper classes experienced a spiritual awakening after the Tsar Alexander II had freed the serfs in 1861. For a time aristocratic men and women, young Guards officers and their sisters, took to working among the peasants to bring about educational and social amelioration. It was in 1862 that Count Leo Tolstoi, after serving in the Crimean War and engaging in travel, married and settled down upon his estate near Moscow, to devote himself to literary and social work. His epic novel of Russian society in the Napoleonic period, *War and Peace*, came out in 1865–72; *Anna Karenina*, the picture of Russian high official life, in 1875–77. Dostoievski was depicting lower grades of Russian society with sombre realism. In France a grimmer realism was coming, of which Victor Hugo's novel of revolt, of the outcasts, *Les Misérables* (1862), was the first and greatest. Even in contemporary English literature there was more than a trace of the novel of revolt in George Eliot's work. The realist or ' naturalist ' school had its most artistic expression in Flaubert's *Madame Bovary* (1857), the *bourgeois* tragedy of life in a small provincial town; and it reached perhaps its grimmest in Zola's *L'Assommoir* (*The Drink-shop*) (1877). *Germinal* (1885) is a story of the coal-miners of the northern departments. "By a happy combination of these two subjects with his brutal talent M. Zola has put into these two novels more truth, a closer and more precise observation, than in the others."[1] He wrote many others—a *comédie naturaliste*; some people called the series *comédie bestiale*.

Into the grimness and materialism of the Industrial Revolution John Ruskin brought an ideal of beauty and a sense of artistry. To the Victorians he appealed as a greater prophet than Carlyle. For so much of Carlyle's criticism was negative, destructive of democracy, contemptuous of modern political, social, and economic development. Even Macaulay, the greatest literary name among the Whigs, whose magnificent and enthusiastic history of the English Revolution began to appear in 1848, had nothing but despair for the ultimate results of complete democracy.

John Ruskin had a better, at any rate a more comforting, message than this. He believed that England could remain beautiful; that a factory could have architecture; that large-scale production, if it had to be undertaken, could be undertaken with artistry; and that political economy, rightly understood, was not just a soulless science, but was also, or ought to be, an ethical system. The son of a prosperous London wine-merchant, he was given a private education, and was frequently taken abroad by his parents. The family travelled in their own carriage, through France, Switzerland, Italy, never in a hurry,

[1] Lanson, *Histoire de la littérature française*, p. 1062.

doing their fifty or sixty miles each day before four o'clock, so that they had plenty of time, besides dining, to look at the church or town hall or general lay-out of the place where they stopped. Weeks spent in walking, sketching, reading, at Venice, Florence, or Rome stimulated the genius of the sensitive youth. The great English classics nourished his literary sense. The wholesome domestic life of a good middle-class home was the congenial atmosphere for harmonious development of what otherwise would have been an over-sensitive nature, over-strung temperament.

In 1843 the literary world was astonished at the publication of the first volumes of *Modern Painters* by Ruskin, then twenty-four years old. Originally intended as an answer to an article in *Blackwood's Magazine* attacking J. M. W. Turner, the book as it was written developed into an exposition of the æsthetic of painting, with profuse examples drawn from Old Masters as well as from Turner and the moderns. The sentences were long, but the thinking was never unclear. The language was always vigorous, the style harmonious and balanced, the arguments fully developed and amply evidenced. Magnificent diction conveyed wealth of knowledge. At one bound Ruskin showed himself to be the most eloquent of contemporary teachers, the great exponent of art whom all the world could read. His simple but striking definitions gave the public new visions of beauty. " Speaking with strict propriety, we should call a man a great painter only as he excelled in precision and force in the language of lines, and a great versifier, as he excelled in precision or force in the language of words." After some exposition and illustration of this the public could understand when he wrote:

> Most pictures of the Dutch school, for instance, excepting always those of Rubens, Vandyke, and Rembrandt, are ostentatious exhibitions of the artist's power of speech, the clear and vigorous elocution of useless and senseless words;

while the early efforts of Cimabue and Giotto are the burning messages of prophecy, delivered by the stammering lips of infants.

Modern Painters was followed by *The Seven Lamps of Architecture* (1849) and *The Stones of Venice* (1853). These works are far more than expositions of their particular subject—the qualities of the best architecture or the history and works of art of Venice—they are incidentally treatises on æsthetics, on ethics, even on society. *Unto this Last,* which was published in the *Cornhill Magazine* in 1860, and *Munera Pulveris* (1862) explained Ruskin's views on political economy. Regarded as a strict science—he contended that it was no such thing—political economy had inculcated and made universal ruthless competition and the pursuit of material wealth. It was all a misunderstanding. True *political economy* should be a system for regulating the habits or conduct of a state or society, making possible the feeding, clothing, and living together of a friendly and enlightened community, in much the same way as *domestic economy* does this for the family. The object of political economy is thus the multiplication of human life at its highest standard, developing the noblest types of manhood and womanhood, in respect of beauty, intelligence, and character. Ruskin's views, as a matter of fact, have had some influence in modifying some of the arguments of the classical economists, and in promoting the social services. That he raised the tone of public taste, and contributed to the beautifying of towns by measures of town-planning, the creation of parks and gardens, the permanent exhibitions of collections of paintings, is incontrovertible. That he brought taste and artistry into the printing and publishing trades, into the schoolroom and the workshop, is not so obvious, though he had some influence in this direction. William Morris, the great craftsman—painter, poet, writer—would hardly have been possible without Ruskin, whose precepts, consciously or unconsciously, he followed up in his wallpapers, his pottery, his printing and bookbinding, and his magnificent social-economic tract (written as a long story) *News from Nowhere*, which was published in 1891.

What Ruskin was for artistry and taste in general Matthew Arnold was, or aimed at being, in literature—the critic, standing forth against the materialism, the banality, the mediocre standards, of an industrial age. A son of Dr Arnold of Rugby, he grew up in an atmosphere of education and with a taste for it. In 1851 he was appointed an Inspector of Schools, and was a good one, a conscientious and enlightened official. Government service was not incompatible with creative work in literature. Anthony Trollope was in the Post Office, Thomas Love Peacock and John Stuart Mill were in the India Office. There is no reason to suppose that Matthew Arnold would have been a greater writer had he been able to devote himself exclusively to the career of letters, though he would have written more. His poetry ranks high in modern literature, and has stood the test of time. It was through his prose, however, his *Essays in Criticism* (1865) and *Culture and Anarchy* (1869) that he had direct influence on the age.

Matthew Arnold has been called the Sainte-Beuve of English critical literature. Alike in their uncompromising adherence to the standards of literature, otherwise there is little resemblance between the restless, encyclopædic, all-devouring mind of Sainte-Beuve and the fastidious Arnold, whose critical work, important as it is, fills only three slim volumes. Sainte-Beuve's marvellous *Causeries du Lundi* and *Nouveaux Lundis* were articles—long articles—on some present or past eminent writer, contributed every Monday for twenty years chiefly to the *Constitutionnel*, some to the *Moniteur* and the *Temps*. Each study was the outcome of a replete mind reinforced for the occasion by six days of the closest re-reading of his subject and the most careful writing. On the seventh day Sainte-Beuve took a holiday, and on Monday he began work on the next *Lundi*. However carefully he worked, he could not, under pressure of the weekly article, refine and refine his style with the artistry of a Flaubert, an Arnold, or a Pater.

Arnold's critical studies were issued in collected form—*Essays in Criticism*. Written in lucid, beautiful prose, they appealed to people for their excellence in matter and form. Without this charm of expression his criticisms would not have attained the currency which they enjoyed in both hemispheres. His mission was regarded as being the spread of culture and the maintenance of the highest standards of culture—*was regarded*, for he would not have made such a claim for himself. A sunny, even-tempered, outward-looking man, he did not take himself too seriously, but he quietly developed his particular gifts, and spoke out the truth as he saw it. If for him literature was the creation of a small *élite* group—as, indeed, it must always be—this was no reason why everybody should not enjoy it. His gentle but sustained crusade against the ' Philistines,' the uncultured sections of the *bourgeoisie* who drag standards down or prevent them from rising, made him in his lifetime a little suspect to the ordinary reading public, and for some years after his death in 1888. Matthew Arnold is now appreciated at his proper worth—the judge, guide, and example of a grand literature which without him had a tendency to be wanting in symmetry, harmony, restraint.

Great advances were made in education, higher, middle, and lower. Dr Hawkins, later Provost of Oriel, said in 1828 that if Thomas Arnold were appointed to be Headmaster of Rugby, he would change the face of public-school education. Arnold, at the time of his appointment, had relinquished (on marriage) his Fellowship at Oriel, and was a private tutor, coaching boys, in his house at Laleham, on the Thames. Dr Hawkins' judgment was correct. Arnold brought discipline, the discipline of self-government, and moral earnestness into Rugby, and his example and precepts were followed in other schools. He once said when dismissing several boys, "It is *not* necessary that this should be a school of 300 or 100 or 50 boys, but it *is* necessary that it should be a school of Christian gentlemen." He died in 1842, just under forty-seven years of age.

There was good and plentiful university education for those who could pay or who could win—then, as a rule, a not too difficult feat—a scholarship. There were the ancient universities, Oxford and Cambridge, and the new foundations, Durham and London. Elementary education was rather meagrely provided for. Sunday schools, which began long ago with Robert Raikes of Gloucester in 1780, taught boys and girls to read and write, so that they should be able to read and study the Scriptures and also to acquire some general education. Weekday schools were, early in the nineteenth century, conducted by the National Society and the British and Foreign Schools Society. There was, however, no general provision for elementary education until the Act of 1870, passed under Mr Gladstone's first Prime Ministership. Secondary education was still given only in private schools, or in old endowed grammar schools, or in 'public schools,' which were, for the most part, ancient or modern boarding-schools managed by permanent boards of trustees. The greatest reform of English education after 1870 was the provision of secondary schools by the Education Committees of cities, boroughs, and counties, but this did not take place until 1906.

An age of movement and struggle abroad—revolutions of 1848, union of Italy, union of Germany, American Civil War—it was an era of stability and orderly progress in material and intellectual things at home. The placid assumption in those days that, on the whole, all was going well with the world is apt to be a little irritating to historians now. The promise of international peace and co-operation enshrined in the International Exhibition at London in 1851 was certainly not fulfilled, though the ideal of international free trade was not definitely rejected until the inauguration of new scales of protection in the French and German tariffs (1878–79). Karl Marx's *Communist Manifesto* (1848), his foundation of the Workers' International (1864), his publication of *Das Kapital* (1867), were stages in the growth of class consciousness, steps, perhaps, towards a universal class war, which, however, has not taken place. Better than the class war was a movement for orderly and peaceful change, a constructive movement, started by twenty-eight weavers of Rochdale in 1844. Their co-operative store, with an original capital of £28 and a stock-in-trade only of flour, butter, sugar, and oatmeal, became within five years a large general store, with sales of £80,000 a year, a depository of savings, and a source of profits to all its members. Societies similar to that of the Rochdale Pioneers were starting all over the country; and in 1864 a Co-operative Wholesale Society was founded at Manchester to supply the retail societies. There was an opportunity through the Co-operative Movement for all the workers and consumers gradually to become proprietors.

The British had a deep faith in their social and political system. The extension of the franchise in the Act of 1867 and the Ballot Act of 1872 (ensuring secrecy of voting) gave the citizen a sense of participation in the great affairs of his country, a sense which was increased by the smooth working of the ' two-party ' system. There were only two political parties in Great Britain. To be a member of one or the other was considered to be a citizen's duty and also his pleasure, for there was very little bitterness in British domestic politics until the struggle over the First Home Rule Bill in 1886. The citizen was more interested in domestic politics than in foreign. A momentous political movement like that of the union of Italy—the statesmanship of Cavour and the exploits of Garibaldi—was for the contemporary English a great pageant, not events to affect their security or peace of mind. Even the idea of empire did not move them very powerfully; indeed, in spite of the Durham Report of 1839 and the writings and activity of Edward Gibbon Wakefield, the English had not much consciousness at all of the Empire, how it came about, and how it might go on, until Seeley in 1883 published the *Expansion of England*, and in 1886, the year before the celebration of the Queen's Jubilee, James Anthony Froude published *Oceana*.

A few years earlier (1875) George Meredith, in the opening pages of *Beauchamp's Career*—the fact that he placed the scene of his novel a few years still earlier is immaterial—wrote:

> The returns of the census of our population were oppressively satisfactory, and so was the condition of our youth. We could row and ride and fish and shoot, and breed largely; we were athletes with a fine history and a full purse; we had first-rate sporting guns, unrivalled park-hacks and hunters, promising babies to carry on the renown of England to the next generation, and a wonderful Press. But where were our armed men?

It was not seriously thought that they would ever be needed, apart from the small professional Army and the Navy, whose control of all the sea communications of the world was not only acquiesced in by other Powers, but was generally accepted as a silent agency of world-wide order and stability.

Chapter XVI

NAVIES, ARMIES, AND FOREIGN POLICIES

IN the fifteenth century the feudal 'system' decayed. Instead of being a consequence of land-holding the bearing of arms became a career; soldiering became a profession. From the sixteenth until well on into the nineteenth century the ordinary citizen did not take part in wars; these were conducted by wage-earners, who spent their whole lives in the business. The soldiers of the eighteenth century were, almost without exception, long-service men. If, for reasons of economy, they were discharged from the Army of one state, they made no scruple about accepting employment in the Army of another state. In war-time when the professional armies of one side were beaten the war ended. In 1792 the French Revolutionary Government, beset by the armies of 'Old Europe,' invented the *levée en masse*, and threw the whole citizenry into the war. This system, however, universal compulsory military service, was not established or generally adopted in Europe before 1870, and even then by no means completely in any country.

After 1815 throughout the rest of the nineteenth century and down to 1914 Europe was at peace. Now and then there was a war, brief in duration of time, absolutely localized in one district or one country. The European peoples lived all the time without general international tension. Not until 1920 and the following twenty years was there general and continuous international tension in Europe, the result of the shock given to society by the World War, and of the strains left behind it by the War.

The Napoleonic War, on the other hand, was not a shock comparable with this, nor did it bequeath to the following period enduring international strains. The Napoleonic War lasted intermittently for some twenty-two years, but, except on the French side, it was fought by professional armies until at any rate 1813. Only in that year was something like a *levée en masse* adopted in Prussia. Throughout the whole twenty-two years of the Napoleonic (more accurately French Revolutionary and Napoleonic) War social life remained practically normal outside the area of the battlefields. When in 1814–15 peace was made society was resumed or went on along the normal line without sense of shock or strain.

Thus the nineteenth century, indeed, the whole hundred years after 1814, was an era of the belief in progress, the belief that society was advancing, and would continue indefinitely to advance, in politics, law, morality, trade, industry, and all the amenities of life. The belief in progress was the foundation of the civilization of the nineteenth century, particularly of the Victorian Age in England or abroad. It conditioned all the policies—military and foreign policies—of the Europeans of that time. They assumed unquestioningly that they fought or negotiated for limited results within the framework of general progress. They never thought for a moment that their political or military adventures could endanger civilization, could lead to the collapse of European society, to a return of the Dark Ages. They could risk a war without the fear of such apprehension, without foreboding of such a horror, because war was a professional business, controlled and localized, just an occasional and exceptional act of policy, marring, but only briefly and in spots, general, inevitable progress. Underfoot the ground was solid.

It is possible to overemphasize the rationality of the peoples and governments of that age. They were not, for instance, too rational to use war as an instrument of policy. They did not call their navies and armies ' defence forces,' nor did they employ them simply for defence. They used their navies and armies to advance their interests, as well as to defend them. War was the last thing to which they resorted in a conflict of wills, but they always kept a reserve for this purpose, as a means of exerting pressure in a controversy, not simply for defence. It was so used by the Italians in their movement for national unity; and by Bismarck in making the German Empire, although he always managed that the opposite party began the war. It was so used by the Americans in opening the treaty ports in Japan, and by the British and French in opening treaty ports in China. War was an instrument of policy freely, though not frequently, used because it could be localized and limited. Nobody thought of ' total war,' of a war carried on until *all* the national resources were exhausted. War went on until the professional armies of one side or the other were beaten, and then it stopped. Even the war of 1870–71 was scarcely an exception to this principle. After 1871 the Governments of the Continental Great Powers passed all their physically fit citizens through the Army, but there were numerous exemptions, so that a large portion of the population never bore arms, or only bore them for one year. The British and United States armies were voluntary, professional, and small; so were the British and United States navies. Even among the other Powers, although a kind of conscription could be enforced, the navies were practically on a long-service and professional basis. A Victorian parent remarked that he never expected any British fighting to have to be done except by the professional soldiers. Even on the Continent the ' nation in arms ' was not a fact in peace-time; it was only an aspiration of chauvinists.

The British Navy was one of the great conserving forces

of the nineteenth century. Its main concerns were defence, communications, the slave trade, and general helpfulness. Defence, of course, was the Navy's primary business—to ensure that neither the British Isles nor any British colony could be invaded by sea. Canada, British Honduras, and British Guiana were the only colonies with land frontiers, but they had no neighbour ever likely to wish to invade them by land. The British people never thought of being invaded. Probably this was the reason, still is the reason (in spite of the 'air menace'), for their fundamental tranquillity. The feeling of being on an island is not by itself enough to produce a serene outlook. For this it is necessary to feel that the island is safe. The British people had no doubt concerning the ability of the Navy to prevent invasion of any of the islands. This was no illusion. It was never tested between 1814 and 1914. In 1914–18, however, even a military raid from the Continent into England was proved to be impossible. The great Moltke, the architect of the German campaigns of 1864, 1866, and 1870, is said to have been asked once whether he could invade England. He replied (according to the story, perhaps apocryphal) that he had several plans for passing an army into the island, but none for getting it out again. Actually even the first stage, the entry into England, was not practicable, as Napoleon had found out at Boulogne in 1805.

Equally important with its task of making and keeping invasion impossible was the Navy's duty of ensuring communications. A map of the communications of the British Empire, such as was often shown in geography text-books or on classroom walls, had scores of lines crossing from every quarter of the globe, all concentrated on the spot called England. None of the lines ran anywhere overland. They came from America, Australia and New Zealand, the Far East, India, Africa, and from all the coasts of Continental Europe. They came over the

Atlantic, the Pacific, the Indian Ocean, the Mediterranean, and the North Sea. The British Empire was practically all insular, and was spread about the world in spots and patches with almost exclusively sea communications; the British Empire was a water empire. There was only one land link in this world-wide system of inter-Empire communications—the piece of land between the Mediterranean and the Red Sea, between Port Said and Suez. This was in Egypt, under the sovereignty of Turkey. In the eighteen-fifties the Peninsular and Oriental Steamship Company was conducting a steamship service between London and Port Said, and another from Suez to Bombay, with an overland donkey service along the hundred miles of sandy plain between Port Said and Suez. It was by this through route that Lord Roberts, as an ensign in the East India Company's army, first went out to India. Previously the regular route between England and India was not through the Mediterranean, but over the Atlantic by way of St Helena and the Cape of Good Hope into the Indian Ocean. This route continued to be a commonly used alternative to the Mediterranean until the opening of the Suez Canal in 1869.

The British Isles between 1845 and 1875 became the chief workshop of the world. With population rapidly increasing, the home-grown grain and other home-produced foods became steadily less sufficient. Ships were full both ways, inward and outward. The outward ships carried manufactured goods and coal; they brought back raw materials and food. Not only did British ships use British coal—there was practically no other available—but the ships of other nations used British coal too. Vast stocks of the fuel were maintained at various points all over or about the oceans, in practically every port. British firms at Lisbon, Cadiz, Marseilles, Port Said, Suez, Bombay, all around India, through the Straits Settlements, in all the Chinese treaty ports, in the islands of the Pacific, in the ports of South America and Canada, earned good money continuously selling coal to all the ships of the world, while the British mercantile marine earned equally good money by carrying it. Yet coal—bulky, heavy, profitable—was just one item in the vast carrying trade of the British. The advent of oil has altered the situation. To-day British shippers do not export coal even for themselves: they buy oil abroad and have to carry it home.

Except in the Black Sea and Caspian, which were open only to warships of the riparian states, the British Navy had to guard the vast British maritime trade over every sea. It had to guard the shipping not only against the potential danger of war: it had to keep an eye on the shipping all the time to prevent piracy, to help ships in distress, to represent the interests of British shipping in foreign parts. The efficiency and ubiquity of the British Navy were a moral support to all British shipping, and often to the ships of other nations. An earthquake or a revolution or a war found British ships either on the scene or arriving within an incredibly short space of time. The flag, the White Ensign, was everywhere, and was the only one commonly seen on all the seas. There was no need to concentrate the British fleet in any one sea, in the North Sea or the Mediterranean. It was just one great patrol—ceaseless, ubiquitous, all-seeing. Such it was when Captain Marryat and W. H. G. Kingston wrote, and down to the end of the century, when Joseph Conrad was writing. Yet Conrad just mentions the Navy here and there; its presence was felt, but its deeds were not sung, for they were quiet deeds, helpful but unromantic. Its story is a saga still unsung.

When Queen Victoria came to the throne the days of Pirate Teach were long past; nobody who sailed on the sea expected to have to walk the plank. Yet piracy was always liable to reawaken; and there was still a nefarious, internationally banned slave trade which was not far removed from piracy. The British Navy throughout the rest of the nineteenth century prevented the revival of piracy, and it gradually got the better of the slavers. That the two horrors of piracy and slave-running disappeared off the high seas was due not, indeed, wholly—for the French and United States Navies did something—but largely to the British Navy.

Even the general political stability of the world has been placed to the credit of the work of the British Navy. For the world was politically stable in the Victorian Age. There were serious revolutions in Europe. There were civil wars in Spain and the United States. There were great wars in Europe—Crimean, Austro-Franco-Sardinian, Schleswig-Holstein, Austro-Prussian, Franco-German, Russo-Turkish—following each other in quick succession between 1854 and 1878. The Second French Empire made a great military adventure into Mexico. Cavour and Bismarck tore up the statutes of Europe, the famous treaties of 1814–15. Communists and anarchists, Pan-Slavists and Pan-Germans, agitated peoples. There was perpetual unrest, sporadic fighting, in the Balkans. Yet the general peace was preserved, and, what is more, nobody feared that there would be a general breakdown. Jules Verne did not even imagine such a thing. He only imagined more and more inventions, fruitful inventions, increasing man's control over nature, encouraging his powers of co-operation. All society felt politically, fundamentally, stable. What was the secret of this?

There was no world war because every conflict was localized. It could not be otherwise so long as the British Navy 'commanded the seas.' This vague phrase really only means that the Navy controlled the lines of sea communication. As long as it did so there could be no general war, because British 'command of the sea' could stop communications between countries which were separated by salt water. Accordingly the nineteenth-century nations could indulge in revolutions and in earth-shaking movements like the union of Italy or the union of Germany without the convulsion spreading over the world.

It was a beneficent lordship of the seas. A navy can hardly be an aggressive force. It cannot climb on to the land: it could not even, in the then existing conditions of armament, do very much damage to people and property on land by gunfire from the sea. Its functions were protective, its duties helpful to all people who went down to the sea in ships. Never had the world such a kindly master; but it was only a mastery of the sea that the British Navy wielded. Nobody can be trusted with a land mastery; and the pernicious submarine has endangered sea mastery. The British Navy swept the surface of the seas clean of piracy, and it was in a position to stop any aggression from anywhere to anywhere across the seas. The submarine, however, has made possible underwater piracy, such as appeared in the Mediterranean in 1937. No problem of this kind, however, troubled the Victorian Age. It was the age of British naval mastery.

The international temperature favoured this condition of British naval command of the sea. Nobody was jealous of it. Disturbing ambitions of European nations were all on land, and mainly on the continent of Europe itself. There was scarcely even a colonial problem. The Germans did not seriously begin to look for colonies before 1879. When colonial competition began to appear dangerous an international conference held at Berlin in 1885 amicably settled the rules for the partition of Africa. Nationalism, 'tariffism,' Pan-Slavism, and Pan-Germanism were, none of them, very intense, or at any rate had not yet become very aggressive. The task of national consolidation occupied the political energies of the Germans and Italians, and the French too, after the Franco-German War of 1870–71 and the foundation of the Third Republic. The Russians, checked in their advance towards Constantinople by the Crimean War, turned their attentions to Central Asia. Even the Russo-Turkish War of 1877–78, which in its final result was rather a failure for the Russians, did not stop the Russian penetration of Turkestan. Merv in Russian hands seemed to Englishmen, who used only small-scale maps, an outpost on the way to India. The English had an attack of 'Mervousness' until the tranquil Lord Salisbury advised them to look at a larger-scale map. Anyhow, the Central Asian advance of Russia involved no *naval* tension with the British people, was no challenge to British control of sea communications. Not until the German Fleet Law of 1898 went through the Reichstag was there the beginning of a naval challenge which was to disturb international relations until the outbreak of the World War of 1914.

The satisfaction of the British people in the unquestioned position of their Navy perhaps accounts for the popularity of sea-stories in the nineteenth century. Captain Marryat was one of England's men of letters, and he has an assured place in English literature. W. H. G. Kingston was a lesser light, but his series of novels from *The Three Midshipmen* through their successive promotions were the companion books for thousands of English boys, and were a green memory in their minds when grown-up. Clark Russell was a minor literary craftsman, yet his *Wreck of the "Grosvenor,"* though forgotten now, had a prolonged vogue in the later period of Queen Victoria. Only in the United States were sea-stories read with anything like the relish that they met in England. The Americans had stirring sea-writers in Herman Melville, Fenimore Cooper, and Charles Dana. Because their paths crossed frequently and they spoke the same language men of the British Navy and of the United States Navy associated easily with one another (as they still do, perhaps, more than ever), so that something of a community of sentiment grew up, a kind of vague idea that there was an Anglo-Saxon sea hegemony.

'Militarism' is quite a different thing from 'navalism.' Navies can hardly be aggressive; armies easily become so. The military mind almost inevitably thinks in terms of invasion, and of being the first to strike. A preponderant army, on a continent of mutually accessible states, easily becomes an 'instrument of policy.' Clausewitz, who was a Prussian general in the Napoleonic War, but whose book on war was not published until 1832, asserted the principle that "war is a continuation of policy by other means." Cavour understood this principle, but its greatest exponent in practice was Bismarck. He made appropriate political moves towards his object, and then the last step was taken quickly and decisively by war. In 1864 long negotiations, which placed Denmark diplomatically in the wrong, ended with the Schleswig-Holstein War and the loss of the two Danish duchies. In 1866 long negotiations for the 'reform' of the Germanic Confederation (of which Austria was the head) ended in the Austro-Prussian War, the defeat of Austria, and the destruction of the Confederation. In 1870 negotiations with the French over a 'Hohenzollern candidature' for the Spanish throne ended in the Franco-German War, the loss of the two French provinces Alsace and Lorraine, and the proclamation of the German Empire. Bismarck's three wars were all "continuations of policy by other means."

Among the Great Powers of the Continent militarism was fairly strong, and tended to increase. Monarchs seldom appeared in public in anything but Army uniform. Count Beust, who was Austrian Chancellor in the early seventies, once asked his master, the Emperor Francis Joseph, to make a public entry into Vienna in civilian clothes; Francis Joseph silently, but quite decisively, brushed aside the request. Military men were very influential in the Austrian Court. In 1866 Francis Joseph is said to have been ready to accept the offer of the Italian Government to purchase Venetia, the last Austrian possession in Italy. At the last moment, however, some military men persuaded him that it was against his honour to transfer territory in this way. So he fought the war of 1866, and lost Venetia without compensation and with the sacrifice of many of his people. In the later years of Francis Joseph's reign Field-Marshal Conrad was continually pressing political advice upon the sovereign, invariably, of course, in a militaristic direction.

In France the soldiers were kept in strict subordination to the civil authority from the fall of the first Napoleon to the fall of the second, and, indeed, for a good many years afterwards. Only between 1887 and 1900 can militarism be said to have been strong in France and to have influenced politics. This was first when General Boulanger was a popular figure, a *Saint-Arnaud de café-concert*, as Jules Ferry called him, and later when the Dreyfus affair nearly rent France in two. Dreyfus had been wrongly convicted of espionage by a military court. The high military men regarded the question of the reopening of the Dreyfus case as an attack on the Army. The controversy became, in effect, a struggle between the civil and military authority for control of the country. When the Waldeck-Rousseau Government in 1899 decided to reopen the case at whatever cost or risk the civilian authority was vindicated. Politics were soon practically eliminated from the French Army.

The Prussian Army always kept itself outside politics. Unfortunately the Government itself was a little apt to be military minded. Even the great Bismarck, who thoroughly understood the need for preserving the predominance of the civil authority, on one occasion allowed himself to be persuaded over a political question by the soldiers, against his better judgment. This was when, at the end of the Franco-German War, he took Metz from the French. It was a political blunder, he told the Marquis de Gabriac some little time later, but the military men insisted on it. As a rule, however, the Prussian Government maintained its independence of the soldiers, and kept them in strict control.

Russia, despite its huge army and numerous generals, never had a military Government. Russia was really governed not by Tsar, nor by nobility, nor by soldiers, but by the bureaucracy, the vast Civil Service from whose influence no one could escape, through which every public act had to be done. The country where generals really ruled was Spain. During the Peninsular War Spanish generals seem to have become politically minded. Nearly all the Spanish revolutions and *coup d'états* were made by officers. Generals Prim, Narvaez, O'Donnell, in turn held the chief post of government under the Crown. Generals Primo de Rivera, Berenguer, and Franco, makers of political history in 1922–39, were only following an established tradition. It was a tradition which the Spaniards shared with their kinsmen in South America, where political generals have made revolutions and *coup d'états* in one republic or another throughout the last hundred years and more.

The British Army being small, the number of officers was also small. The term ' officer corps ' or ' officer class ' was never used in Great Britain, and was not understood. Having no solidarity among themselves, the officers had no political influence. Although mainly drawn from aristocratic or wealthy families, the officers were very seldom the heads of their families, or if they were they did not remain in the Army for long. An exception to the general custom that officers came from wealthy families was the Indian service. Sons followed fathers as officers in the Indian Army for generations. They were never wealthy, but they could go into the service, because in the Indian Army an officer could live upon his pay and retire with a much larger pension than British Army officers could claim. Indian Army officers had no effect upon political policies, which were kept strictly in control by the Secretary of State for India in the British Cabinet, and which were administered by the Indian Civil Service—a body of university-trained men, none of them with any military experience or interests.

Although British Army officers as such had no political influence, they were, according to one of the curious paradoxes of British public life, frequently Members of Parliament. Not only did retired officers stand as candidates for Parliament, but officers on the active list could obtain leave to do so, relinquishing their military duties for the time being. The custom enabling officers to do this came down from the eighteenth century, when it was very frequently taken advantage of. It was not, however, common in the reign of Victoria; most of the officers then in the House of Commons were on the retired military list. Officers who were peers, however, were always full legislative members of the House of Lords. Nobody has ever suggested that soldiers had any influence upon policy, although Queen Victoria once wrote to Lady Wolseley, asking her to use influence with her husband, Lord Wolseley, so as to force the hands of the Cabinet.

The United States Army officer was even more remote from politics, if that were possible, than the British officer. He was more specialized than the British. He spent four years at West Point as a cadet, as against the British Army cadet's two years at Sandhurst or Woolwich. After his long, specialized, and very vigorous training at West Point the American officer passed his active career in one military post after another, always on the 'frontier,' where conditions of life were hard, and hazardous operations, though on a small scale, against Indians were not infrequent. From the military point of view the vital factor was not the Canadian, where political conditions were quite stable, nor even the rather turbulent Mexican one, but the internal frontier—the thousands of miles of shifting, zigzag line of settlement from north to south, marked by the 'westward movement' of population. The frontier was steadily advanced until in 1890 it met the existing settlements in California. The census enumerators of that year could find no 'front' of migration. The frontier had disappeared, and the U.S. military posts were all surrounded by their own people. Before that, however, they had stirring times, and not always favourable. In 1876 General Custer and nearly a whole regiment of cavalry were wiped out by Sitting Bull and the Sioux Indians near the Little Big Horn River, in Montana.

That the United States Army was capable of making a big effort was proved in the Mexican War of 1844–46. The Civil War of 1861–65 was not fought by professional armies, although nearly all the high officers on both sides were 'West-Pointers.' The regular army was submerged in the larger forces which the Union Government had to raise from its citizenry. The armies of the South were wholly extemporized out of the Southern citizenry. The people of the United States had a long spell of large-scale fighting with 'nations in arms.' In 1865 they returned to normal conditions of life, and the little old professional army reappeared; but between 1865 and 1914, and again between 1920 and 1939, few people in the United States ever saw a soldier.

The stable 'frame of life' in the Victorian Age was due to many factors; among them three can be picked out as particularly notable. These are the British naval control of sea communications, already mentioned, the Monroe Doctrine, and the 'European States System.' The Monroe Doctrine, except during the five years' aberration (the American Civil War), kept North and South America clear of foreign intervention and imperialism. The European States System helped to keep European frontiers stable, or, if they were being revised, it helped to localize the shock. The 'System,' which was perfectly understood by all the statesmen, comprised three things—international law, the concert, the balance of power.

International law was a body of treaties, customs, and opinions of learned jurists which were generally recognized as binding. The content of international law was subject to revision and development, but its fundamental principle remained the same, and was universally accepted—namely, that there were certain rules binding independent states in their relations with one another. Even the sovereign state, or, rather, its supreme authority (for the state has no personality), never claimed to be a law to itself. The European statesmen were able to trust one another; they never questioned that there were certain limits of policy beyond which no statesmen would go. They took it for granted, for instance, and they were justified in doing so, that any treaties or other engagements that were made would be kept.

The concert of Europe was an understanding among the statesmen of the Great Powers that when a serious crisis was developing, or when anything important involving the interests of many states had to be done, they would meet in conference. This understanding or custom was well established since the Congress of Vienna of 1814–15. It was very seldom that the Government of a Great Power, though it might feel strongly tempted to do so, refused to go to a conference. Bismarck did so in 1866, when he was remodelling Germany, but, though he complained loudly, he did not refuse in 1878, and actually presided over the Congress of Powers that met in the summer of that year at Berlin in order to redraw the political map of the Balkans.

The balance of power was the third element in the European system. This was not a balance between one league or group of Great Powers and another equivalent league or group. There was no such kind of balance before 1904, when the Dual Entente was made, thus associating Great Britain, through the French, with the Franco-Russian alliance. In the Victorian Age the balance was between individual states. Each of the five Great Powers (Great Britain, Austria, Russia, France, and Prussia)—after the union of Italy there were six—was considered to be strong enough to ensure its own independence. A combination of four or five Great Powers against one could probably have been fatal to the one, but no such combination was ever expected or threatened to come into existence. The Great Powers balanced one another. Even the formation of the Austro-German Dual Alliance in 1879 or the Austro-German-Italian Triple Alliance in 1882 was not regarded anywhere as upsetting the balance of power. The essence of the system of balance was the existence of Austria, or, rather, of the whole Habsburg monarchy of Austria, Hungary, and Bohemia. "If there were not an Austria," the Bohemian historian Palacky remarked, "Europe would have to make one." The Habsburg monarchy ensured political stability over a great area of Central Europe which without the monarchy would be perturbed, unstable. And even when in alliance with Germany it was generally an effective balance against that Power, for Austria was a grand empire; its directing class, and, indeed, all its peoples, were proud of its prestige and independence. The disruption of the Habsburg monarchy in 1918 destroyed the balance of power in Europe. The League of Nations was instituted to take the place of the balance of power.

The nineteenth century had a number of political assets which the twentieth century has lost: the concert of Europe, the balance of power. It also had an "international of monarchs." Every Great Power except France after 1870 was a monarchy. The sovereigns were a sort of caste, an aristocracy above all the other aristocracies. In spite of competing nationalism they recognized, if only out of self-interest, a certain degree of solidarity with one another. In the early years of the century after the fall of Napoleon they had formed a Holy Alliance of themselves. In 1849 the Tsar Nicholas I of Russia sent his troops to help the young Emperor Francis Joseph of Austria against the insurgent Magyars. The house of Coburg, into which Queen Victoria married, had very numerous royal relationships. These were greatly increased when the Queen's eldest son married Princess Alexandra of Denmark; for the Danish house of Glücksbourg was also widely connected, particularly with the Romanoffs. Many royalties met together on family visits at Copenhagen, Osborne, Berlin, and Darmstadt. Just how much this aristocracy or 'international' of European monarchs helped to maintain peace and good feeling among the jarring states of Europe it is impossible to estimate. It was just one of several factors that contributed to keep Europe stable.

There was not only a monarchical class: there was a ministerial class. For the peace and happiness of Europe as a whole the important men were the Foreign Ministers. They all belonged to the same social class, came of 'good families,' had received much the same type of education at school and, with few exceptions, at a university. Europe was governed by gentlemen, most of whom knew one another personally, and all of whom knew the modes of thought, the aims, and the limits of action of one another. Not all of them could be said to be strictly scrupulous. Not one of them was completely unscrupulous. On the contrary, they all had the scruples of their class, and they could be counted upon to adhere to certain principles and to observe certain limits of action in their conduct towards one another. Metternich, Bismarck, Gortschakoff, Walewski, Clarendon, Salisbury, all belonged to the same social *milieu*, and if they had all met together or corresponded would have easily understood one another's minds.

And with all their limitations, the limitations of a

rather closely guarded governing class, they were big men. They knew their business, to look after their countries' interests, primarily national, but secondarily European. Whatever their egoisms or ambitions, they would never have plunged Europe into a general war, as their successors did in 1914. They played with the fire of war, but they controlled it. When their armies were defeated they made peace. It was taken for granted that at the end of a war the defeated state, at any rate if it was a Great Power, would still exist, with sufficient reserves and prestige to go on much as it had done before the war. The frightful barbarism of total war was wholly alien to these aristocrats; they did not wish, and in any case they had not the power, to stake the entire resources of their people in the struggle. They would not all have said, as Metternich did, " Europe is my country," but most of them, while placing national interests first, recognized a certain claim upon them to be good Europeans. They were not lofty idealists. It is easy to exaggerate their virtues; nevertheless, it was government by gentlemen.

There was plenty of adventure in the Victorian Age. Life was felt by the ordinary man to be something of a struggle, probably much as it is felt now. There was never a keener, more daring age of exploration. There were socially restless and, from the point of view of existing society, dangerous elements—Bakunins, Marxes, anarchists, communists. Nevertheless society was gaining slowly in serenity, in the assurance that well-being was on the increase, that in nature and in politics the ' good ' was, on balance, getting the better of the ' bad.' A simple, recognizable proof of the advance towards serenity of mind was the growing disuse of passports. In the last years of the nineteenth century and the first years of the twentieth British visitors to France or Germany or Italy did not require to take passports, and this facility was also afforded to foreign visitors to the British Isles. The overseas world was open too, open for visit, open for permanent settlement without waiting-list or 'quota.' There were large free-trade areas—the British Isles, the British Crown Colonies, India, Holland, the Dutch, Portuguese, and German colonies, Belgium, the Congo Free State, Norway, Switzerland, China. Elsewhere tariffs were low, relatively to the value of goods moved, low compared with present-day schedules. During the World War Governments inevitably closed their frontiers, and since then conditions have not been favourable for a general reopening. Thus the twentieth century reversed a process that had been continuous throughout the nineteenth century after 1815 —the process towards an open world. "When I went round the world in 1900," writes M. André Siegfried in his book on the British Empire, "I did not have to show my passport once."

Some moralists believe that human nature does not change much from age to age. The profound difference between the Victorian Age and the present may perhaps be due not to alteration in human character, but simply to physical facts. In the Victorian Age the world was open; to-day it is closed. In the Victorian Age there were unoccupied lands to be colonized, the United States and the great British colonies—especially the United States —beckoning to hundreds of thousands of willing immigrants. The present is an age of a closed world. It is a much smaller world too than the Victorian, owing to the great 'Revolution of the Twentieth Century,' the revolution in speed of communications. The people of the Victorian Age had to deal with the problem of adjustment between the nations in an open world; now it is the problem of adjustment in a closed world.

INDEX